D0875637

THE NOBLE SAVAGE

By the Same Authors

PORTRAIT OF VINCENT
A Van Gogh Biography

THE FOUR BRONTËS

NECESSARY EVIL
The Life of Jane Welsh Carlyle

MARIAN EVANS & GEORGE ELIOT

GORDON: THE STORY OF A HERO

The Noble Savage

A LIFE OF PAUL GAUGUIN

By

Lawrence & Elisabeth Hanson

"*I come from the Borgias of Aragon . . . but I'm also a savage.*" GAUGUIN

READERS UNION
CHATTO & WINDUS
LONDON 1956

This RU edition was produced in 1956 for sale to its members only by Readers Union. Full details are obtainable from Readers Union Ltd at 38 William IV Street, Charing Cross, London, W.C. 2, and at Letchworth Garden City, Hertfordshire. This edition is set in 12 pt Bembo and has been reprinted in Edinburgh by T. & A. Constable Ltd, printers to the University. It was first published by Chatto & Windus Ltd in 1954.

AU
BAR DES THEATRES

Preface

When we were preparing to write our biography of Vincent van Gogh we naturally examined the materials dealing with Paul Gauguin. We discovered that little of this material had been translated into English, that it was of great interest, and that considered as a whole it presented a man far removed from the general impression of Gauguin.

We had long admired the work of Gauguin. His letters and writings and the writings of those who had known him gave us an interest in his personality. We felt that some attempt should be made to give in English a complete and balanced portrait.

This is a study of Gauguin the man. But as a man cannot be separated from his work we have, where we thought it necessary, dealt at some length with his development as an artist. To a professional art critic our comments would doubtless and rightly appear elementary. But we are not professional art critics and the book has not been written for them. It has been written primarily for those who, like ourselves, get pleasure and inspiration from a work of art and are eager to know more about the artist—this being in our experience one certain way of understanding his work better. We have used only words which can be understood by any reasonably intelligent man and woman. If, as we hope, some readers are led beyond our simplicities, many excellent critical monographs exist on Gauguin as painter.

We also believe that this book may appeal to another type of reader—he who, with no particular interest in art, is nevertheless interested in the life of the artist. To such a reader Gauguin's life, we feel, may well be revealed as one of the most fascinating ever lived by a painter. We must admit that we should feel pleased if this book does something to destroy the misconceptions—the "Gauguin legend" as they are known—which the cinema, the novel, the careless critic and even certain of Gauguin's acquaintances and friends have foisted on the world. Gauguin is not the man that he is widely held to be in England and elsewhere; he is, we believe, vastly more interesting. If we have not succeeded in making him so the fault is in us and not in him. In that case we must hope that this book, if it does nothing else, will encourage another biographer, more skilled and more far-sighted, to improve on our efforts.

A word about Notes. We considered the possibility of adding notes and references. They would have run to some fifty pages of text at the end of the book. But it has been made abundantly clear to us that almost all of our readers, and most of our critics too, either resent or at least do not appreciate these additions. We have therefore incorporated into the main text all notes deemed essential. And, as almost every one of our references would have been to books and manuscripts in French, most of them unobtainable in England, we have omitted them. The bibliography will enable the student to trace and check all references.

We have made free translations, our aim being to express the essence of the thing said and the manner of saying it. Ninety per cent. of these translations have been made from the original manuscripts. We should perhaps add, for the benefit of students unable to consult the originals, that wherever we have checked these with printed versions the latter have usually proved to be well edited.

A word should be said about the illustrations. We were faced with a difficulty. Should we print personal photographs, etc., customary in a biography; reproduce some of the better known pictures on which we had printed Gauguin's comments; or, which we should have preferred, reproduce lesser known canvases that we believe are as good as many of the more famous? Ideally we should have wished to do all; practically it was impossible. We have therefore tried a combination of the three. Our aim has been, as in the text, to show the development of the man and the artist. We therefore include photographs not hitherto reproduced in England, self-portraits, an illustrated letter, examples of his work in painting and sculpture in wood which we consider both great and significant and on which he has commented, and finally, to please ourselves, we have each chosen for reproduction a picture which we believe to be the best of his lesser known work and deserving of greater attention. We cannot, of course, reproduce in colour, and colour reproductions are in any case suspect. But we would urge readers to see as many original canvases as possible; with Gauguin more than with most painters the colour is all-important. We give a list of publicly owned Gauguin pictures at the back of the book; the list is not intended to be in any way comprehensive, but may help readers in Europe.

We have many to thank for helping us with this book. Our first mention must be of the friendly interest of Madame André Joly-Segalen, who put the Gauguin collection of her father at our disposal, entertained us and helped us in more ways than we can mention; of the Comtesse de Goldschmidt-Rothschild, who made us free of her collections, helped us to trace scarce canvases and manuscripts and offered a much appreciated hospitality; of Monsieur Michel-Ange Bernard, who entertained, showed us his father's collection, and explained at length his views on the question Gauguin–Emile Bernard; and of Monsieur and Madame Roland de Margerie, who have been most encouraging, hospitable and kind and have helped greatly to make our Gauguin research a pleasure. To these and to the following we owe our grateful thanks for permission to examine, to quote from manuscripts, to reproduce pictures and photographs: Madame Huc de Monfreid; Madame Jeanne Schuffenecker; Madame O. Sainsère; Madame Emile Bernard; Ir. V. W. van Gogh; M. Dominique Denis; M. Alfred Dupont; the Home House Trustees; Mr W. Church Osborne; Mr A. Conger-Goodyear; the Directors of the Bibliothèque Nationale, the Bibliothèque d'Art et d'Archéologie, the Louvre, the Musée d'Art Moderne of Prague, the Ny Carlsberg Glyptotek of Copenhagen, the National Gallery of Scotland and the Gemeente Museum of Amsterdam. We wish also to express our appreciation of the work of M. Malingue and M. Jean Loize on Gauguin which has so greatly helped us. And for various favours we must name Madame M. Perin, Madame Alice Penkala, Mr and Mrs J. Baljeu and Miss B. Carpenter.

Paris,
1954

L. H.
E. M. H.

Contents

	PREFACE	Page vii
Chapter		
1	PAUL GAUGUIN AND METTE GAD	15
2	SUNDAY PAINTER	37
3	*ETUDE DE NU*	55
4	ROUEN	62
5	COPENHAGEN	66
6	PARIS	74
7	PONT-AVEN	87
8	MARTINIQUE	97
9	DECISION	108
10	ECOLE DE PONT-AVEN	120
11	EMILE BERNARD	130
12	VINCENT VAN GOGH	144
13	THE VOLPINI EXHIBITION	161
14	LE POULDU	169
15	THE SYMBOLISTS	181
16	THE DROUOT SALE	193
17	TAHITI	207
18	LAST FLING	230
19	THE FINAL YEARS	252
	EPILOGUE: MAN AND ARTIST	285
	BIBLIOGRAPHY	287
	SOME GAUGUIN PAINTINGS IN EUROPE	293
	INDEX	295

Illustrations

PLATE		FACING PAGE
1	METTE IN 1879. Marble by Gauguin	56
2	ETUDE DE NU. 1880	57
3	GAUGUIN IN 1888. Photograph	128
4	LA RONDE DES TROIS BRETONNES. 1888	129
5	LA VISION APRES LE SERMON. 1888	144
6	LETTER TO EMILE BERNARD. 1888	145
7	LE FAUTEUIL DE GAUGUIN. 1888. Vincent van Gogh	160
	GAUGUIN PAINTING IN SCHUFF'S GARDEN IN 1889. Photograph	160
8	BONJOUR MONSIEUR GAUGUIN. 1889	161
9	SOYEZ AMOUREUSES. Sculpture in wood. 1889	208
10	EMILE GAUGUIN AND ALINE. 1891. Photograph	209
11	MANAO TUPAPAU. 1892	224
	OTAHI (SEULE). 1893	224
12	SELF-PORTRAIT "à mon ami Daniel de Monfreid." 1896	225
13	LES SEINS AUX FLEURS ROUGES. 1899	256
14	CONVERSATION A TAHITI. 1900	257
	VILLAGE BRETON SOUS LA NEIGE. 1903	257
15	GAUGUIN'S STUDIO AT ATUANA with his last "vahine", 1903. Photograph	272
16	THE LAST SELF-PORTRAIT, 1903	273
	METTE IN 1905. Photograph	273

Chapter One

PAUL GAUGUIN AND METTE GAD

1848-1873

I

PARIS, spring 1873. The pension, near the Bourse, of Madame Aubé, wife of the sculptor. Two Danish girls had just arrived from Copenhagen for their first holiday in France. One of these girls was Marie Heegaard; her part in the story was brief; her father, a well-to-do industrialist of Copenhagen, had paid for her best friend to accompany her on the trip. This friend was Mette Sophie Gad.

Mette was then in her twenty-third year. She was a tall, wide-shouldered, well-developed blonde, with a determined chin, a prominent nose and clear skin. Her features were too strong, too masculine for beauty, but her vivacious manner and the direct glance of her fine blue eyes—a challenging glance—made her a striking and somewhat formidable young woman. To her very soon the charms of Paris narrowed themselves to a young man who dropped into the pension for an occasional meal. Despite his powerful shoulders and a heavy body, this young man appeared taller than he really was (he was under six feet), chiefly because of his high, narrow head. But he also held himself upright and had the manner of a tall man. He walked slowly, deliberately and with a slight roll in his gait as though he were a sailor. But that he certainly could not be; he was dressed in a black business-suit and went off to the Bourse every day with an air of importance. To an experienced observer the young man would appear to be wearing his sober clothes with rather too much of an air, as though he had not worn them for long and was not at ease in them. There was, in fact, something a shade flashy about him. But Mette, attracted and curious, and whose experience of men was limited, was chiefly anxious to find out who he was. This was not difficult because he, interested too, began to stay on after dinner. He was, it appeared, a valued member of the staff of Bertin, the stock exchange broker; his name was Paul Gauguin; he was unmarried.

Gauguin's promising position in the stockbroking world was matched by his appearance and manner. He was not handsome in any recognised form, but gave an immediate impression of solidity and power. He was a heavy-faced young man with dark hair grown long over a bull neck. His high, well-set cheekbones, long firm chin and the suggestion of heavy jowls conveyed forcefulness. He wore a red-brown moustache. His complexion, like his manner, was hearty and coarse. He had a generous mouth, large and full in the lower lip, tending to a supercilious curl in the upper. When he smiled, which was not often, the supercilious expression changed to one of irony—but a gentle irony. He had a pleasant smile.

The least satisfactory part of his face was the narrow forehead, but neither Mette nor any other woman wasted more than a moment on it—the eye went instinctively to the two features, his nose and eyes, which made the rest appear almost ordinary. His nose, a great beak broken at the bridge, jutted from the long space between brow and mouth with the arrogance of a pirate chief; it was positively rakish, it could with difficulty be reconciled with the Bourse, the bank, the black clothes. And his eyes! Almost covered by heavy lids, they seemed at first small and dull; then one would catch a gleam of blue-green and realise that they missed nothing. He made no effort to raise the lids, glancing lazily from under them. But there were moments — and as he looked at Mette, more frequent moments—when the iris was exposed, the dullness disappeared and the glance became a bold stare, difficult to meet.

He talked, as he walked, slowly, deliberately. He talked little, and with an ironic undertone. He raised his voice, as he raised his lids, rarely. He had no need of emphasis; the strong face, the beaked nose, the hooded gaze, the powerful body, the authoritative delivery—Mette found them extraordinarily impressive.

She would have described herself as practical, and so she was, but for the moment she behaved like one bemused. A flattered woman is not usually the best judge of character, and Mette was no exception; she saw the handsome, powerful face, but did not read the signs implicit in it, she read only the obvious signs of growing admiration. The admiration of men was not new to her. She had even had an unhappy love affair. But this man! That bold stare was an insult and compliment in one. What woman could resist this challenge? Not Mette. If she had misgivings they were overborne by the comforting thought of a lover at once romantic and successful—for Gauguin was gambling with assurance on the market, Bertin was proud of him, he was plainly a coming man. That confident pronouncements could cover a childish optimism, that his way with her was too adroit to be the way of a man with his first woman, that for all his outward respectability he was not respectable, Mette was too inexperienced to perceive.

Gauguin opened his campaign in conventional fashion; he advised the Danish girls what to see and how to see it; then, the charm of Mette gaining ground, he accompanied them, walking magisterially between them along the Paris streets and through the gardens. His attitude to both indicated, to those who wished to see, what kind of feminine company he had kept. But Mette and Marie were too charmed to be cautious: to have a male escort and such an impressive one overruled whatever native shrewdness they possessed. When despite his gallant inclusion of Marie it became clear that he was seriously concerning himself with Mette, Marie obligingly began to drop out and the conversation changed; no more was Paris extolled, but in strict keeping with tradition they began to talk about themselves.

Mette's story was soon done. Nothing could be less remarkable, and not even an admirer could make much of it. Gauguin did not try very hard. He listened to the slender reminiscences of the Gad family, civil servants to a man for generations past. He heard about the magistrate father on the island in the Cattegat; of the family's removal after his early death to the Copenhagen home of the maternal grandmother—the domineering, sharp-tongued daughter of a blacksmith; of the two younger and prettier sisters and their conquests among the visiting cadets; of the two still younger brothers; and of Mette herself leaving home at seventeen as governess to the children of the President of the Council, Estrup. He heard all about the kindly Heegaards. He missed the salient facts (or like Mette allowed them to be pigeonholed away)—that Mette's life at home had been one long struggle to remain respectable and to rule the house; that there was next to no talk of books, music, pictures, but a flood of comment on the difficulties of making do on a small income, on the peculiarities of her family, friends and neighbours. A man does not always hear clearly when he is looking at a pretty girl. Small beer, but how charming—that would be his thought. Small beer. But what matter? His own history was extraordinary enough for two, for a dozen. He became positively talkative when the conversation turned on himself and his people. Mette, it soon appeared, liked nothing better than to watch and listen. He talked slowly, solidly. The days passed, the weeks: neither tired; he talked on.

2

It was a strange story. He talked mostly of his ancestors on the maternal side. When he spoke to anyone on this subject he would say impressively, "I come from the Borgias of Aragon," He would list the Viceroys of Peru provided by this noble Spanish family, tap his great chest, lift the heavy lids slightly and repeat, "I come from the Borgias of Aragon." And that was not the end of his claims. In his veins, he insisted, ran the blood of the Incas and—who could tell?—of the Marquesans too.

Was there a twinkle in those half-hidden eyes? Hard to say; there was much about this man, then as later, that Mette did not understand. Others—for Gauguin was free with his genealogy—looked sceptical when he launched into a rhapsody on the Borgias, and Gauguin, with a huge and lazy shrug of the shoulders, would reply, "If I tell you that on the maternal side I'm descended from a Borgia of Aragon, Viceroy of Peru, you say it's a lie, that I'm a boaster. But if I tell you that the Gauguin family is a bunch of scavengers you despise me. What a life!"

But to him the Borgia, the Inca and perhaps even the Polynesian strain in his blood (for a Viceroy of Peru had sent an expedition to the Polynesian islands of Marquesas more than two hundred years earlier), though conjectural, was a reality; he was proud of it, and because of it he felt himself to be in some way set apart from the French businessmen about him.

To Mette by this time he was also set apart, though for a different reason; he was the man with whom she was falling in love. Had she been familiar with the French, the Peruvian Spaniards and Indians and the men of the Marquesas, she would perhaps have been struck by Gauguin's unlikeness to the first and resemblance to the others, particularly in the shape of the head and the bony structure of the face. As it was—and she thought it sufficient—she admired the face of a man who might take her for ever out of family quarrels, the teaching of other people's children, shortage of money, a man who could give her a home and children of her own. So thinking, she gave way willingly to the confident tone and regal manner. He was not to be gainsaid in person; and Mette, fascinated, had no wish to gainsay however much she might question when he was not there. In any case, what did it matter? There was he, there was she—that was reality.

But if his claim was a fantasy it was a harmless one. Much more alarming to a well-regulated mind was Flora Tristan—for that Flora Tristan had existed and that she was Gauguin's maternal grandmother could not be denied. And he admired her even though, as was his way, he expressed it by banter. He was for ever talking about her. "A socialist-anarchist blue-stocking," he would say. "A bit of a scream, my grandmother." Then he would add, "A genius if you take Proudhon's word for it."

Her full name—which, like her married name, she never used—was Flora Tristan y Moscoso. Gauguin rolled it round his tongue as he explained that she had in her veins (and therefore he also) the blood of France, of Peru and of royal Spain. Her father, Don Mariano Tristan y Moscoso, a colonel in the Spanish army in Peru and a friend of Bolivar, made a romantic marriage to a young Frenchwoman and was promptly disowned by his family. Their daughter Flora, born in Spain in 1803, was pretty, ardent and utterly uncontrollable. Taken to France in her teens by her widowed and almost penniless mother, she rushed into marriage at seventeen. She had been forced to go out to work, found a job as a colourist in the studio of André Chazal, a lithographer from Orléans, fell in love with him and married him. He was poor—far too poor for a girl brought up in the luxury of Lima—but he was also as passionate as Flora, madly jealous and possessive.

The marriage was a succession of appalling scenes. After a few years, in 1825, she left him, taking with her the only living child of the marriage—a boy. She took refuge with Chazal's elder brother Antoine, a painter who specialised in flower and animal studies in the Jardin des Plantes, where he afterwards became Professor of

Iconography. Her daughter was born a few months later. For some years she struggled to keep herself and the children, working at anything that offered itself. By the time she had saved enough to visit Lima and persuade the family to give her an allowance, she had made up her mind about her future. Her hardships as a woman trying to maintain herself had opened her eyes to faults, grievous faults, in society. She knew what she must do and knew it with a frenzy. She had discovered the Comte de Saint-Simon and his crusade. She threw herself into the work with ardour, travelling throughout France and visiting England preaching the gospel of class equality, sex equality, the rights of all to the good and happy life and so, by a natural transition, of free love. But free love of a noble kind. This, which she practised fearlessly, became one of the three main planks in her platform; the others being a matriarchal government and (with a somewhat startling reversion to the practical) the formation of trade unions.

She not only talked to the people in every town and village she visited, she discovered a flair for writing; pamphlets and books hurried after one other, each more urgent and inflamed than its predecessor. She was in the tradition of the early feminists—of Mary Wollstonecraft, whose books she had read—desperately sincere, embarrassingly emotional, welcoming suffering and discomfort in the cause—but in her there was also a particular detestation of moderation; she lived in a perpetual whirl of passion and sacrifice. She was loved by the common people, loathed by the bourgeoisie and regarded with amusement by her own class, but all agreed that she had extraordinary pluck. Nothing could move her from her course—insult, laughter, desertion, physical assault. Her energy—she was a small frail woman—was prodigious, her eloquence fiery. She did not hesitate to whip up her audience by examples from her own life, nor was she above embroidery when indignation overcame her; her husband was a brute, a blackguard, a monster of cruelty, the very incarnation of the masculine reactionary forces. What she had suffered! What all women suffered!

Meanwhile Chazal was biding his time. He fought her for custody of the children and eventually she was forced to hand over her son. Not content with this, he abducted his daughter from the school in which Flora had placed her. The child was recovered, stolen again, bandied about between the maddened parents until her mother finally won the case and kept her—in theory, for she was too busy travelling about the country to see her for more than a few days in the year. But Chazal had not yet given up hope of persuading his strong-willed wife to come back to him. If she would not, he was determined on revenge. At last, in 1838, he caught her outside a house she had taken in the rue de Bac. There was a violent scene. He begged her to return—he loved her still. She refused. He threatened her. She taunted him. Beside himself, he shot her. She was seriously wounded, the ball passing just below the heart. His trial was one of the sensations of the year—Paris had been thrilled by the report that he had shot George Sand (whom Flora had visited that day), and the courtroom was crowded. He was sentenced to twenty years' hard labour.

Flora forced herself back to a semblance of health and, triumphant, continued her Saint-Simonian exertions with exceptional ferocity because the movement had been banned. She continued especially her attempts to set up trade unions and did at last help to establish one. But she never recovered fully from her wound; she died at Bordeaux in 1844 and a monument put up by the grateful workers now stands over her grave. She died four years before the birth of her famous grandson, four years before the outbreak of the revolutionary movements throughout Europe which she had tried so vigorously to help on their way.

3

To the prim Mette from a respectable family in Copenhagen this story was disturbing, even disgusting. Gauguin, one may be sure, did nothing to lessen the blow. He had only to see a shocked or disapproving face and he was off, not sparing invention to give the finishing touch to a tale—and to the expression opposite. Everyone was fair game; and Mette's comments in later life give some idea of her feelings. But the thought that the handsome young stockbroker who told the story might have inherited some of his grandmother's characteristics did not seem to occur to her, and one cannot wonder at it—anybody further removed in manner and person from the tempestuous Flora would be hard to imagine. Flora was so obviously disreputable and Gauguin so blissfully unaware of it—that was the trouble; or, worse, being aware of it, took unseemly pleasure in the recital. Or was he just a prodigious tease? It was a puzzle. Certainly his "Ah, she was a deuce of a good woman, a true-blue socialist" was no reassurance at all; Flora sounded anything but good, and as for socialist, well, in Denmark in 1873 that unsavoury spectre was best forgotten. Nor did his "She was a very pretty and noble lady" convince; pretty she might have been, but she was no lady. Mette had to look long and often at her admirer in his sumptuous black suit and to recall the Bourse, Bertin, the mounting bank balance.

She had to recall them many times to carry herself through Gauguin's day-by-day recital. As he talked on, Mette began to wonder how he had ever come to his present happy pass. Everything seemed to be against it. Yet there he was as large as life stretched massively in a chair or walking by her side with deliberate step, the picture of reliability and, to a fond eye, of respectability, telling her the most incredible stories. Incredible? After Flora, how could she doubt them? The one sensation she could safely enjoy was gratitude that he had been so miraculously preserved for her and the life civilised.

From Flora the story passed to her daughter. Aline-Marie was not at all like her mother; she was proud of her Spanish blood and looks, and she had her share of Spanish pride and temperament, she could be capricious and gay, but fundamentally she was gentle, dependent, feminine in the more obvious way. She remained unmoved by the unsatisfactory state of the world; most of her thoughts were given to the young man whom she had met at the pension where Flora had left her during the last Bordeaux crusade.

This young man was Clovis Gauguin, like André Chazal, from Orléans. He came from the *petite bourgeoisie*—his father was a wine merchant—and was chiefly remarkable for his courage, or obstinacy, in remaining a staunch radical in face of a conservative family. He took up journalism, and when he met Aline-Marie had just been appointed political correspondent to the *National*, the liberal paper founded some fifteen years earlier by Thiers, Mignet and Armand Carrel. When Flora died, they married and settled in Montmartre at 56 rue Notre-Dame-de-Lorette, where their children were born: in 1846 a girl, Marie; on June 7, 1848, a boy,

Eugène-Henri-Paul. The first days of the boy's life were lived against a background of battle; the Commune had risen and the sound of desperate street-fighting was only too clear in the Gauguin house until government troops put down the rising.

The *National* survived the struggle, but Clovis Gauguin scarcely lived up to his resounding christian name; he remained unknown; no article appeared over his signature. But if he had not the gifts of his companions, he shared their convictions. When Louis Napoleon staged his *coup d'état* in 1851 Clovis decided to preach liberalism elsewhere. The elsewhere was inevitably Lima; there at least he and his family would find sanctuary. Peru was not perhaps the happiest place for a reformer, but he, poor fellow, never had his principles tested in this far-away new land—he did not reach it. As the ship was sailing through the Straits of Magellan he had a heart attack. The captain put him off at Port Famine, but he died before landing. In that dreary spot he was buried and his young widow and her two small children were carried on to begin their new life in Peru.

Gauguin, as he told the story, anathematised the ship's captain—"a terrible fellow"—who, he declared, had caused his father's death. As in so many of his accusations, the effect was the thing. Effective it was, and Mette had no difficulty in showing the desired indignation and horror. But of his father's ominous burial-place Gauguin perhaps did not make enough. Port Famine! But no hint of forewarning disturbed him.

One can imagine his languid tone quickening as he went on with his tale, for at Lima his true life began. His great-great-uncle, the head of the family, lived on, a man much to Gauguin's taste—eccentric and over-lifesize, particularly in his appetites—and he was given to pronouncing the name appreciatively: Don Pio Tristan y Moscoso. When the Gauguins arrived in Lima, Don Pio was reputed to be more than a hundred years old (for good measure Gauguin made him a hundred and nine) but full of life. By that Gauguin meant that the ancient man still had an eye for a pretty woman. And his niece Aline-Marie was pretty; not only pretty but charming—her son's portrait, taken from an early photograph, makes this clear—and, more important, most gratifyingly Spanish; not a tinge of the misalliance appeared in looks or manner to disturb the old man's admiration, and more than a tinge of his long-dead brother, Don Mariano. Her French father was in a distant prison, her French husband was dead—what could be more suitable? She was given a great welcome.

She and her children were received in a house which, although one of the biggest in Lima, hummed with life. At eighty, widowed but indefatigable, Don Pio had taken another wife and peopled his great house with a second substantial family. He could even offer children young enough to play with the newcomers. There was room for all and money for all—Don Pio's guano and saltpetre kept him wealthy—but that was not the way of a grandee; this favoured niece must have a house as well as an income of her own. Paul and his sister soon found themselves in a handsome home with a little negress as their maid and a Chinese boy to wait on them. They wanted for nothing.

The Gauguins lived in Lima nearly four years. In this time the boy was submitted to decisive influences. A more perceptive woman or one less fascinated by the teller of the tale might have taken warning by the way in which he spoke of these years. He spoke with unusual animation. He spoke nostalgically of things which to his listener seemed better forgotten. But he had forgotten nothing. Mette lived before the day when one looked to the child to find the man; to her, Gauguin was merely indulging a masculine weakness by talking about himself. She couldn't approve, but what had that little boy in Lima to do with the man looking admiringly at her in Paris? She discounted Lima in him as she discounted Flora Tristan. She listened, but learned nothing.

Lima in the eighteen-fifties was a blend of high civilisation and barbarism, of luxury and squalor. Grandees lived back to back with the dregs of the city; their carriages bore them, scented, exquisite, through stinking streets; vultures and chickens pecked at refuse heaped against the walls of splendid mansions; negro and Indian padded past palaces through mud and offal to hovels unfit for animals; the howls and cries of lunatics chained to the flat roofs (they were kept as a form of taxation) every now and again rose above the laughter and quarrels and bartering far below.

The contrast heightened the boy's pleasure; everything fascinated him. The aristocrat in him welcomed the elegant formality of life in the big houses; the glowing canvases and tapestries on the white walls; the shining silver, the piled candles, the native vases with their bright geometrical patterns; the swish of silk dresses across floors of brilliantly coloured tiles, the gleam of jewels on bare necks, the proud swing of the high mantilla. He relished his sense of importance when on Sundays and Saint days the little negress preceded him up the aisle of the church with its great dome of fantastically carved wood and laid down the special rug on which he and his sister might kneel without soiling their clothes. He loved to watch the Chinese boy at work on the interminable household laundry, to hear the hiss of the iron, to see the pigtail slowly swinging.

But that other, stronger strain drew him to the world whose shouts and smells broke into his home. He loved the garish Carnivals, the dances and games and rainbow-coloured processions. He lingered in the street or leaned from his window admiring the sashes and headwraps of the half-naked women, hectically bright against their glistening black and brown skins. He watched enviously the games of the naked coloured children, their bellies queerly distended, as they played noisily in the dirt. He was happier with his little negress than with his sister, with the Chinese boy than with his cousins.

The country about the city was dramatic; the enormous dusty plain; the mountains, sheer, fantastically ribbed to north and east; to the west, the illimitable blue sea. But even more remarkable to the little Parisian were the hot dazzling glare of the sun by day and the sparkling of the moon and stars in the pure night air. Everything he saw was big and bright: the vividly patterned moths and butterflies, the brilliant fruits, the flowers thickly massed and throwing off perfumes so heavy that the senses drowsed.

There were horrible things; lying in bed, he saw his uncle's portrait on the opposite wall give a sudden lurch—an earthquake; two madly gleaming eyes peered in at his window one moonlit night—the lunatic had broken from his chain on the roof. But when the horror had passed even these seemed part of the exciting life of this colourful land. And the good things were so many and so good. The spice shops were a particular joy with the aromatic scents that set him dreaming of ships and islands across the sea where the spices were gathered. And the sweetmeat stalls! He spoke, as though it were yesterday, of himself discovered by the Chinese boy between two barrels of molasses sucking a fat sugar-cane after the manner of the negro children and brought back to a mother who slapped the truant's face then covered him with kisses, her tears pouring down.

Since the death of her husband the young Aline-Marie's love of her son had naturally become possessive. She suffered when he was rebellious, when he was long out of sight, when she suspected that she had a rival. But Paul was not to be possessed. He loved her in his way—but it was not her way. He was independent, critical, his first thought, then as ever, himself. Even in these early years he watched and remembered her tantrums with amusement; with pride too, for her heel-tappings, her face-slappings, her haughty voice were to his mind all outward shows of that inward aristocracy of blood of which she told him so often. He was proud of her. He loved best the irresponsible child in her. He laughed at the trick she played on the officer dining next to her at the banquet of her cousin President — she had concocted for him a special dish of the strongest sweet pimentos, and laughed uncontrollably behind her fan every time he, scarlet in the face, assured her that the dish was nectar. And when she came upstairs to kiss Paul good-night and to share the joke, looking, in her mantilla and gown, both beautiful and roguish, he would melt into love and admiration.

But, his mother gone, he moved happily into that other world. The little negress slept with him and his sister; she was naked to the waist; she taught him a love he was never to lose, a love of the coloured body. "Oh, that penetrating animal scent, that tropical savour!" he was writing in the last year of his life.

Perhaps the negress taught him more than this. At any rate just before he left Lima the boy tried to rape one of his cousins. Or so he said, jauntily. Absurd? Or if true, meaningless? Neither, with a Gauguin in whom the child is very much father of the man. The sexes mature early in South America; he, surrounded always by women, took enormous pleasure in them; and it was in keeping with the later Gauguin that as a child he should respond to the sensuous influences all about him. Did he tell this story to Mette? Knowing Gauguin, one would say yes, he would do so. Of delicacy, as Mette would think of it, he had no trace—he despised it as hypocrisy, just as he despised the conventional view of considerateness as cowardice. With him a spade was a spade and should be called so. The accompanying laugh, and the charm, must not be forgotten. Even so, Mette would scarcely be amused. At seven years of age! And actually to boast about it!

4

Only the fringe of this subject had been touched; Gauguin had much more to say. But first there was the return to France. The idyll of Lima came to an end in 1855 when his paternal grandfather died in Orléans. His mother was summoned back for the disposal of the estate. She went—foolishly, Gauguin afterwards thought; Don Pio had bequeathed her a substantial legacy, but on his death a few months after she left Lima his family found means of disregarding it. Gauguin rounded off the story by telling how, later, the son of the President Echenique came to Orléans to suggest a small payment as compensation which his mother immediately rejected with a proud "All or nothing." And nothing it was.

So Aline-Marie and her two children—Marie now nearly ten, Paul nearly eight—gave up Lima and the legacy for a somewhat pinched and provincial existence in Orléans. Whatever she gained from the estate of her husband's father, it was insufficient for her to set up a home; she and the children continued to live at his house, now the property of his son Isidore. This bustling little man, known as Zizi, was kind in his peculiar way, and the family settled down to unspectacular years. No more dinners and receptions at the Presidency, no more coloured servants, silks and satins, fleets of carriages, no more bowings and scrapings wherever she moved—for a woman still youthful and pretty this must have been difficult to accept. But Aline-Marie was proud, as her son repeatedly emphasised, and she was loving; fixing her mind on her children, she gave up luxury and position without many qualms. It is even possible that she welcomed the change, worried by the effect of the life in Lima on a boy naturally extravagant, imaginative and self-willed.

The young Paul did not take kindly to the limitations of provincial France. At his day school his master said, "That boy will grow up either an idiot or a genius." So Gauguin told Mette and others, and dismissed the prophecy with a careless "I'm neither one nor the other" that did not sound entirely convincing. The master's remark has been heard before and will be heard again; but in this instance it was at least true that Paul Gauguin was not behaving like an ordinary child of Orléans. He spoke Spanish and learned French with difficulty. He had grandiose ideas in keeping with his boasted ancestry but unsuited to an Orléans day school. And he did strange things. He would be seen in the garden stamping up and down and flinging handfuls of earth and sand into the air. When asked what was the matter, he stamped all the harder and shouted in anger and despair: he had fallen short of his ideals and was busy punishing himself. That was rightly considered to be peculiar, and so in another way was the incident of the nut tree: the boy lying motionless in an ecstasy under the tree, waiting, he explained, for the nuts to fall.

His mother, realising that the boy was exceptional in some way, wondered what this way could be. She wanted him to grow strong —he remained weedy and rather delicate—but she looked for something more than strength. His hands were particularly slender and nervous. What would they do? One day a neighbour answered the question. Paul was discovered whittling away with a knife at the handle of a dagger. He often did it, he said. He carved queer designs on the wood. The neighbour announced with confidence, "He'll be a great sculptor." That kind of remark has also been heard before and will be heard again, but Aline-Marie chose to believe it and her son did not forget it; he repeated it now to Mette with a deprecating "she was no prophet".

In his mother's mind were no doubts, and the boy was greeted with fury when he returned from school one day with a set of strange marbles for which he had traded his rubber ball. "Traded!" she exclaimed contemptuously but also with fear. It was true, this boy had a head of a kind for business: to get something for nothing or next to nothing, that was smart, that proved him the better man.

But was it the dagger handle or the dagger? The dagger was missing from the handles he carved, but he hankered after it. He was descended from the Borgias of Aragon, he insisted, but he was also a savage. The Borgia blood had mingled with the native blood of Peru; and the native blood of Peru—who knew what mystery was hidden there, what far away race had its share in him? He was as proud of the one as of the other. And he was never likely to forget either, what with his mother's reminiscences and the appearance of his home—for Aline-Marie had transformed her rooms in that most French of houses in Orléans into an exotic imitation of a Lima interior; furniture, rugs, curtains all Peruvian, with a collection in which she took much pride of silver figurines and Inca pottery.

He was for ever running away. That scene in Lima after the barrels of molasses had not discouraged him. Anything would set him off. Once it was no more than the picture of a traveller with a stick and bundle over his shoulder. The young Gauguin—he was nine—promptly filled a handkerchief with sand, fastened it to a stick and walked out of the town. He was found in a nearby forest by the family butcher and brought back, but his mother was troubled; would his restlessness never end?

For a few years she was given a respite. At eleven he went into the secondary school. It suited him; he was small for his age, but he had an imperious manner and was able to hold his own; his flow of Spanish gave him a sort of glamour; and as he could make anything with his hands he soon had a little court of followers. He learned useful lessons, he said: to hate treachery, meanness and above all self-righteousness. He learned these lessons well. He also learned, he claimed, to follow his own judgment. This lesson he learned almost too well. Finally he learned "to concentrate myself in myself, always watching what my teachers were up to, making my own playthings, my difficulties too and the responsibilities they carry with them." In a sense, learning this, a boy may be said to have learned nothing. Gauguin realised as much: "In general I think the experiment is dangerous"; but "mine was an exceptional case".

It was. Already he had the beginnings of that inseparable mixture of arrogance and authority that was felt alike by the boys at school, by Mette to whom he told these things, and by almost all who came to know him.

At seventeen, after an unsatisfactory year or two as boarder at the Lycée, he followed his instinct, making the first of the abrupt decisions (if his runnings away are excepted) which were to be characteristic of his life. He wanted to go to sea.

His mother was appalled. She pleaded with him. He was immovable. She yielded, but begged him at least to join the navy; she saw him, if he must do this mad thing, as an officer. For that more schooling was necessary. He refused; he wanted to go at once, and go he did; he went to Le Havre and engaged himself as pilot's apprentice on the *Luzitano*.

He had his reasons. The home with Uncle Zizi was not an entirely happy one. Zizi himself was an eccentric recluse who never went outside the house and did not exert his authority inside, wishing simply to be left alone. The women ruled. His mother alone Paul might have accepted, for her rule was one of love, tiresome though it could be. But there was also his sister Marie. This girl, hot-tempered and domineering at the best of times, was embittered by her mother's preoccupation with Paul. She opposed her in everything, and when her back was turned took out her spite on the still undersized Paul.

No doubt his sister's tyranny, his mother's idolatry, increased in the boy the ambivalent attitude towards women that the man never lost. But why to the sea, if he must escape? He was neither strong nor healthy. The sea was not in his blood. No, but the "savage" was, and the *Luzitano* plied between Havre and Rio de Janeiro. What were six years of provincial French schooling to one who had read his Rousseau, and whose own dearest memories were of warmth, colour, clear skies, a life lived close to nature? He believed that the negresses of Lima, the Indians in their colourful squalor, were wise with a wisdom that so-called civilisation knew nothing of. He went.

5

Mette at last understood the rolling gait so incongruous in the businessman. He had been apprentice, stoker, third-class seaman, steering-room assistant, second-class seaman up and down the oceans for six years, explained Gauguin, and—no doubt with his ironical smile—it had made a man of him. The second part of these six years had after all been spent in the navy, where he did his military service—not as his mother had dreamed, pacing the bridge in gold braid, but stoking in the sweaty, airless Hades far below.

He had kept mostly to the South American run, but had been as far east as India and occasionally to northern ports. It was near one of these, Copenhagen, that he heard of the outbreak of the Franco-Prussian war in 1870; his ship, the cruiser *Jérôme Napoleon* (which incontinently changed its name to *Desaix* when the Empire collapsed), was stationed for a time in the Cattegat. Every day he must have seen the island on which Mette was born and had spent her girlhood.

The war over, he gave up the sea as abruptly as he had taken to it. But the sea had done its work. It had turned him from a weedy boy into a powerful man and confirmed his sense of superiority. It did more. On his maiden voyage he was told by the first mate how through a mischance he had spent two years on one of the Polynesian islands—two halcyon years. Why did he ever come away? the man asked mournfully; and the young Gauguin, standing by him at the wheel, had a vision of magic islands with an unspoilt race of people, with women for the asking, food for the picking, sun beating down the whole day through.

His ships did not, it seems, call at any of these islands, but he saw enough of the tropics to convince himself that his joys as a child and his intimations in after years were no illusion. And although he was tired of the hardships of life at sea and longed for money in his pocket, a comfortable bed to lie on and intelligent talk in cafés (for he discovered, perhaps with surprise, that he was a Frenchman as well as all the rest), the impressions remained, of scented nights, blatant days, of men and women walking a world old and new in one, old in the mysterious depths of tradition, new in the opportunities it afforded all who lived its unspoiled life. But there must be some other, easier way. A Gauguin, a Borgia tied to the deck of a ship, disciplined, abominably paid, offered glimpses of paradise then snatched from it—no, that was not the life. He was glad to leave it.

When he went to sea his mother could endure Orléans no more. She longed for Paris. She had friends there in her mother's admirers, the Arosa family; she moved near them, to St Cloud. But she did not enjoy Paris for long; she died there while her son was still at sea, died young like her mother. Gauguin came back in 1871 to find himself without a family and without a home; his sister had married a Chilean merchant, Juan Uribe; his mother's house, like the Arosa mansion, had been burned and pillaged by the victorious Prussians—all the family papers had been destroyed, all the valuables brought back from Lima had been stolen.

But he did not come back to nothing. His mother's last thought had been for him; before she died she begged Gustave Arosa to look after Paul. Arosa, a wealthy banker, did so in a more far-reaching manner than Aline-Marie could have dreamed possible. At first he gave practical help; he spoke to his son-in-law, a director of the firm of Bertin. On April 23, in his twenty-third year, Gauguin began work in the rue Laffitte and at the Bourse and took on the mantle of respectability.

But the anecdotes with which he was accustomed to enliven the story of his years at sea were anything but respectable. He had "committed my first sin" at Le Havre just before making his first voyage. He went on with gusto to describe the "sins" which followed thick and fast. Two will do. His predecessor on the ship handed him a letter for his mistress, a Madame Aimée who was singing Offenbach at one of the Rio theatres. Gauguin delivered the letter in person and the singer promptly threw overboard the absent for the present. "How handsome you are, my dear! Let me take a good look at you." She took a good long look—it lasted the full month the young Gauguin was in port: "An absolutely delightful month," he said. "I became a great rascal."

Madame Aimée taught well and had found a naturally gifted pupil. On the return voyage Gauguin stole from under his captain's jealous eyes the affections of a "fine fat Prussian". He and his Prussian "found a charming nest" in the sail locker and employed his spare hours in dalliance there. She, said Gauguin, was "deeply smitten" and begged for his home address. La Farcy, rue Joubert, Paris, he told her—the address of a well-known brothel. He was, he admitted with a grin, "a remarkable liar", although at the time he had felt twinges of conscience.

Whether he told these incidents to Mette is not known and is not of much moment. Like most men he had the displeasing habit of boasting to his chosen woman of earlier adventures in this kind. Men do so usually (whether they know it or not) to enhance their value in the eye of the beloved and to bring jealousy to support whatever attractions they may have. Gauguin, too, no doubt, although his manner of telling the stories differed from most. But the effect on Mette did not differ; she had to take reassurance where she could find it. That she understood Gauguin's love affairs, as she would have called them, was unlikely. It is an instinct of self-preservation in a loving woman to picture the young man led astray. But Mette was mistaken. To Gauguin all willing women were fair game. He was big, strong, healthy, he slept with women, as he ate his meals, to satisfy a large appetite. In like-minded company he never spoke of it—the fact was taken for granted. But when he scented squeamishness, disapproval, all the schoolboy in him came to the surface, he boasted of his conquests, enlarged, exaggerated, made the very worst of this, to him, most ordinary event. He did not spare Mette. "Oh, I was a great rascal"—that, with a sleepy twinkle of the half-hidden eye, was his attitude. What harm had he done? Those who dislike promiscuity will think considerable harm. Looking at the matter from his point of view he was no doubt right; as long as a woman kept out of love with him all was well.

6

But Mette had fallen in love. Or if that phrase is too strong—it is undoubtedly abused—she was flattered, attracted, excited. To her, marriage was the only freedom; the man who seemed likely to offer it at any moment appeared more eligible than she would have dared to hope before she left Denmark. If she mistook physical attraction and a substantial bank balance for love, it is a mistake often made. She listened as Gauguin's past was spread before her—something hidden, as something is always hidden, but enough revealed to warn her, not only in the facts but in the manner in which they were presented. She listened, but she would not be warned. She did not like much of what she heard though with an effort it could be dismissed as a romantic past. She made the effort, never considering that the past can become the future, that her suitor's ancestry, his admiration for Flora Tristan, his nostalgic memories of Lima, his wandering life—this and much more shouted aloud for caution. But no: men must talk about themselves; let him talk; rather out than bottled up inside, to explode later. Had he not long since of his own free will abandoned all but talk? And with the unconquerable vanity of the admired and fascinated woman she promised herself that he would find in her home and the family she would give him all the adventure he needed.

True there were, unavoidable even to the favourable eye, characteristics in this man which were to be regretted. There was that tendency to coarseness in convivial moments. There was more than a hint of what must be called irresponsibility. There was his—lust was the only word for it. Distressing, all of them. But were they not, and especially that last failing, a challenge to her, the good pure woman, the steadying influence? She thought so. She perhaps remembered the prettier and younger sisters at home, both of them engaged to be married. She could scarcely forget her own worrying age—for twenty-three and unmarried was in the eighteen-seventies a reproach. She agreed gladly, promptly, to an engagement. She agreed to marry him that same year, in November.

7

And Gauguin—what can be said of him? Like Mette he wanted a home. Visits to the homes of other men were as much irritants as pleasures; he was never a good guest and, homeless, was a difficult one, adopting the airs of master of the house, lazily expecting all to do his bidding. He was tired of living in rooms, he had endured two years of them after six years at sea. He longed, as the born wanderer will, for stability and security. He had a vision, visionary indeed but natural and in character, of himself surrounded in this home of his by a devoted wife and adoring family. He too wanted children, he was never at a loss with them. He had the wish, he had the money, he lacked only the woman. He was ready, more than ready, but nothing happened. He was not a society man, he detested small talk, he was ill at ease in drawing-rooms, his language when he did speak slipped only too often into the language of the fo'c'sle. He rarely met marriageable girls, his women were of another kind.

Then Mette appeared. With his limited experience of the respectable she seemed to him a charming revelation, intelligent, possessing a neat sense of humour much to his liking and a liveliness that contrasted happily with his stolidity. Physically he could ask for nothing better; he relished the strong, full-bosomed woman—Mette was this and handsome too. He pressed his suit. He won it without difficulty. He was exultant. To Madame Heegaard in Copenhagen he wrote letters, typical of his day and age, of his luck in "stealing so rare a pearl from Denmark".

He behaved like any other lovesick young man. He was lovesick (more so than Mette as time was to show) but he was not any other young man. He was not even a fool, but he was inexperienced in the ways of the respectable, he was vain, he was as always absurdly trustful, and his optimism almost passes belief. All intuitions, all observations were waved away.

Mette was cold, her blue eye was chilly despite its loving glances. Very well: who better fitted than Paul Gauguin to melt that ice? Mette was conventional. He saw that too. But like all men who break the conventions at will he sometimes hankered after them. Might not such a woman be just the woman for him, always ready to kick over the traces? Would he even want to kick over them any more? Gambling on the exchange—and successful gambling at that—was surely sufficient safety valve for that restless demon within. He wanted to think so. He thought so.

Mette was self-opinionated. That also was clear to him. The years without a father, the need to work early and support her family, the struggle with an imperious grandmother had strengthened her character but had hardened her too. But the most self-opinionated of women is usually willing to make the motions of submission to a man before marriage. Such arguments as they had would appear to Gauguin as merely an exciting challenge to the master he would soon become. Like all men he contributed to his own confusion. Normally he could not bear contradiction, he liked his women strong physically but mentally pliant, but as lover he affected a humility and sweet reasonableness which he could never maintain and he laughed delightedly at the obstinate, self-willed flashes in Mette without understanding that they were no lover's gambit but uncomfortable revelations of the truth.

Mette was a philistine. Not for nothing did she come from a family of civil servants; for all her charm, her education, she was a philistine. Her one true interest was a man and a home, prosperous, respectable, which she could run with efficiency and to the admiration of all neighbours. And with that home would come the one true love of her life—children. Even this did not escape Gauguin, but its implications were lost on him. His remedy was the remedy of an ostrich. He talked long and often to Mette. All his past history was opened before her—all but one apparently small item. Of this recent development—one that he could not possibly hide when married—he said not a word.

"*I had no idea* that he had a leaning towards the arts," complained Mette years afterwards—a typical remark, typically phrased. Not a word did he say of his interest in painting, not a hint did he give of his own tentative efforts to paint.

Why? She was bound to know. He never explained his silence; the cause of it must be sought in his subconscious. Somewhere in that rather bounderish stock exchange gambler something leapt up in protest and said No. And he obeyed and kept silent.

He obeyed but did not understand. Had he been told, "You are a serious man, she is not a serious woman," he would have laughed incredulously. Later he was to become preternaturally conscious of the blasphemy of exposing his feelings about his work. In the summer of 1873, when he believed that Mette was the wife for him and the Bourse his true vocation, an instinct wiser than the man enforced the strange silence; and Mette went back happy and triumphant to Denmark for her last few months of unmarried life ignorant that her lover had another love, and that one her deadly enemy.

Chapter Two

SUNDAY PAINTER

1871-1881

I

WHEN Gauguin joined Bertin in 1871 he met Emile Schuffenecker. Schuffenecker was a small dark-bearded Alsatian with large soft eyes shining behind spectacles, a mild and hesitant manner, a speech that broke easily into a stutter. He was timid and he was prudent.

At first glance he was not at all the man for Gauguin except for the appeal of one's antithesis, and this alone cannot explain the friendship. Gauguin not only did not suffer fools gladly, he did not suffer them at all; nor did he suffer prigs, prudes and bores. And Schuffenecker was often a bore; he was platitudinous, he had not an original idea in his head. But he was kind, he soon became devoted, he had a comfortable house and in that house he had, like so many plain and inconspicuous little men, a pretty, temperamental and unsatisfied wife. Gauguin began to make himself at home and the relationship between the two men took shape like most of Gauguin's friendships; a patronising affection on his side, an admiration not far from worship on the side of Schuffenecker.

"Schuff", as Schuffenecker naturally became, immoderately proud of this lordly young man, spread all his treasures before him. Chief among these was an enthusiasm for painting, which he practised in his spare time. He persuaded Gauguin to visit the galleries with him, the Louvre and the Luxembourg of course, but also the few galleries (at first only Durand-Ruel) which had the courage to show the moderns—the much abused Manet and his few admirers, Monet, Degas, Camille Pissarro, Renoir chief among them. And he was soon urging Gauguin to try his hand.

Gauguin needed little persuasion. He was not a stranger to good pictures. Arosa, a cultivated man, was forming a useful collection, including Delacroix, Courbet and Daumier, which Gauguin saw often at St Cloud during his week-ends at the re-built house. He could claim, moreover, that the blood of painters of a sort ran in his veins; he had, after all, though he did not talk about it, a grandfather who had been a lithographer and a great-uncle whose flower and animal studies had won limited praise.

More to the point, perhaps, he had leisure, he had money, he had boundless physical and mental energy which was not being used up in this new, respectable existence of his. He was taking to fencing at the Salle Hiacinte like a duck to water, he liked his game of billiards at the cafés, he liked his woman, he read an occasional book—the Bible, Shakespeare, Balzac were his standard fare—all this, yet time could hang. Schuff's suggestion was welcome and, in the light of the future, providential. For of course boredom was not all. The idea appealed to him. It struck a chord. He could not have said why and, being a man of deeds, did not waste time wondering. He wanted to, that was enough, and he got on with it. It was good fun, and within reason he was quite willing to hear the admiring Schuff telling him, without much obvious reason, that he had a gift for it.

By the time he first saw Mette at Madame Aubé's he was in the thick of a not very exhausting struggle to become a painter in fact, and he had begun to drop into the painter's cafés of an evening. He said nothing to her about it until after they had been married on November 22, 1873—married twice over, ironically enough, according to the custom of each country—at the town hall of the ninth quartier in the rue Drouot, and at the Lutheran church in the next street, the rue Chauchat.

Mette made no objection to this new interest. Every man is safer with a hobby—that is one of the first laws of the suburban wife; if her husband wished to be a "Sunday Painter", as the amateurs were named, he was welcome. Moreover, the ground for objection was taken from under her feet by the marriage of her sister Ingeborg to a Norwegian painter, Fritz Thaulow—no Sunday Painter, but a professional. And she liked and trusted the gentle Schuff, who was plainly neither restless nor reckless nor a genius. She may have had her doubts about his wife, whose looks were too good and whose manner to Paul was perhaps a shade too intimate, but Paul did not seem unduly interested, as indeed he was not by that time. So she agreed to his suggestion that they should take a small apartment near the Schuffeneckers, then in the rue Boulard in Montparnasse.

When, in August of the next year, she bore her first son, named Emile after Schuff, and less than two years later, in 1876, a daughter Aline, and watched the unmistakable pride and affection of their father, she must have thought, if she thought at all, that he, just as she, now had all that he could wish for. A loving wife, a growing family, a good friend, a prosperous job—what more could a man ask?

What indeed, except a reason for living. Gauguin continued to feel a steady affection for Mette (he did not look elsewhere, so far as is known, for some years), he was charmed with his children, he relished the pleasures that came from having plenty of money in his pocket, he even found something extremely satisfactory in domesticity although he proved to be not at all, in Mette's sense of the words, a ladies' man, and resolutely avoided parties and domestic chatter. Few people can resist the charm of a first home, and he made no attempt to. If he were to be judged by his few letters, he would indeed be all that Mette could wish. He wrote, as he had first talked to her and Marie Heegaard, with conventional sprightliness—quite the pillar of society. Coy compliments—"Why doesn't the fair Marie honour us?"; coy complaints—"Allow me to turn my eyes towards Denmark, where I see with sorrow two young girls so indifferent that they don't often answer our letters"—this was Gauguin the married man. One such intended in the same vein held, as these remarks often do, a truth that Gauguin was to find particularly unpalatable later on: "As you know, when she is unwell she hasn't exactly all the courage of a Christian martyr." This was Mette.

For the moment, however, he was like a man playing with toys. None of these things touched him deeply except perhaps his children. Yet he was not a trivial man, however much he liked to appear as one; he had strong feelings, and from two directions these feelings were so roused as to overwhelm all that had been built up in the peaceful years since 1871.

Schuff, a mild agent of destruction if ever there were one, played, all unconscious, the villain's part. He was very fond of Mette, the last thought in his mind was to come between her and his hero. He had no overwhelming ambitions and detected none in Gauguin.

All he saw was a talent greater than his own—a talent that it would be unfriendly in him not to encourage. Without difficulty he persuaded Gauguin to spend an evening or two with him each week at the nearby Académie Collarossi where they could draw and paint from the model.

That perhaps would have been sufficient to decide Gauguin's destiny. But within six months of Gauguin's marriage Thaulow paid a visit to Paris. He could and did advise. He looked at the sketches, spoke his mind, and Gauguin, not yet sure of himself, accepted criticism with uncharacteristic humility. He and Thaulow went over to St Cloud. The talk was all of painting. Thaulow gone, Gauguin continued his week-ends with Arosa. He brought his sketches. He made studies of the house. At home he sketched the children, he tried his hand at Mette and the children in the garden. Mette could not cavil at this harmless hobby. She was busy with the home and the children, she was proud of her steady husband who continued to make money hand over fist. She even humoured him, writing verses at the foot of one of his canvases in praise of his painterly skill.

But Gauguin meant business. They thought well of his work at the Collarossi, he began to think well of it himself. Pastime it might be, but one could excel even in a pastime. And he liked to excel. He was one of the smartest men on the floor of the Bourse, he was one of the best fencers in Paris, he could hold his own with the best at billiards, he could knock back his drink and keep a cooler head than most—why, then, could he not rival those nincompoops from the Beaux Arts? Within two years he had eyes on the Salon. As always when meditating a vital act, he kept his own counsel; in the next year, 1876, without a word he sent in a canvas, *Paysage à Viroflay*. It was accepted. It was no more than competent, like the pictures surrounding it.

This was the high-water mark of respectability in Gauguin's life. The conventional gesture over, he looked ahead. He too could see that the exhibits at the Salon were no worthier than his own. Was he a genius like the rest of the Ecole des Beaux Arts? Such a thought was enough to lessen the triumph. The Salon, however, had done what he wanted; it had answered his question, am I a painter or no? For the rest he had a keen nose for the pretentious. Not there his future.

A meeting at Arosa's house settled the matter; he was introduced to Camille Pissarro.

2

Pissarro had first become prominent—notorious would better describe the general attitude—two years earlier, in 1874, when thirty men and one woman ("Independents" as they called themselves) exhibited their work at the Nadar gallery. Though not the greatest among this company, Pissarro was the driving force in it. But for him there might have been no exhibition.

Gauguin, of course, had heard all about this exhibition—no one living in Paris and interested even mildly in art could have failed to hear about it—and although he nowhere says so, he must have seen it with Schuff and no doubt again with Thaulow. Gauguin's comments on the reception of the exhibition by the critics and public would have been amusing for their pungency if for nothing else, but he wrote few letters, and no records of his conversation at this time have been kept. He would be familiar with the name Impressionist—given to the group in disparagement by the critic Alfred Leroy because Claude Monet included a picture *Impression, Soleil Levant*. It was the big joke of the day. He would have read or have heard of the painters' protests against this nickname; but he, like everyone else, continued to use it; the name stuck. It is possible that he jeered like most of those who saw the exhibition, and agreed with the critics' conclusions—"aberrations", "infantile", "insanity". He may have relished the music-hall skit *La Cigale* on an Impressionist painter, greeted with an appreciative roar the cartoon showing an Impressionist picture upside down—just as sensible that way as any other, the newspaper declared—and read with a chuckle the novel written to make the movement a laughing-stock. All things are possible to a successful stockbroker and a man who, if not exactly buried in domesticity, has one foot in it. Certainly he was to exhibit at the Salon two years later, and the champions of the Salon were the bitterest opponents of the new movement.

And yet a doubt, or a hope, must remain. Impressionism was not, as its enemies implied, a movement springing from nowhere and breaking all tradition. It was a spontaneous and inevitable expression, in music, letters and the theatre as well as in painting, of the period—the period of renewed interest in the life and doings of the everyday man and woman, in science, and in that popular manifestation of science, photography. Its work criticised by implication not the masters of painting, to whom it owed much, but the reactionary and effete painters of the day—the members of the Beaux Arts who in the latter half of the nineteenth century were still busily painting and exhibiting pictures far removed not only from their own times but from life of any kind; pictures glossy, rigid and of a stultifying formality, modelled all too faithfully on the bygone masters, of Grecian nymphs, of battles long since forgotten, of famous nonentities, all painted in the dull tones considered appropriate to the dignity and venerability of the subjects.

Against this kind of thing the Impressionists rebelled. They were not Impressionists, they declared, they were *plein air* painters—they painted in the open air instead of the studio, they painted what they could see before their eyes instead of indifferently imagined versions of what no living man had seen; and what they saw as truly representing republican France was not the Sunday parade of the wealthy in the Bois de Boulogne but washerwomen, street-menders, boys and girls dancing, railway trains, jockeys, ballet girls; not Versailles or the rue Royale but Montmartre or the Rive Gauche. Their concern was with their own day and age and preferably with the little-regarded section of it; why look, they asked, to dead and gone times for inspiration when the world about them was so alive, so charming, so marvellous to paint? Their concern was to reproduce what they saw, not photographically but as the camera taught them to see it—that is, to reproduce light and the effect of light on objects.

But they were also Impressionists, deny the name though they might; the critic who christened them had chosen better than he intended; for the cardinal point of their art (and an essential one under the conditions in which they painted) was to seize at once and put on to canvas the effect of light as seen at a glance—the momentary effect of sunlight before clouds swallow it, for instance. This sprang directly from the photographs which for the first time isolated a moment of time. But the camera, though an instantaneous eye, was not an individual one. The individual eye was Impressionism, and perhaps its most important achievement, for it presented a unique work—the vision of one man at one particular moment, never again to be repeated. This encouraged at once the development of an eye for the transitory effects of nature—often the most beautiful—and of technical means to express these quickly and truly.

This double revolution, in subject and in treatment, was greeted with howls of derision: these men, declared the critics and the conventional painters, had not only deserted the dignity and beauty of their art by dabbling with unromantic subjects, but had produced paintings execrable in themselves—for to portray light the Impressionists had lightened their palettes to an extent undreamed of and had broken up the tones by applying their paint in tiny dabs of the brush.

But the lead of the critics and the academic painters was scarcely needed. The public gazed incredulously at canvases of a horrid lightness which when approached closely dissolved into a bright blur of tiny brush-strokes; and, reacting promptly and in the strictest tradition to the unusual, expressed uneasiness, alarm and lack of self confidence with anger and abuse. Who wanted to look at paintings which, when visible, showed nothing more exciting, romantic or noble than the common people and the common scene? The wretched Impressionists were mad, debased, dangerous. They should be suppressed. Was this what France, the land of great painters, had come to!

Of all this Gauguin heard much—the papers were full of it each time the Impressionists exhibited, in the spring of 1874 and again two years later; the conversation in every gallery, every café where artists gathered, turned inevitably and often with high words to the innovators. Even in the Bourse, where there hung proudly but unregarded a picture by Gérôme, one of the contemporary masters, for which fifty thousand francs had been paid—even there the Impressionists were good for a laugh.

But there was another side to the question and Gauguin heard it. He was familiar with the forebears of the Impressionists in Arosa's collection at St Cloud and in the galleries he constantly visited—and he found in the Arosas admirers not only of Courbet and Corot but of their legitimate descendants. Gustave Arosa often spoke about Pissarro and his friends, he had bought some of his canvases and his brother was about to commission a large work from him. Now there was Pissarro, in the Arosa drawing-room.

3

Camille Pissarro was a bulky, middle-sized man who looked more than his forty-six years because of the vast black beard that covered half his face and spread well down his chest. His father was a Portuguese Jew born in the West Indies and married there to a creole. His son's race was apparent in large dark eyes, hooked nose and easily impassioned manner. He usually wore a soft wide-brimmed black hat and a capacious but soiled and tattered black ulster which drooped comically about his broad shapeless figure. He looked what he was, with the disorder and the fire in his eye and the mane of bushy black hair on his neck and the beard stirring massively as he gesticulated and opened thick lips and shook an impatient head. Camille Pissarro was an exhibitionist in the better sense of the word, impulsive, generous, hot-tempered, good-hearted. He became known as the father of the Impressionists because he was so much the senior of most of them; he looked and sounded fatherly except when he became excited; but it was also a true title because of his indefatigable struggles to weld highly dissimilar men into a movement—he urged, wheedled, cajoled, argued his fellows into one exhibition after another. His enthusiasms —for he moved easily from one to another—were difficult to resist.

Gauguin did not say what he thought of him until years later when they had parted and his judgment had become suspect. But for all his sharp words then he remained grateful, as he ought. To dislike Pissarro was difficult, to feel impatience easy; but Gauguin wanted to learn; this fat, jovial Jew, breathless with emotion, great arms flapping, had much to teach. Gauguin listened.

And Pissarro? Pissarro loved and hated in breezy, choleric bursts. But chiefly he loved. A friend of the Arosas must be a friend of his. This large young man who sprawled about the chaise-longue at St Cloud was a dilettante, but a talented one. He was not perhaps as likeable as one could wish, nor as humble, but he wanted to know more about painting, that spoke well for him. He had exhibited at the Salon. To Pissarro that word was like a red rag to a bull. The Salon! But here was an exhibitor repenting of his stupidity and sin if not in so many words at least by listening. And this young man was made of money if Pissarro's eyes did not deceive him; he moved with the lazy assurance of the well-to-do, his clothes had cost a pretty penny, he was on the stock exchange. Here was that rare bird a purchaser in the making, a man who could commission pictures, a man who would meet an Impressionist without insult.

Poor Pissarro had long since learned to swallow his pride. He began to speak. He had much to say: the Impressionists had suffered for their faith, and not only in spirit; although almost all had been at starvation point during the past years, and could not sell their pictures, they would not paint in any other way; Sisley would never be the same man again after his privations; Monet's model had just died of hunger. He could name a dozen other cases. He, Pissarro, had lost one child, he was at his wits' end to know how to feed and clothe the three remaining. There might be others, and his wife scolded him and said "Why paint? Why not a decent job?" and he was often so short of cash that he could not even find the fare to Paris. And when he did find the fare?—Ah! life was one long round of begging trips, borrowing here, borrowing there, haunting the galleries of likely dealers, the clubs of the rare rich sympathiser. Hour after hour of exhausting, humiliating tramps about the pavements with the stomach rattling unless one had been lucky enough to find a friend in temporary funds. He looked plump—well, fat if you like. That was his misfortune. It was not the sign of a square meal every day—no, and not every week. He walked the streets hungry. The next day the same. And the next. Eternally.

But the game was worth the candle. All of it! At such moments the ludicrous in Pissarro disappeared; he was superb, godlike, his rotundity, his shabbiness were as nothing, he was a man with a mission. Impressionism—if the fools must call it so—was not finished, it was scarcely begun. Why, he and Monet were still hard at work trying to thrash out the truly scientific palette. They had cleared the palette. In their pictures so far they had used pure colours side by side, the three primary colours and their derivatives. They had done away with muddiness, they had let in the air, but there was far to go. Look at the shadow, for instance. Black said the simple, black painted the academical fools. But there was no black. It didn't exist. A black shadow was nonsense; a shadow in nature contained the colours of the spectrum. The effect of light alone gave it the appearance of blackness. How paint it in truth? And the bounding line; more nonsense, there was no such thing. Again the effect of light. How to convey the impression of a bounding line? All a question of the palette employed. And if it came to that, how and what did one see? What was perspective, what the illusion of solidity, of reality, but the effect of light?

Ah! there was much yet to be done—the scientific palette was still far away. But they would reach it, the Impressionists would find it, perfect it, and the generations to come would praise their name and the painters after them would build on the foundations they had laid. And not only the painters: in their own sphere the musicians with Debussy at the head were to discover a new world of impressions; music would take its tone from them in future ages. And the poets too were creating impressions in words. Revolutions all; a second and greater French revolution, for this was the enduring world of art that was being transformed—a world without frontiers and without end.

4

Gauguin, eyeing the perspiring Pissarro, felt—what? His actions are the best guide. He invited Pissarro home, visited him, bought a picture from him, he cleared his own palette and began to paint after the Impressionist manner. Pissarro was pleased—for an amateur this Gauguin showed promise. He encouraged him to begin collecting Impressionist canvases, to help the pioneers and eventually to help himself when the prices rose. He took him to the Nouvelles Athènes on the place Pigalle to hear the great ones talking, endlessly talking as the glasses slowly emptied and the fumes of tobacco, beer and coffee grew thicker.

There was Manet, the best-dressed painter Gauguin was ever to see, with his well-cut suit fitting the square shoulders and narrow hips in English fashion, the bowler hat pushed back on the fine forehead, the long pipe smoking far down in the sensitive left hand; one of the best-looking painters, too, with the wavy chestnut hair and frizzy beard slightly tinged with grey. He was plain spoken but good tempered, the man "whom no one annoyed". Gauguin heard his "the chief person in any picture is the light"; heard him laugh goodnaturedly at the sensation following the exhibition of his *Olympia* and *Déjeuner sur l'Herbe*, at the subsequent abuse—he was a monster, a rascal, a fiend—and the interview with the journalist out for scandalous copy. Manet told the story well, the attractive creases at the corners of his mouth broadening when he described the journalist's loud "M. Manet! M. Manet!" as he rose on tiptoe to peer over the heads of the customers, looked right, looked left, and ignored the small man sitting quietly, inconspicuous, immediately before him on a little chair, the picture of harmlessness. Then came the mild "Here I am, Monsieur," from the small man as the journalist was almost on the point of stepping over him; the journalist's pause, astounded, and his confused, "Ah! Pardon! I expected to see a giant, and I was looking everywhere for the grinning face of a jailbird."

A photograph of *Olympia* was pinned to the wall of Gauguin's workroom (he had no studio); he greatly admired and tried to follow it; evidently with some success, for when Manet one day looked at a canvas of his with a "Very good" and Gauguin answered deprecatingly "Oh, I'm only an amateur", the master replied with a decided "No. The only amateurs are those who make bad pictures."

Gauguin never forgot this encouragement, and listened with additional respect to the man who had given it. Sitting back, behind the masters round the marble-topped tables, he heard the repeated grate of the door on the sanded floor every time a customer came in, the chatter of the bodiless group at the bar whose hatted heads shifted about behind the glass-topped partition, but his attention was given to Manet and the others, and at first to Manet particularly. He stored up the comments: "Colour is a matter of taste and sensibility. For instance, it's necessary to have something to say; without that—*bonsoir!*"—"No one is a painter unless he loves painting more than everything else. It isn't enough to know your *métier*, it is necessary to be moved by it."—"Science is good but for us imagination is better"—and, when he had just come back behind the engine on the Versailles train, "What a magnificent sight, these two men, the driver and stoker! Their sangfroid, their assurance! These people are the modern heroes. I shall make a picture of them."

Not all thought like Manet or were so considerate to the outsider brought along by Pissarro, but fortunately for him they came less frequently to the Nouvelles Athènes. There was Monet, for instance; Monet for ever talking of the Manet exhibition which followed *Déjeuner sur l'Herbe*, the exhibition which brought him to the feet of the master and virtually began the Impressionist movement; Monet of the bluff, handsome face, the all-seeing eye, the coloured half-Tam O' Shanter, half-beret perched on the grand head of black hair, the big foursquare black silk bow at the neck, the hint of coming corpulence below. Monet did not care for Gauguin and made little secret of it; he didn't approve of amateurs and professionals mixing, he said. Perhaps, for he was a proud man, the thought of Gauguin's money made him distant; but the young stockbroker's manner grated on him too. Gauguin could be difficult even in such company; scenting dislike or patronage, he would rouse himself from his schoolboyish reverence and break arrogantly into the discussion with some wild statement.

Possibly this aspect of the visitor alienated Renoir also; for the delicate, ascetic-looking Auguste Renoir who painted studies of robust women, the mournful-faced Renoir who put, as no other man had done, youth and happiness into his *Moulin de la Galette*—he too shied away from Gauguin after a while. He may have suspected that this amateur was not serious; he was neither the first nor the last to be deceived.

But Degas rather took to him. Degas had money and could afford to be lenient, Degas had a sarcastic tongue and could relieve his feelings. He sat there like a patrician eagle—more like a lawyer than an unorthodox painter, said Gauguin, with his rounded shoulders, his eyes shielded by blue glasses, his umbrella, glossy top-hat and pepper-and-salt suit—and he dealt out sharp blows at the academicians. "La peinture avait d'abord été le café noir," he would say in his precise, cultured voice, "le café au lait, maintenant c'est le lait." For that matter he would spar with anyone handy; he and Manet were often at odds; he would reply to Manet's "Degas was painting *Semiramis* when I was painting *Modern Paris*" with a "Manet is in despair because he can't paint atrocious pictures like Durand and be fêted and decorated; he is an artist by force not by inclination." Gauguin would smile; this was humour of his own kind—one of his kinds at least. Degas smiled occasionally at his own tentative thrusts, and that was a compliment indeed. Degas after a time inclined to agree with Pissarro that the persistent young man had talent.

With some at the Nouvelles Athènes—Caillebotte and the melancholic Sisley, for instance—Gauguin had little to do. They were more of an age with him, they had not the stature of the masters, and they resented him. But he sat often with Pissarro's friend and pupil, Armand Guillaumin, an amateur like himself though more advanced. Guillaumin was a likeable man, lively and cheerful and exceptionally optimistic, looking week by week with touching faith to the national lottery to deliver him from his stool at the Department of Bridges and Embankments.

The effect of these evenings was soon seen. Gauguin began to haunt the gallery of Paul Durand-Ruel and Père Tanguy's paint-shop in the rue Clauzel where he could also see Impressionist canvases and the work of that mysterious figure, Paul Cézanne. He began to buy these pictures—they were an investment, he told Mette. He bought Monet, Pissarro, Manet, Renoir, Cézanne, Sisley Guillaumin as well as Daumier and Jongkind. Within a year or two he reckoned that his collection was worth fifteen thousand francs. The business sense on which he prided himself may have been satisfied by the purchases, but it was not the main reason why he made them. He hoped to buy himself into the favour of the group—a not unreasonable calculation and typical of him at that time. But most of all he admired and wished to study the Impressionist technique.

He did study the canvases thoroughly and at ease, for in 1877 he moved his growing family to a large apartment at 77 rue des Fourneaux, off the interminable rue de Vaugirard and still close to the faithful Schuff. There he could put up Pissarro and provide more space for the children. But chiefly he moved because the new apartment had a room that could be made into a studio. He made it into a studio. He painted, painted, after the Impressionist manner. Perhaps he hoped that he would be invited to hang a picture or two at the Impressionist exhibition of that year. He was not invited. Pissarro no doubt would have wished it, but Monet and Renoir would not exhibit with an amateur, and certainly not with Gauguin. Gauguin, disappointed, turned his hand to other uses. The owner of the apartment lived next door; he was Bouillot, the sculptor, a friend of Aubé. Gauguin took lessons from him, was soon modelling in clay and shortly afterwards was working direct in marble. Bouillot was delighted with these works—busts of Mette, Emile and Aline. But Gauguin's sensitive hands and sure sense of form were put to best advantage when he began to work in wood; a statuette of Mette shows even so early how he was to master this material.

5

Mette, who now had two children and was expecting a third, was beginning to grow uneasy: where was this business acumen of which she heard so much? To invest money in the work of men who were blackguarded up hill and down dale seemed queer if not absolutely crazy. But then her husband was plainly infatuated—not with another woman—that she could have dealt with—but with an idea; and, as she discovered, one cannot lay hands on an idea. Did Gauguin dream of becoming a painter? Was he so mad? Yet what could she think when he was off evening after evening to classes, to exhibitions, to that café across the river where those new cronies of his talked on and on about a discredited theory? Except for one, she had never seen these men, she had only read abuse of them, but that one was enough to damn the whole lot. Camille Pissarro might be the fine artist her husband claimed; all she could see was that he made an undesirable guest; he was shabby, far from respectable, almost certainly a cadger and, what was most serious, he was leading his admirer astray, filling his mind with absurd notions. She could keep an eye on him when he came to her house, distasteful though it was, but what of Gauguin's week-ends at his home in Pontoise—what went on there?

Gauguin was a good husband, a good father; he kept her and the children almost in luxury, he worked hard. He was obviously fond of her, proud of his fine home, absurdly wrapped up in the children. But there were the spare hours swallowed up, every one of them, the hint of bohemianism in his clothes of an evening, the impossibility of talking to him. For he simply would not talk; he shut up like a mule on this subject. Kicked like a mule too, with those savage ironies of his. And Thaulow was a thorn in her flesh. He never forgot his brother-in-law Thaulow. There was Schuff; she could talk to him. But Schuff, though kind, was a broken reed; he had followed Gauguin to the Salon in 1877 and was now busy following him in the Impressionist manner. All he could do in the way of reassurance was to point to himself: he painted; could he be considered as reckless or even injudicious? No one could consider the mild and cautious Schuff as either; a steadier, a more devoted family man never existed. Mette had to get what comfort she could from that. His wife led him a pretty dance, it was true, but that, Mette saw, had nothing to do with his painting. But Schuff was not Gauguin.

What Gauguin really thought Mette could never find out. He was a silent man at the best of times after that one outbreak of story-telling, and he remained as close as an oyster. That he was becoming obsessed by this hobby of his was clear, for in 1879 he moved again a few hundred yards away to a house in the rue Carcel—a house owned by the painter Jobbé-Duval—with a huge studio so that he might have more room to paint and entertain his painter friends.

By 1880 his cultivation of Pissarro had its effect. Pissarro after gigantic efforts arranged an attenuated Impressionist exhibition. He wanted to invite Gauguin and was supported by Degas, who had watched the amateur's progress with approval. Monet and Renoir refused to exhibit, the threatened presence of Gauguin providing sufficient excuse: "the small church," declared Monet, "has become a banal school which opens its doors to the first dauber who knocks." Both men moved over to the Salon, where Monet's work met with unexpected approval. Without them the fifth Impressionist exhibition opened in April in the rue des Pyramides. Gauguin was represented by several landscapes: *Pommiers de Vaugirard*, *Ferme à Pontoise*, *Pommiers de l'Ermitage*, *La Sente du Père Dupin*. They created no stir; all that was heard of them was the verdict of the critic J. K. Huysmans that "in landscape M. Gauguin's personality has hardly escaped yet from the influence of his master, M. Pissarro."

6

This was just; what it did not and could not be expected to recognise was the achievement of this amateur, virtually untaught, in raising himself to the level of such company. That he appeared by merit and not because of his money can be verified by anyone who studies his entries. These paintings are pleasant but undistinguished because Gauguin had not found himself as a painter, he had not, in the jargon of that time, discovered his individual vision, his "sensation".

But he was satisfied for the moment; he had been recognised, he was a painter. He was also doing very nicely on the Bourse. Could he have the best of both worlds? It seemed that he could; and it was a man in good spirits who the following year, 1881, spent his holidays at Pissarro's house in Pontoise. Guillaumin was there too, using his free time in the same way. Cézanne was also painting in the village.

Gauguin, like many another, thought Cézanne a queer bird. "His face resembles an ancient from the Levant." To others he looked like a cross between peasant and shop-keeper, bourgeois to the core in his clothes, his speech, his caution, his closeness, his crustiness– in everything in fact but his art. And even there he managed to turn art into a medium for quarrels. He seemed to go out of his way to be contentious, would exhibit nowhere but at Père Tanguy's shop after 1877, presented a scowling face to all advances. Gauguin's charm, such as it was, ran off Cézanne's back; all the persevering stockbroker got for his trouble was a grunt, a slight raise of a black eyebrow above small suspicious eyes, and a tighter clamp of the obstinate lips. Only the genial and persevering Pissarro had managed to keep on good terms with him, though even Pissarro could not bring him back to the Impressionist fold.

But what an artist! Gauguin, who had not hung about Père Tanguy's shop for nothing, found a strength and simplicity in Cézanne's work that appealed enormously to him. Put beside Pissarro—they painted studies of similar subjects—Cézanne had a spare, vigorous attack that made Pissarro's delicate treatment appear weak and fussy. Already Cézanne, applying a watercolour technique to oils, was abandoning impasto, painting with thin, clear brushstrokes of flat colour that lightened and strengthened his work. Already he was stripping his pictures of inessentials, conveying the bony structure of a scene. Already, to emphasise his forms, he was experimenting with an outline, usually of pale blue. As a rule he took away the blue, but something remained, the faintest indication of a bounding line.

Gauguin saw the effect, but the method escaped him. How did

Cézanne do it? But the man resembled his work; he was not forthcoming; he was developing his "*petite sensation*" and he was not passing it on. If other men wanted to find their "sensation", let them work for it as he did. Gauguin, rushing in with a blunt question or two, tried the taciturn man's patience; Cézanne thought him an ass, then a dangerously prying ass; for when Gauguin reached home he scribbled off a note to Pissarro: "If Cézanne finds the recipe for compressing the exaggerated expression of his 'sensations' into a single, unique procedure, please try to make him talk in his sleep by administering one of those mysterious homeopathic drugs and come to Paris as soon as possible to tell us all about it."

The expansive Pissarro, incapable of keeping anything to himself and not above a bit of gossip, passed the note on. The result was quite alarming. So! This fool of a Sunday painter was trying to filch hard-won secrets! From that moment Cézanne had done with Gauguin and never had a good word for him—least of all when the later Gauguin proved himself both great painter and admirer. To Cézanne, the man was a thief, a poseur, a trifler: he never forgave the note, he never forgot the hours when Gauguin was not painting; the bawdy jokes, the cognacs tossed off with indecent speed, the fo'c'sle language, the talk of women—yes, and may be not stopping at talk. He, a painter! Yet Cézanne was mistaken; Gauguin was in this matter a serious man, as serious as Cézanne himself. In Cézanne he had found his second outstanding influence, an influence minor only to Pissarro.

Even Pissarro, though encouraging, saw no future for Gauguin as a painter. Talent he had, he had made strides; but he remained derivative, he showed no obvious originality; Huysmans had said the last word on him. Sunday painter he was, Sunday painter would he remain. It was a common judgment; and there is nothing to show that Gauguin then thought otherwise; he was, he felt, a stockbroker first, painter second. Yet he had already, in the months preceding the Pontoise visit, given the lie to himself and the others.

Like most important events, this arose casually. Gauguin had followed the Impressionist lead in subject as in technique; they were primarily landscape painters, he would be one too. Then, egged on perhaps by Degas, who was more versatile than his companions, or by Manet's recent *Le Tub* and *La Toilette*, he decided to try his hand at the nude. At this point Mette, mother now of a third child, Clovis, and expecting a fourth, put her foot down. Gauguin might paint in the rue de Vaugirard, by the banks of the Seine or even at Pontoise if he insisted; but bring models into her house he should not. And he, possibly dubious of risking a struggle about nothing more than an experiment, gave way. Or was it that he had discovered that a one-time model was actually living in the house with them? Justine, the new children's *bonne*, had posed in the nude for Delacroix. And so it came about that Justine, sitting in the nude on her bed, was his next subject.

Chapter Three

ETUDE DE NU

1881-1883

I

A FAMOUS art critic has described *Etude de Nu* as one of the greatest studies of the nude in the history of French art. He did not exaggerate; but if the unrewarding game of comparison is abandoned, the effect of this picture on the future of painting the nude, like the effect of the mature Gauguin, remains enormous, incalculable. But the mature Gauguin is at least explicable; this nude of 1881 is not; it came into being like a bolt from the blue, without rhyme or reason; at one moment Gauguin is painting as one would expect him to paint at that early stage, at the next he is painting a masterpiece.

How did this nude—his first—differ from almost all nudes that had preceded it? The composition—well contrived—and the execution—simple, a little severe—good though they are (remarkable in fact when one considers the limitations of the artist), are less interesting than the question: how was Gauguin able to give this nude what no other painter of his time had done? Gauguin applied to the nude the principles applied by the Impressionists to landscape. It is an essay in naturalism. And as technically he was far behind his great contemporaries, his triumph is not first and foremost a technical one. It is best understood by looking first at the nude in the hands of those who had painted before him.

At first sight one would say that familiarity would apply to the nude as to any other subject. But it is not so; the painter is a man like any other, brought up in clothes and to clothes. To him the female nude, paint it a thousand times though he may, is always a woman unclothed; he may not be interested in his model, but her nudity is not a natural state in the civilised world. He may not be aware of his subconscious feelings—habit is a powerful deceiver—but they act on him whether recognised or not. And he knows that to the public, for whom he is painting the picture, nudity is even less of a natural state. As a result his nude is always and obviously a woman posed. Indeed, the painter made a virtue of it; he posed his model heroically, in the classical style. The result is not inspiring as intended, because it is lifeless; these women, even when the painter paints them in abandoned or inviting attitudes, are no more than dummies.

And as if to make sure of artificiality the painter deliberately painted and posed his model out of nature, far removed from reality. Her flesh is firm, flawless, her buttocks half concealed or slimmed, her belly flattened, her shoulders elegantly drooped (with the breasts partly concealed) or braced beautifully, but as no woman naturally stands or sits so that the breasts are pulled firm and shapely. But even here the painter was not satisfied; the breasts, tautened though they are by this artificial shoulder-straightening, remain as all breasts must remain, with an unmistakable sag, increasing with age, above the nipple. This sag the painter ignored, giving his models impossibly firm round breasts. So in two respects—in his subconscious attitude towards the nude and in his deliberate idealisation of the nude (the one a logical outcome of the other)—the artist set up a convention in this genre. The convention had been established through centuries and accepted for centuries. Then, with a single study, Gauguin shattered it.

He painted Justine sitting on her bed mending her chemise. Her shoulders droop almost to the point of being hunched, her breasts (in full view) sag, her belly protrudes, the girth of her buttocks is emphasised by the sitting posture. Her flesh is a little slack, slightly muddy. Her face is neither beautiful nor plain, her expression in no way remarkable. She is, in fact, a woman, any reasonably good-looking woman in the late thirties caught in repose, making no effort, taking no trouble to appear at advantage. The effect, in words, is unattractive, even formidable. In the painting it is not so; there the effect is one of beauty because it is life; this woman thinks, talks (probably with an indifferent accent), she can be an angel, a devil, she relishes a good gossip, she probably darns well, she has capable hands, she has a sharp tongue but a kind heart, she is past her best but, being French, she has not lost hope. There she sits, slightly slumped—a living, breathing woman. One would swear that she is not posed but had been seen unawares by Gauguin and painted at once. And that, indeed, is more than likely. That Gauguin could live in a house with a woman as attractive as Justine and not make her his mistress is unlikely. What more probable than that, after lying with her one day, walking about her room dressing himself, he turned to see her sitting thus on the bed, her chemise in one hand, a needle in the other, about to sew up the tear, thinking —what? And the artist in him leapt at the chance. What a picture! She had been a model, she could hold the pose if pose it could be called.

Stay as you are! Gauguin would shout. Just like that. He fetches his things, hangs a mandoline on the wall to give the necessary balance, looks through narrowed eyes—eyes bright for once. Magnificent! What a picture! That is supposition with a strong tinge of likelihood. What is certain and obvious is that the picture is a triumph of naturalism. The background is contrived, but nothing else. But why? And why from Gauguin—of all people, one might add without thought—the sensual Gauguin, the Gauguin who delighted in smutty stories, the very man who might be expected to produce a suggestive picture when he tackled the nude.

But Gauguin, though his sexual habits resembled those of many men, was not as they. He was sensual, but he was also cold. And he was not prurient. To him a nude woman was everything but also nothing, she was exciting but she offered no surprises. An ordinary man sits down to a good dinner with an appetite. His salivary glands begin to work, he is filled with pleasurable anticipation, but he does not get violently excited; he has seen and tasted food for as long as he can remember. He enjoys without wonder and certainly without embarrassment. So it was with Gauguin; he lay down with a woman as he sat down to his food. In a sense he did not think of her as nude; of course she was nude—how else should he lie down with her? And that was the beginning and end of his thoughts on nudity except—and it is a vital exception—that as an artist he saw its possibilities as no other man had seen them.

How did this come about? Nothing could be simpler or more obvious. Gauguin had been accustomed to nudity as to food since his childhood. Lima had left its mark; there nudity and semi-nudity was the rule amongst the poor and the native servants; no one considered it. The child Gauguin played with the half-naked girl, slept with her naked. All about him he saw nakedness. Four years in the life of a child can be decisive for the man. In this respect it was so for Gauguin. He was not only accustomed to the nude and unaffected by it, he also held it in his mind as the very reverse of what it stood for amongst all the men he mixed with; to him it was the normal state, a state urgently desired, a state to revert to at the earliest possible moment; to him it was the symbol of freedom, health, sanity. "I'm a savage," he would explain later. "I come from the Borgias of Aragon, but—I'm also a savage." And it was true.

These thoughts had been pressed out of sight by years of "civilised" life; perhaps he was no longer conscious of them, he might be thought to have "grown out of" them; but they were there, and when, as now, he was suddenly taken with the wish to paint Justine, they expressed themselves wordlessly. The *Etude de Nu* is a great painting not only because it is the first naturalistic nude, forerunner of a new trend not yet exhausted, but because it is the expression of Gauguin's innate and passionate conviction.

2

Etude de Nu was included in the Impressionist Exhibition of 1881 (again without Monet and Renoir) and was at once hailed by Husymans as a masterpiece; "I do not hesitate to affirm that among contemporary painters who have worked at the nude not one has so far struck such a relevant note of reality, and I don't except Courbet whose *Femme au perroquet* is as little true, as little orderly, as little flesh as the *Femme coucheé* of Lefèvre or the cream *Vénus* of Cabanel. Here is no show, this is a girl of our own day and one who doesn't pose for the gallery, who is neither lascivious nor simpering, who occupies herself usefully by mending her clothes. I am happy to acclaim a painter who has felt, like me, a strong disgust for mannequins with round rosy breasts and flat hard bellies, mannequins posed according to a *soi-disant* good taste and drawn according to the rules learned by copying plaster casts. . . . Up to now Rembrandt alone has painted the nude."

Degas was particularly struck by the canvas. If Gauguin did get an inkling of the naturalistic treatment of the nude from anyone it was certainly from Degas, whose pastels of women at their toilet, though not strictly nudes, show a similar objective view of the model for a very different reason, since Degas was not sexually interested in women. But all in the circle were congratulatory and Pissarro positively ecstatic.

This, surely, was fame. But Huysmans apart, the critics ignored the painting as, virtually, they ignored the exhibition. Gauguin's satisfaction remained limited. Perhaps, as he expressed no resentment, he did not realise what he had done. However, everyone who had seen the nude waited, some with curiosity, others eagerly, according to their view of Gauguin, for his next work. They had to wait some time, until the next Impressionist exhibition, for Gauguin was not communicative.

After a struggle more prolonged even than usual (Monet and Renoir held out through a full and heated month of argument before they could be persuaded on the casting vote of Degas to exhibit with Gauguin) the exhibition opened in March 1882. It should have been a great occasion, with the return of the two great men and the mystery of the wealthy stockbroker painter of *Etude de Nu*, but as far as Gauguin and his well-wishers were concerned it was a wretched anti-climax. To the general astonishment he exhibited nothing but landscapes in the Impressionist manner with the Pissarro influence once more heavily in evidence. Huysmans, greatly disappointed, dismissed his entries with a short: "No progress here, alas. This year, nothing worth while. At most I will quote as being more valid than the rest the new view of Vaugirard church. As for his *Intérieur d'Atelier*, the colour is dull and scurfy."

Why had Gauguin gone backwards? No one knows. That Mette was at least partly responsible can be confidently assumed. Justine sat no more as model. Justine lived no longer in the rue Carcel. The nude was banned.

Whether in addition to intervention from Mette there was some indecision, some falling away of purpose in Gauguin cannot be known. But from that moment his future was settled. "Dull and scurfy!" "No progress here!" He never spoke to Huysmans again, but he took his judgment to heart. It was not so much a judgment of the canvases he had exhibited as of the double life he was trying to lead. Had he received more praise, who can tell how long he would have continued this life? But praise had come to an end; he was once more a Sunday painter, a shadow of Pissarro.

During the next few months he was silent. He continued to paint, to drink and play billiards at the cafés, to fence, to buy pictures, to amuse himself with his children, to sleep with Mette and perhaps not with Mette alone. But a struggle was going on. It was now clear that there could be no compromise; if he chose to live on the fat of the land, then a Sunday painter he must remain. And he knew now that he was not a Sunday painter. He was a painter. He would be a great painter. Manet's "No one is a painter unless he loves painting more than everything else" was a warning and a challenge; he had ignored the warning, now he was confronted by the challenge.

Still he hesitated. No doubt he thought of Mette, for she represented the substantial, conventional life that he was by no means anxious to cut himself off from, she had been loyal, she had given him a good home, she loved him after her fashion and he her. He thought of his children. There were four (Jean had been born the previous year) and there would soon be five. He loved them all, Aline and Clovis particularly, but all. But chiefly he thought of himself. He was thirty-four, going on thirty-five. He had had nearly eleven years of easy living. He liked putting his hand in his pocket and living up to the superior being he felt himself to be. He liked the hail-fellow-well-met atmosphere of the Bourse, he liked his reputation as a daringly successful stockbroker. How did he know that he would succeed as a painter—the Impressionists had struggled for years and most of them were struggling still to make enough to eat? Was he greater than they? Had he not begun too late? Perhaps intimations of the future troubled him.

But in the end the optimist, the vain, the proud, the adventurous, the selfish, the strong—in a word, Gauguin the artist—had his way. Mette with all her virtues was a philistine, and a hostile philistine at that. Look at her reception of the nude, her attitude to painting, to art of any kind, the sneers at Pissarro, the indifference to the exhibitions! Perhaps she would love art when she had been chastised through art. The children would grow up, go their ways—was he to sacrifice his future for them and give them a hypocrite for a father?

And Gauguin being Gauguin, was it not fantastic to imagine anything but success? Had he ever failed at anything?

When he acted, he did so as always, suddenly and secretly. He said nothing to Schuff, nothing to Mette. He waited until Mette was safely over the birth of her fifth child, Paul, then, at the beginning of the new year 1883, he came home with his news; he had resigned from Bertin's; he was going to be a painter.

Chapter Four

ROUEN

1883

I

"NOW," said Gauguin, "I will paint all the time." This was no more than an anticipation when he said it, for he had burnt only half his boats. He had arranged to lend Bertin a hand for one year, until the beginning of 1884. This gave him plenty of time to prepare his plans. And he had been offered his job back if he wanted it.

He thought this cautious, businesslike. He was always to consider himself the businessman turned artist, but never more so than now. Schuff talked of leaving Bertin and giving himself more time to paint—Schuff, who had scarcely a grain of genuine talent! The argument was understandable but false: Schuff no longer needed Bertin; Schuff had two children and would have no more; Schuff saved his money, invested it in property, prudently bought and sold on the Bourse. Schuff really was a businessman.

The idea of a return to Bertin was, of course, little more than a sop to the alarmed and angry Mette. As a serious thought it was revolting to Gauguin's pride, unthinkable and in any case quite unnecessary; he was going to make money by painting as he had made it on the Bourse. How unthinkable a return to Bertin or to business in any shape really was he then had no notion; he was still, consciously, the "sharp" one, always a step ahead of the crowd; he was merely changing the crowd, that was all.

He began by experimenting with designs for Impressionist tapestries—the first stage of a larger plan, to transform industrial art. He was so full of the money to be made that when he went in the summer to Pissarro (now at Osny) for some weeks of painting his comments on the untimely death of Manet were almost perfunctory. Even his condolences on the failure of the one-man exhibition Pissarro had just held at Durand-Ruel fell some way short of adequacy. What did it matter? was his attitude. Trust me.

Here's a fortune going begging. You people have been painting for years, but you've had to wait for me to come along and exploit you. And I will. "Do something revolutionary," he urged; and Pissarro, who would try anything, still desperately hard up and awed by Gauguin's manner, promised hopefully. Perhaps he really would lead them all to financial success.

They sketched each other and painted together as before. Pissarro was encouraging—his bursts of optimism were more infectious than sound—and Gauguin's enthusiasm for industrial art began to cool. Looking at the studies they had made he was inclined to agree with his host—they were pretty good, and his not always the less good. He would exhibit at the next Impressionist show and perhaps he would surprise one or two people. He went home determined to spend every spare moment at his easel.

Later that summer Pissarro moved to Rouen to paint. In Paris he and Gauguin had both met a queer friend of Guillaumin, Eugene Mürer. This man, a chef by profession, had for some years given meals to the half-starving Impressionists in exchange for canvases. He wrote a novel, dabbled in painting, and finally took shares with his sister in a hotel in Rouen, showing there as a free advertisement his now extensive Impressionist collection. His praise of the town as a painter's paradise brought Pissarro there posthaste.

All this Pissarro reported glowingly to Gauguin—altogether too glowingly: the views were superb and, an afterthought, the people seemed to have plenty of money. Gauguin fixed his mind, as befitted a businessman, on the afterthought. People with money! Mürer with his permanent exhibition had familiarised them with the Impressionist technique. What could be easier than to relieve them of some of this money in exchange for Impressionist pictures painted by himself? Should they not buy all, the exhibition in Paris that Pissarro was arranging would benefit by their stupidity.

The thought was no sooner in his head than it became an accomplished fact. He would soon be free of Bertin; the Impressionist tapestry designs—well, the idea had not worked out too well, the manufacturers were "imbeciles" hidebound beyond belief, the public taste was unbelievable. No other money-making scheme had occurred to him, he had savings enough for a year, he would be wise to give up the big house and leave expensive Paris—and of course he wanted to try out his arm in fresh surroundings. Durand-

Ruel told him that Pissarro's work had improved greatly at Rouen. He wrote off to Pissarro; he would come down, scout out the ground. He warned Mette: Rouen was likely to be their new home.

Pissarro received the news with dismay. He was painting better at Rouen—that was true—but he was not a penny the better off for it. In fact, he had run so short of cash that he had been forced to turn to the obliging Mürer, who gave him a room for a pittance. "Gauguin is planning to take Rouen by storm!" he cried ironically to his son Lucien. How could the man be so naïve? And not only naïve: "He disturbs me greatly, he is so deeply commercial. . . . I regard it as a waste of time to think *only* of selling. One forgets one's art and exaggerates one's value."

To Gauguin, however, he proposed to say nothing—"I haven't the heart"—but of another matter he had to talk, though with reluctance. The exhibition in Paris was not to be. Like Pissarro and Sisley, but with more success, Monet and Renoir had held one-man exhibitions earlier in the year. They had done with group showings. Even Pissarro, disheartened for once, called a halt: "We have had enough exhibitions." But Gauguin had to be told: Pissarro knew the hopes he had placed on showing the works painted since his decision to leave Bertin: "What will Gauguin think, what will Gauguin say! The fact is, he has his reputation to make. I really don't know what to say to him."

What he said or how he said it is not known; but when Gauguin visited Rouen in November the blow glanced off him. He found a house, all would be well. Rouen would fall to the invader.

His attitude annoyed Pissarro. They differed ostensibly about Gauguin's politics—he favoured (or so he informed the too easily baited Pissarro) a jingoistic foreign policy, praised the taking over of Annam and Tongking by the French, the sending of Gordon to the Sudan by the English. Pissarro, a strong radical, rose to the bait without a struggle. "He's always on the wrong side of the bastards," he growled after an evening of argument. But what really annoyed him was Gauguin's vanity. For a man not yet even a professional painter to breeze into a town and announce that he would sweep the board where his master had considered himself lucky to sell two or three pictures, would educate a public that had solidly turned its back on the great Impressionists—no, it was too much.

But perhaps it was best to laugh. Pissarro, never far from a guffaw, shrugged huge untidy shoulders. Let him get on with it: he had not forgotten the fiasco of the Impressionist tapestries, he had long thought Gauguin too cocky, and he had a suspicion that Gauguin was beginning to think him old-fashioned. Very well; let them see what up-to-date business methods would do for a painter who had still to learn his a b c—and not least, that painting and business didn't mix. He went back to Osny soon afterwards and left the would-be conqueror to his spoils.

It is not difficult to imagine Mette's feelings during this year, and her later attitude confirms imagination. She did not believe in her husband as an artist, she thought him selfish, thoughtless, cruel. But her resentment often wavered into sheer bewilderment. For Gauguin had no doubts: he would not only paint the pictures, he would sell them. His manner was so assured that even after ten years of marriage Mette more than half succumbed to it. He was a masterful man, decisive and resolute. Was he a genius after all? Nothing that she saw suggested it; but she must have asked herself whether a man who had no genius would be so mad as to throw up so good a job, or so rash as to uproot his wife and children and plunge them all without reason into a strange town and a new life. Could vanity alone account for it? She did not know. She had been married for ten years, but she now realised for the first time that she did not know her husband. He was as confident about the success of his painting as he had been about the rise and fall of shares on the Bourse. The shares had risen and fallen as he predicted. She could only hope against hope that he had not lost his gift for prophecy. And in that mood of doubt, fear and hope, she packed and moved with him and the children to Rouen in January 1884.

Chapter Five

COPENHAGEN

1884-1885

I

In less than a year—by November 1884—the Gauguin family was in Copenhagen. Rouen had not fallen to the invader; it had resisted his business attacks with such determination that not one Gauguin picture entered a Rouen home and not one Rouen franc entered a Gauguin pocket. Instead, Gauguin francs were spread liberally amongst Rouen shopkeepers—so liberally that in spite of economies by the shocked Mette the savings melted away; Gauguin's year shrank week by week; by November he was well on the way to beggary.

He went to Copenhagen and not to Paris and Bertin because the period away from the Bourse had been decisive. The pictures that Rouen rejected, though still Impressionist in manner, had begun to show a certain strength and simplicity—partly the effect of a growing admiration for Cézanne but also a sign that an individual painter was asserting himself.

Even more was the painter asserting himself in determination. He had far to go; his figure work in particular was uncertain—to the end of his life he sketched over the pencilled squares used by every beginner. But when one remembers that he had never had regular tuition in his life, that the occasional evening at the Collarossi and a few odd weeks of instruction from Pissarro represented all the outside help he had been given, the fact that he could paint at all well is significant of much. He did not miss the significance; it encouraged him to such an extent that the Rouen rebuff, instead of bringing out all the businessman, merely roused all the artist. There was vanity in this, of course—vanity was mixed with most of Gauguin's motives—but vanity was overridden by conviction of another and nobler kind. He was a painter, he would be a great painter.

Rouen, after all, was only a miserable little seaport. When the harassed Mette said, "We must go home," Gauguin saw in the suggestion not an acknowledgment of defeat but the opening of an opportunity greater by far than anything Rouen could offer. In Copenhagen he had friends—no, why mince words, admirers in the powerful Heegaards, and he flattered himself that he would charm the Gad family as he had charmed them. In Copenhagen the Impressionist technique was unknown, they were still painting a hundred years behind the times. And he was on his own! No rivals, and the chance to convert an entire country, to win quick fame, to make a fortune. He set off into exile with positive abandon.

But alas, a successful stockbroker and an unsuccessful painter are two very different men. The Heegaards saw in the painter only a man who had deliberately given up an honourable position for a mad and egoistic whim. The Gad family contemplated with frigid disapproval the ne'er-do-well who landed himself and wife and no fewer than five young children on them, not through misfortune (they flattered themselves, perhaps rightly, that they would not be backward in such a case) but through sheer selfishness and, they suspected, a sneaking hankering after the idle and dissolute life. They recalled his past, but with a new emphasis—no more that nonsense about the Borgias, Incas, Presidents of Peru and suchlike, but the facts, the six years at sea, the notorious grandmother, the jailbird grandfather. No wonder! They even blamed him for the loads of canvases, furniture, linen, silver and bedding which Mette brought with her—every stick of the Gauguin effects. All very nice, no doubt, but it meant the taking of a house; and what was the use of furnishing a house when you couldn't pay the rent? More inconsiderateness by this flighty Frenchman who had snared their Mette. And who, pray, would pay this rent and for the food, the clothes, the education of the children? There was only one answer, and the Gads, gritting their teeth, prepared grimly to get their money's worth. They would pay; but they would bring Mette back to the fold and would make sure that the five children were Gads, not Gauguins. As for Gauguin himself—well, they hoped that they knew their duty.

For the time both families lived in the Gad house. The friends and relations who called in to see this monster in the flesh were pained in fair relation to their probable liability should he prove a permanent charge. The one question that interested all was when and how he would earn a living. Not at painting—one look at his canvases was enough. Surely he would not stand idly by and watch his poor wife resume the French lessons she thought to have done with when she married. No one said as much, but the atmosphere spoke for itself. Mette herself was not backward with reproaches: to watch her family disapproving of the man she had chosen—this humiliation stirred all the acid on her tongue. She cared for him, but she cared even more for appearances, for right dealing. She had been a good wife to him; could as much be said of him as husband? And what of the children? She was a mother before all else.

2

Gauguin, his optimistic dreams collapsing, made outward motions of contrition. He too would give French lessons ("me giving French lessons!" he says in an aside to Schuff, "you'll burst yourself laughing"), he would earn the beastly money that was all the Gads seemed to care for. He would even ape the respectable; he got a job as representative in Denmark of a French manufacturer of tarpaulins and canvas blinds. But the desire to paint, driven underground, grew to a passion: "I am tormented more than ever by art," he told Schuff at the beginning of the new year, 1885, two months after he had reached Copenhagen; "tormented by lack of money too". He had soon taken the measure of the Gad family, who pursed prim lips at him, but surely there were some in this godforsaken country who would know an artist when they saw his work. He drew and painted in every spare moment. And he did not hide his opinion of the Gads; he ostentatiously kept away from them and when obliged to sit at table with them he maintained a stiff contemptuous silence. He dreamed of Paris and his work, he wrote out his dreams to Schuff, to Pissarro, to Guillaumin, but chiefly to Schuff.

He talked a great deal about the "sensation" he was seeking. He wanted his pictures to be a unique representation of his reaction to a scene. "All is there, in that word," he declares. "For a long time philosophers have reasoned about phenomena that seemed to us supernatural and of which one has nevertheless the *sensation*." Raphael had found his sensation, Cézanne was finding his: "In the Midi he passes whole days on the top of a hill reading Virgil and looking at the sky. As the horizon lifts his blues become very intense and his red is like a loud shout."

Gauguin knew well enough that he must take from the Impressionists as from his other masters only what his own "sensation" demanded. But what exactly did it demand? That, to a man subjected to a strong and congenial influence, was perplexing, it was complicated. There was no easy way, no sudden inspiration. It was a matter of thought and of contemplation. "For me the great artist is the expression of the greatest intelligence; through his brain there come to him the most delicate, the most intangible feelings and intuitions."

This, cloudy though it might be, was the language of a man in love for the first time. And in the spirit of one who, however wretched ("I haven't a sou, I'm up to the neck in trouble, so I console myself with dreams") and however perplexed, had found himself, he not only unburdened himself to Schuff, he proffered fatherly advice. A few years earlier Schuff had helped to found the Salon des Indépendants. Why not come in with us? he now asked to cheer the exile. But the exile did not react as expected; he became the Olympian, the man who had preceded Schuff into the true though abhorred Salon, who had since been received in a manner into the councils of the Impressionists themselves. They had better take care, he said impressively from the depths of a cultureless Denmark, that the little society did not incur the misfortune of winning the critics' good words and become overwhelmed by popularity. No societies for him, no societies for Schuff if he were wise. No, "work freely and madly; you will make progress, and sooner or later your worth will be recognised". "Dare everything": that was his advice and his aim.

3

For some time his own daring was confined to the little room where he struggled in odd hours to express his "sensation". All the rest of the time he suffered—dependent on the Gads, people whom he despised, detested—forced to listen to their puerile talk: "You come from such a big country, you must find us behind the times, we are such a small country. What do you think of Copenhagen, the museum? Of course it won't seem much to you"—then the pause for the denial, the polite raptures. The museum, Gauguin soon found, had next to nothing in it, and the fine Copenhagen mansions with their wonderful mediaeval tapestries, their unregarded Turners and Rembrandts, smelt of mould and were littered with accessories, the contribution of the present owners: "You sit down on a red velvet cushion shaped like a snail. Covering the priceless table is a hideous cloth that cost a few francs at some cheap store. You see a photograph album and flower vases on the same place." Gauguin looked, listened and inwardly raved. "Vandals!!!"

And these people were as dead as mutton. Dead, dead. He was sitting, eating, visiting with the dead. Malicious dead, too; behind their routine chilly enquiries was the wish to wound this large stranger with his superior manner and contemptuous, heavy-lidded look. How nicely that brother and son-in-law was doing; perhaps if he listened, watched, followed, in time he too . . . Oh, unbearable insult!

Thaulow was thrown in his teeth. Thaulow! No longer, as on that first Paris visit, the admired professional but a nothing, a conventional ass who perpetrated wishy-washy stuff with one eye on the popular market. One thing after another. A second brother-in-law made his appearance—George Brandes. He was going far, this earnest student of literature; everyone could see that, everyone said as much with meaningful glances at the one who was plainly going to the dogs.

For Gauguin wasn't proving himself to be a first-rate commercial traveller. This was scarcely surprising since his mind was rarely on the job. And when he did force it to the job his temperament was on the verge of ruining every prospect. No one more suited to impress a client than this bulky figure with the imposing delivery. So one would have thought. But the only kind of business that interested Gauguin was his own. His pride revolted against trade. The horror of Aline-Marie when her son came home with the marbles had passed to him at last. A Borgia and an artist to cringe before some insignificant Dane, to beg him to buy a few yards of canvas! How to control himself? He did not always control himself; and when, his fury overcoming him, he threw a glass of water over one of his most influential customers, his work as commercial traveller dwindled to the writing of letters promising large returns in the future. But the family enquiries, punctilious but penetrating, exposed his shortcomings in all their nakedness: successful he might have been, they implied, in gambling on the Bourse, but when it came to honest hard work. . . .

They expected him to look on while they taught his children to grow up as Danes, to speak the ugly language as their mother tongue, to attend the prim churches and, worse, to think in the Danish way—the conventional, goody-goody, characterless way so different from the French and a million miles removed from the way of his own childhood. They actually encouraged the children to ask him for money in the hope—or so he believed—of shaming him into hard and honest work.

And there was Mette frowning at him across the table or casting beseeching looks. He began faintly to have an inkling of the woman he had married. Yet no more than an inkling; he could be generous in other ways than lashing out with his money, and in his fashion he was loyal. What he chiefly saw was that Mette's family had raised all the Dane in her (all the Gad would have been a more charitable conclusion) and he fixed his loathing on them and their country.

4

If life was difficult for him, he went out of his way to make it more so. Winter wore into spring, but the atmosphere in the Gad house grew ever more icy and he took a sardonic, childish pleasure in living beyond his reputation. They thought him a useless Bohemian, the self-righteous Lutheran prigs—they disapproved of the naughty French? They should not be disappointed. He ignored Mette's glances. When he deigned to speak it was to utter pleasantries in his best lower-deck manner. He shattered one convention after another. He haunted shady parts of the city. He consorted with queer characters. He ignored the family friends or showed his true opinion of them by some unmistakable gesture—as when, wearing only a shirt, he walked into the room where the women were enjoying a comfortable gossip, said coolly, "Don't disturb yourselves, ladies," walked across to the bookshelves, took a book and walked out again.

This story may be apocryphal, but is worth repeating because it accurately expresses Gauguin's attitude and his actions. He longed to be rude, to shock, and if he did not do it exactly in this way he did it in other ways. He made a scandal by hiding behind the women's bathing-place on the beach (men and women bathed naked) and standing up with a broad grin and appreciative eye as the pastor's wife walked out of her bathing-hut down to the sea. "Her white body made a good effect." But better was to come. Her daughter, hearing Gauguin move, cried out, and her mother turned horror-struck and ran back to the hut, "thus showing me all the front after having shown me the back". It was about the only bit of genuine pleasure he got out of Denmark, but it showed what a pernicious thing was this misnamed civilisation with its conventions and clothes. Away with them! Away with Denmark too: "I hate the Danes, I hate the country, I hate the climate." No exceptions: "The Danes are not to be judged in Paris but at home. With us they are sweet as sugar; at home they are pure vinegar."

But Denmark took its revenge. After months of hard work Gauguin managed to arrange an exhibition of paintings. It was a complete failure; within five days it closed. It was possible to see victimisation behind this new humiliation, and Gauguin was not the man to miss it. His exhibition, he told Schuff, had been summarily closed by order of the Academy. Those people would stop at nothing; all favourable notices had been suppressed "by the old Academic clan". The very frame-makers banned him: "I was forced to get a frame made by a joiner, the frame-makers would lose their clientele if they worked for me." "And this," he added disgustedly, "in the nineteenth century! But if we are nothing, why all this fuss? To feel that one is an element, imperfect but still an element, and to find the doors closed everywhere! It must be admitted that we are the martyrs of painting. A young concierge who had been a pupil of Courtois for two years would get more consideration. Bah! The stupidity of the human race is almost as great as its vanity."

Gauguin's contemptuous attitude towards all things Danish and his manner, growing more lordly the worse his state became, set people's teeth on edge; frigidity was met with frigidity; few stirred a hair's-breadth out of their official channel to help him. But, this apart, there was no cause for surprise in the failure of the exhibition. No one remotely akin to the Impressionists had ever managed to get a foot into the circumscribed cultural life of Copenhagen. The city, accurately reflecting its country, stood staunchly by the conventional rendering, the unmistakable story with a moral twist, the dull colours finished in a high gloss. Gauguin's canvases appeared to such an audience as a cross between madness and immorality. As London was to disgrace itself by a typically boorish rejection of the Post-Impressionists in 1910, there was no particular reason to expect Copenhagen to be more forthcoming nearly thirty years earlier.

The failure of the exhibition—the disgrace they would have said—settled the Gad family once and for all. This haughty incumbrance who ate their bread with a grimace and an insolent stare had been given his chance. He said he was a painter; the experts of Copenhagen replied that he was not. He was, in fact, no good—he couldn't paint, he wouldn't work, he was and would always be a dissolute slacker. Their disapproval became biting. One sister-in-law spoke out. She it seems by Gauguin's venomous references to her was not overawed by his manner and her tongue matched his own. "For six months I haven't said a word," Gauguin cried to Schuff with pardonable exaggeration. "I am completely isolated. To the family I am of course the monster who never earns a penny. And that, in the present age, is the standard by which one is judged!"

His complaints no longer ended with the Gad family. Mette did not escape. Why did he stand this intolerable situation, why martyr every decent instinct in himself for a woman who repaid him by refusing to reply to friends' letters, telling him that he must do it; and who ranged herself with his enemies? "She is not kind at the moment," he tells Schuff. "Misery has completely embittered her, especially in her vanity (in this country where everyone knows everyone) and I have to put up with all the reproaches. Naturally it's because of my painting and because I'm not an eminent stockbroker, etc." For once he gave an indication of his intentions. "I'm beginning to have enough of it and I'm thinking of dropping everything and coming to Paris. Working at Bouillot's as an assistant sculptor simply for my keep, I shall be free."

This was in May 1885. A few weeks later, after more plain words from the sharp-tongued sister-in-law and a violent scene with Mette ("Oh the wicked passions that parted us!" he was to write later), he suddenly decamped to Paris, taking with him his favourite son, the six-year-old Clovis.

Chapter Six

PARIS

1885-1886

I

GAUGUIN'S break from Copenhagen has been freely represented as the turning-point in his life. It is the best known; thousands—perhaps millions—whose knowledge of him is otherwise scanty are aware that he left his wife and children to be a painter. One cannot wonder at this: the idea of the artist abandoning all for his art is dear to every romantic heart; and when that all includes a family, numerous elements rush in to give the story what is popularly known as human interest—rousing approval, disapproval, shocked pleasure, resentment and envy in those who have neither the courage nor the excuse to do likewise, and a hundred other emotions. No: one cannot wonder at the interest; yet the fact is that Gauguin's act was neither so dramatic nor so final as has been assumed.

There has been much discussion in print about the rights and wrongs of it. The moralists have condemned him for abusing the marriage vows and portray Mette as the victimised wife. His biographers mostly see him as a man from whom the impossible was asked and censure Mette for failing to follow him. But the flight from Denmark was inevitable from the moment that Mette suggested going home; she was truly going home—and there lies the explanation of everything else. The suggestion, however wise in her eyes and whatever Gauguin's immediate reaction to it, was a declaration that she put her faith in her family and that she had no faith in him. Sooner or later that lack of faith would openly break up a marriage which in any real sense had already ended, if indeed it had ever begun.

Yet Mette's suggestion had to be made even though it implied that the marriage had been a mistake and admitted that she had married Gauguin not for himself but for what he could give. That is no basis for marriage, but Mette could not help herself. No doubt she would have preferred to stay with her husband if only for the sake of appearances, but she did not believe that he was capable of supporting his family at all, and certainly not in respectability. She believed her first duty to be to her children—which with her meant to give them a regular, secure, orthodox upbringing, even though it had to be a fatherless one. Not for one instant did it cross her mind that Gauguin was aiming high and nobly for the first time in his life; she had not that kind of mind. She could see in his actions since leaving Bertin only avoidance of duty, awful hints of the disreputable, debts, disaster, disgrace. And Gauguin, being what he was (or what he was rapidly becoming), could no more stay in Copenhagen than he could fly; the wonder is that he endured six months of it.

To say this is to say simply that they should never have married. Many of Mette's motives for marrying were suspect, and Gauguin ought to have known better, but they were not biographers writing a life of Gauguin fifty years later, they were human beings living at that moment and subject to all the temptations and errors that the meeting of an attractive woman and an interesting man, both ripe for marriage, can bring about.

Having married, and Gauguin having made his choice for the future, neither could accept the position, admit their mistake, separate amicably and go their ways, making the best of a new life alone. To Mette he was not so much a husband as a man who had vowed to keep her and hers all his life. To him she was a woman whose life work was to stick to him and support him whatever he did—and never more so than at that time when he was trying to discover the greatness in himself. To both, divorce was anathema, and even separation unnatural. There is no sign that they considered it at any time, and certainly not at that point. For there was a fondness on both sides—of habit naturally, but also more than that.

It is a convention that a man who leaves his wife cannot love her, but Gauguin did not leave Mette in 1885—he left her relations and her country. The parting, though inevitable to the eye of today, was not so to them, and specially not to Gauguin. He wanted Mette and the children to live with him—but not in Denmark; he declared again and again that he would set up a home for them all when he had made enough money. He meant what he said; he tried many times to persuade Mette to join him; but she would not,

He was foolish to ask, and one likes him for it. Mette was wise to refuse, and one does not like her for it.

Curiously enough, while many words have been lavished on Gauguin's behaviour in leaving Mette at Copenhagen, his abduction (for that is the word) of Clovis has gone almost without comment. Yet here was a truly selfish and irresponsible act typical of Gauguin at his worst. No doubt the child relished the prospect of such an adventure, and no doubt Gauguin persuaded himself that he would demonstrate through Clovis the falsity of Mette's complaints that he could not keep his family; but at best Gauguin behaved stupidly, and, as events turned out, purposelessly.

2

For his plans came to nothing. Still full of confidence, he had not prepared the way, he had based all his hopes on a casual remark of the sculptor Bouillot, and, arrived in Paris, he found that Bouillot had no work for him. And not only Bouillot; no one had work for him. He could not sell his paintings. He had next to no money, no clothes except those he stood up in, nothing. He found shelter for a moment with the carter's wife "Mère" Fourel in the impasse Frémin, close to his old apartment in the rue des Fourneaux. She had called him out in the night years earlier with a scream of "My husband has hanged himself." Gauguin had cut down the still warm body, and she, unaware of his amusement at dinner the next night when his guests clamoured for souvenir pieces of the rope, was ever afterwards grateful for his prompt help. And she did not mistake him, for Gauguin was one of those men who laugh off their kindnesses and take pleasure in showing themselves in a bad light. She also took pity on the small boy. There was not much she could do—a bed, some bread and wine—but she did it.

Jobbé-Duval, his old landlord, helped him a little and his wife took Clovis off his hands for a few days at a time, but they were too pinched themselves to keep others. Pissarro, still poverty-stricken, had a shrewish wife who hated painters. Guillaumin was poor as a church mouse. Degas had money, but he was difficult, touchy. Schuff, his investments prospering, was the best bet of all, but Schuff had a wife with a good memory and who liked to rule the house. The moment Gauguin came into it she was no longer master or even mistress. For the sake of Clovis and to humour her husband she gave them food and shelter, but not graciously. Their visits were short, and Gauguin predicted gloomily (but not inaccurately) that the Schuffenecker marriage would "end in ruin or suicide". Schuff, he told Mette, "is a good lad, but unhappily he is getting more and more fed up with his wife who, far from being a companion, is growing into a regular harpy".

For the first time in his life Gauguin began to know what it was to go hungry. He was soon answering Mette's reproaches with reproaches of his own. He was tormented by the canvas manufacturers for money advanced on prospective sales—the only way he had been able to raise the fare from Denmark to Paris. He was being tormented—and why? Because Mette's relations had promised him orders they had never taken up. And for her to reproach him for leaving Copenhagen! He took a high line. "No free and honourable man could stand life under such conditions. Your sister was to blame. My honour was at stake, and the honour of my family. Let there be no more question about it."

And what ridiculous questions she asked when she did write!—for she always, he complained, left his letters for a month or so and never by any chance answered his questions. He had asked her to send down canvases from his collection so that he could raise some money. She ignored the request, asked what he would do with himself and Clovis during the winter? "What can anyone do in Paris without money, a job, a home, furniture or even a change of clothes?" he replied irritably. "With nothing, one does nothing." The subject was a sore one. But there was another and worse. Bouillot kept on saying that he had no work to give him. When one came to think of it, wasn't that a bit suspicious? "Have you been writing to Madame Bouillot?" He knew what she was after: "You want me to go back to the Bourse."

He not only had a wife who was privately urging his friends to discourage him, he had rheumatism. Gauguin, like so many strong men, suffered the minor pains without fortitude. "Another pretty recollection of Copenhagen!" he snarled. Ah, "but if that were all!" It was not all. More dirty work was brewing in Denmark. "Remember, I have a gift for seeing what happens behind my back." At that moment he felt sure that the abhorred sister-in-law ("the most stupid and wicked woman I've met") was planning some new devilry. "But I am a man who can't be kept down—and specially just now."

The confident note was due to movement and a new plan; it was September, he wrote from Dieppe, and he was going to London "where I have some trumps to play". He had left Clovis with his sister, Marie Uribe, and started off briskly. For the time his hopes were again high; all would be well.

At Dieppe he met Fritz Thaulow (no longer the perfect husband but rapidly moving towards a separation from his Gad wife), Degas and Pissarro. The gathering was not a happy one. Pissarro, despite the increasing whiteness of his patriarchal beard, was flirting youthfully with the "scientific impressionism" of Georges Seurat; and with the enthusiasm of the convert he tried to open the eyes of Degas and Gauguin. He received no encouragement. Degas let loose some of his choicest sarcasms; Gauguin, who had heard of Seurat from Guillaumin, thought the young man with his long serious face, his earnest eyes glistening through glasses, his mathematical theories and his canvases covered by the "dot", a pompous young ass who would have been better employed in an architect's office. Pissarro ought to know better at his age; it was rather disgusting. Yet Gauguin needed another exhibition as never before; Pissarro was the only man with enough energy and faith to organise it, and Degas the only man with enough money to finance it.

Annoyed by his dilemma, Gauguin took out his spleen on the absent Guillaumin, who had introduced Pissarro to Paul Signac, Seurat's friend and disciple: he was egoistic, he was common, he was stupid. This display of cattiness didn't commend itself to either man. Pissarro, indignant, burst out in defence of Guillaumin: he had done him the service of his life. Degas called Gauguin to order, giving him a lesson in ironical disparagement—a lesson so sharp that Pissarro forgot his wrath and turned against Degas. By this time his need of an exhibition and his even more desperate need of a loan from Degas had completely left Gauguin's mind; he was being attacked, criticised—that was all he could think of. His arrogance rose to new heights. No money changed hands, no exhibition was settled. He painted one or two seascapes and a portrait, he walked about the town picturesquely—he had reacted with a violence from the Bourse—but the extravagance of clothes flaunted about the streets and the slow, heavy, slightly rolling gait emphasised the expression that came into his face. A doctor who saw him then summed him up as exhibiting all the signs of megalomania. This was perhaps a not unreasonable diagnosis on sight, but the doctor was mistaken. Gauguin's expression was the expression of a man who had begun to suffer for his work, and who resented the suffering as unjust. The worse his state became and the blacker his prospects, the haughtier and more forbidding his appearance.

Did he or did he not go to London? No record of such a visit has been found. All that can be said is that if he went, the purpose of the journey failed. For he was back in Paris by October, chastened and with Clovis on his hands once more; his sister had had enough of him or, as is more likely, of his father. Marie had reverted to the Spanish strain in her blood, but not to its attitude to trade; on the contrary she took with her husband's name a mercantile view of the arts. She was worried by the possibility of this brother sponging indefinitely on her. She had never thought much of him; she thought even less now. Mette, who was giving the Gauguin circle in Paris her version of the break, wrote at length to her. If Marie's heart needed hardening, Mette's letters did it; she would pay for Clovis to go into a pension for a month or two, she said; Gauguin must look after himself. He, disgusted, took Clovis to the Jobbé-Duvals while he looked about for a room. He still had no work from Bouillot, painting was "in a state of crisis", but he had hopes of selling a Renoir and a Pissarro—two of the few canvases from his collection that he had left with Schuff when the family moved to Rouen. Meantime he told Mette that he was going to hunt up a small job—any job—on the Bourse. The concession agonised him and he added furiously, "only until the position for the painter improves". At the moment Degas alone could sell; no other Impressionist painter had a chance, so greatly was the public malice stirred against them.

It is perhaps impossible to convey to those who have never seriously gone hungry the physical effect of starvation—the pain, the dizziness, the fainting attacks. It is an illness, but an illness that no doctor can cure; like every other illness it does not stop short at the body; and its effect on the mind is incomparably the more serious. Gauguin was an optimistic and credulous man—this fact cannot be emphasised too often—and he was excessively proud. He had known hardship at sea, but had never lacked food. For the greater part of his life he had lived in luxury. He had left Copenhagen as he had left Bertin because he must—"it was a point of honour". He came back to Paris believing that he would make enough money by his sculpture and painting to send soon for Mette and the other children; and that before doing so he would supply her regularly with cash from his earnings. This was foolish, no doubt, but he believed it.

The shock of the true situation did him permanent harm. To be forced to write to Mette (and so to her family) for help instead of sending help to her; far from summoning her to a new home, to be unable to keep himself in one, to have to watch Clovis go hungry and know that the boy ought never to have been taken away; to be forced to beg—he, the prosperous successful Gauguin—because he had obeyed his instinct to follow the artist in himself! On a full stomach such thoughts would sour the strongest man; on a permanently empty one they scar the character and disposition. If Gauguin by the winter of 1885-86 was scarcely recognisable for the man of a year earlier there is no cause for surprise; like everyone who goes short of food and worries perpetually about money he became bitter and quarrelsome, his nerves on edge. Fortunately for him he was strong in body as well as in will and he was proud. "Is pride a fault and should one develop it?" he was to ask himselt years later; and he answered, "Yes, I think so. It is the best thing we have to fight the human beast in us." Its value and its dangers his life was to show; but in this dreadful winter the beast if put down in one way reared up in another; his pride kept him alive and sane, but at a price; he found himself in an impossible situation and he too became impossible.

He took a wretched room in the rue Cail near the Gare du Nord, rented a bed for Clovis, packed him off to a day school and persuaded the wife of the concierge to keep an eye on him. Then he tried his luck at the Bourse. But his appearance was so strange (for he had to sleep in his clothes) and his manner so truculent that all he got for his trouble was a quarrel that ended with his opponent sending his second the next day. The affair blew over, but there was no job. Gauguin wrote bitterly, "I'm fine, I have four bare walls to make me gay," and threateningly, "I hope the children won't be brought up in ignorance of their accursed father. But no matter,

I'll change all that." Mette, anxious about Clovis, suggested that Danish friends should call. Gauguin's pride flared up; to be seen in that hovel! "I don't want to set eyes on any Dane." But a Dane did call, nevertheless—none other than Marie Heegaard, now married and in Paris. Times had changed: the gallant young Gauguin was a hungry, embittered man, his flowery compliments had soured into sarcastic comparisons of the visitor's lot and his own. "Your infamous sister-in-law," he told Mette, "was careful not to invite us to her home. All she did was to bring clothes for Clovis and find fault with the parquet floor. Am I expected to clean the thing?" And she had criticised a portrait he had just painted of Schuff: "horribly Impressionistic!" He snatched the clothes and saw her go with a growl. He hated the stuffy *bourgeoise* coming in with her airs and graces and fat useless purse while he was unable to afford a meal or a model and slept on a couple of planks.

Marie's visit roused another suspicion in his mind. Clovis was all right, he insisted angrily, he was all right. And at first Clovis was all right. It was fun to rough it with his father, to eat haphazard on his knees, to cut out paper patterns in one corner of the bare room while his father stood at his easel, to listen to the jokes which he could not always understand of their cheerful blasphemous neighbour the marine and his girl friend. But Clovis was not a strong child and the winter was a terror, freezing day after day from October to April. There was no money for heating, neither of them had sufficient clothes or bedclothes, and although Gauguin ate next to nothing there was not enough to go round.

No work, no money, his friends tightening their pockets and Clovis complaining of headaches, losing colour, his eyes looking bigger his face smaller every day. Gauguin felt desperate. For three days he lived on dry crusts so that the boy should keep up his strength. He had only twenty cents left, the cold was so bitter that he could no longer hold the brush to paint. Clovis sickened, he ran a high temperature, he was obviously ill. Gauguin went round to a bill-sticking firm. "Take me on," he demanded. At first the manager laughed at him. He persisted. There was no resisting him. He was taken on. He pasted bills on the hoardings and walls of Paris. The frost thickened, his hands became chapped, raw. He could scarcely stand for weakness. He was paid five francs a day. "No doubt your Danish *amour propre* will be injured at the thought of a billsticker husband," he told Mette savagely. For Mette was complaining too. She was depressed, she thought of suicide, she must have Clovis back, and why not him too, did they not love each other? That was the burden of her last letter. He could not contain himself at the thought of Mette in her snug comfortable Copenhagen house complaining to him.

"There's nothing to whimper about," he had told her on the return from Dieppe. Now, cold, hungry, humiliated by failure—failure to get a good job, to sell a picture, even to keep the child (for when Clovis recovered Gauguin had been forced to put him into a pension and to beg his sister to pay the first month's rent)—he lashed out. Who was the one to talk of suicide? "You have a house, furniture, children, you can see all the Danes you like, you enjoy all the benefits of marriage without the trouble of a husband. What more can you ask except for more money?"—"I'm still in the soup and by the look of things I shall stay there. I've been driven out of my house, chased from pillar to post, the walls of my wretched room are running with damp, I've got pains in my shoulders." On and on. The children were no longer to speak French: "Your family ought to be content now, winning all along the line." As for her love: "that has just made its appearance as if by magic"—"yes, me too—at a distance. But you are only a mother, not a wife, so don't be surprised if one day I find a woman who will be a real wife. I know very well that you think me without charm, but . ." On and on. Look at the Jobbé-Duvals, wretchedly poor but not wretched. Why? "Because they rise above their misery by *unity of heart* . . . never any acrimony." But "You keep on with your nose in the air, your clear conscience, your duty. There's only one sin for people like you—adultery. Apart from that, all is right. It is not right that you should be driven from your home, but it is right that I should be driven from mine. So don't take it badly if I find another home. And in that one I shall be free to billstick. Each to his own taste."

The pattern is familiar. He differed only from the host of squabbling husbands because he was suffering for his principles. This apart, he showed as much need of his wife as his thousands of brothers of theirs. He could not leave her alone. She doesn't write for two months, he sends a sarcastic note: "What's up? Why sulk? That Danish *amour propre* again?" He had seen Brandes at the Salon and hastened to get in his dig at this favoured brother-in-law. "*He pretended not to notice me*. He didn't notice the pictures much either —was too much interested in the fashionable women." He had also seen his sister "to whom you write long letters. To comfort me she cries to the rooftops that I'm a wretch, that I have left Bertin to paint, that this poor woman without a home, without furniture, without support, has been abandoned for this atrocious painting. I say in effect that the fool is always right, that you are all angels and that I'm a miserable rotter."

Clovis he had not seen. The child was still in the pension outside Paris, but, Marie having refused to continue to pay the bill, Gauguin dared not go near him for fear of being forced to take him away. He hadn't seen him for four months, but he still wrote defiantly, "I shan't send Clovis back, far from it—I'll have the rest one day, it's my right."

He could not leave her alone, he could not do without her. And when May came, the frost disappeared and Pissarro at last hammered out an exhibition, Gauguin hastened to pass that on too. His good and his bad news all had to go to Mette—first the suffering she had caused him, then the triumph she was missing through her lack of faith. For this eighth and last Impressionist exhibition was a triumph, though a small one, for him. It had been a struggle: Monet, Renoir, Sisley all lost for good to the Salon; the very name Impressionist abandoned—Degas had insisted that it be called simply Eighth Exhibition of Paintings; the weirdest collection of exhibitors with little in common except the walls on which they hung—Schuff introduced by Gauguin ("I've seen a still life of his and it's simply terrible," wailed Pissarro); a little band of friends invited by Degas; while Pissarro brought in his son Lucien, Signac and Seurat. All most unsatisfactory, and particularly Seurat with his vast and laughable *Grande Jatte*, executed in his infamous dots— "I can't see the thing," complained Degas, "it's too big." Yet there was the exhibition at that moment at No. 1 rue Laffitte—and in that street where Gauguin had worked for eleven years at Bertin's he now showed nineteen canvases and several works in wood and marble.

How could he help but feel moments of cheerfulness, hungry and resentful though he was—or resist a triumphant shout to Mette after those long, humiliating months? She, like her family, had wiped him off as no artist, as a slacker. Well, let her hear; in spite of every hindrance, of frightful deprivations, there he was in the exhibition with one of the largest showings of any of the sixteen exhibitors—studies of Rouen, of Dieppe, a winter scene of his beloved Vaugirard and its bus, portraits, the Arosa house at St Cloud and, best of all, the browsing cattle in the park beside the house. All this and more—his sculpture—from a half-starving man, from the waster! "Our exhibition has put the Impressionists on the map. I've had a great success with the painters. Bracquemond has bought one of my pictures for two hundred and fifty francs, he thinks my sculpture so fine he's introducing me to a famous ceramist."

Mette was now proposing to come to Paris; to come, he thought bitterly, at the first sign of success. He put her off; it would be a waste of money, he couldn't receive her (he was giving up his room) and couldn't keep her. "You have reason to be cheerful now that you are surrounded by those whom you love, in scenes which remind you of your sweet childhood, valued as you deserve. What could I ever offer you in compensation in this dirty country of France?"

She was given the most favourable view of the painter triumphant—that was only to be expected—but Gauguin also wrote as he felt. It is one of the most endearing and admirable traits of the artist that a little encouragement will go a long way with him—he leaps to supply all the rest out of his own courageous optimism—and Gauguin was then and always a heartening example.

The critics remained unmoved. One of the best of them, the young Félix Fénéon, among the rare defenders of the Impressionists, noticed that "the tones of M. Gauguin are very little distant from one another and that as a result his pictures show a dull harmony". He also commented on Gauguin's habit of contrasting strong colours: "this painter constantly opposes the ruddiness of the beasts and the tiles of the roof to his greens". But how could Fénéon see where this habit would lead? To those who look at these pictures in the light of the future, indications of the later Gauguin are not difficult to find. The critics of 1886 had not that light; they had instead the assertion of Gauguin that he was an Impressionist taking part in an Impressionist exhibition. That the expression of his "sensation" might take him outside the Impressionist circle, that he might be at his greatest only when he had jettisoned Impressionism —this naturally never occurred to him.

The basis of his satisfaction was that from this moment he was acknowledged by men whose opinion he valued as a force to be reckoned with in modern painting. No more deprecatory undertones of "Sunday Painter", but respect, whether in agreement or disagreement. He had suffered for his art, but not in vain. He was, if not a happy, a triumphant man. He thought occasionally of retiring to a "hole" in Brittany that Jobbé-Duval had recommended months earlier where he might work quietly and cheaply. He had not gone for the good reason, which was to become familiar, that he had no money for the fare and nothing to pay the bills; he was also determined, having come to Paris, to get the benefits that Paris alone could give the artist; but he kept the country in mind.

For the moment he rented a small studio near the Vaugirard church; he worked hard and well with the ceramist Chaplet making pottery of every kind, showing the flair with the wheel that he had shown with the mallet and chisel years earlier. The breach with Degas healed (for Degas was particularly struck by his exhibits) and the 250 francs in his purse he once more strode into the Nouvelles Athènes with the assurance that a few good meals and a little money brought back in force.

He needed this assurance. The exhibition had brought into the open the inevitable disintegration of the Impressionists. Not only had Monet, Renoir and Sisley gone for good—the rump split into two camps. The "scientific Impressionists"—the neo-Impressionists as they were to be called—derided as out of date the "romantic Impressionists", as they nicknamed the remnants of the old body—Degas, Guillaumin, Gauguin chief among them. Pissarro, reacting to the criticism of Seurat's work, would argue, expostulate, plead. Could they not see that the logical development of Impressionism was Seurat's synthesis of scientific methods? Could they not realise that this led to the use of optical mixture instead of a mixture of pigments to produce intenser luminosities by breaking up the tones? The "romantics" replied no, they realised nothing of the kind; all they could see was that the vile "chemical techniques" and the hideous dot led to pictures which were devoid of personality, originality or charm. The red-faced Pissarro, blowing furiously through his mane of a beard, insisted that the artist must express himself in the character of the drawing and his vision—not in his execution. The "romantics" derided such a notion—the "scientists" ("chemists" would better fit them, they said) had to find some excuse for their execution or lack of it.

None so scornful as Gauguin of the rebels: Pissarro, who was surely in his second childhood, the perky Signac, covering his canvases with a welter of sickly coloured dots, the prim Seurat, who had nearly turned the whole exhibition into a laughing-stock, and his young followers, the lanky Anquetin, pride of the Ecole Cormon, and the infant prodigy, Emile Bernard. Of these last two he took no notice, they were beneath contempt; but on those who were old enough to know better he had no mercy—his sarcasms withered.

The battle, like all battles of this kind over café tables, had no end. How long Gauguin would have continued the struggle no one can say. But Degas, watching the dialectical progress of his pupil, was so delighted that he voluntarily offered a loan. Clovis was still in his country pension and, the Danish Marie having made up the arrears, could safely remain there. So towards the end of June Gauguin, his fare paid and the question of paying for his keep relegated to the future, suddenly went off to his "hole" in Brittany.

Chapter Seven

PONT-AVEN

1886

I

THE "hole" was the village of Pont-Aven on the south side of the Brittany peninsula, near the mouth of the river Aven and close to the desolate Cape Finisterre. Jobbé-Duval's recommendation had been partly kindness to a friend, partly protection against endless demands from a hungry, jobless man. He described the place as a painter's paradise—he had painted there on and off for twenty-five years—and he held out the attractive inducement: "Go to my pension, the Pension Gloanec. If Marie-Jeanne Gloanec takes a liking to you, you won't have to worry about paying your bills."

Gauguin, helped powerfully by lack of the fare, had resisted the temptation for a year—he felt that Paris was the place for a man with a name still to make. He also hoped to sell several pictures. He was mistaken in this, but he held on. The exhibition released him, or perhaps drove him: he had made a name, but he had not made money. Why not try Brittany? It was cheap, quiet, unspoiled; Arosa as well as Jobbé-Duval had spent much time there.

He said that he felt an imperative call to throw off the artificiality of Paris and to get back to a life lived close to its origins, a sombre life in keeping with his mood. A friend explained later that "he went to this ancient countryside to discover surroundings and an atmosphere different from our excessively civilised world." This has been treated as a picturesque afterthought. However, unlike most of the painters who prated about a return to nature and sat snugly on their café seats in the boulevard de Montparnasse, Gauguin really went and, going, discovered in the country and its people an affinity with the "savage" in him. It is a commonplace that the artist needs the stimulation of frequent change of scene. Gauguin went beyond mere movement; he proved himself equally at home in Paris and in bleak Brittany, living as the people lived, thinking their thoughts. As a complete contrast to Paris, Pont-Aven was as good a choice as could have been made in the whole of France. What Gauguin could not know was that this Breton village was to reveal his "sensation" to him and to establish him as one of the great painters. For that, absence from Paris and the influence of the painters there was essential; and no doubt Pont-Aven, severe unpretentious, but with its own beauty, was essential too.

The Pension Gloanec was a substantial stone building in the Breton style, painted white with black surrounds to the wide central door and the windows. Above the door hung a large painting of Pont-Aven as if to say that here was the headquarters of the art. It said no more than the truth; the pension was already an institution to many painters from America, England and Scandinavia. The French artists were few—they had not yet discovered Pont-Aven or even Brittany.

The painters were ruled kindly but firmly by their hostess, Marie-Jeanne Gloanec, a substantial, upright figure surmounted by the crisp, white Breton headdress. She knew nothing about art, but there was little she didn't know about artists—for fifteen years she had housed, encouraged, rebuked and fed them. She stood no nonsense: she and her maids, the attractive Louise and the plain Marie le Pape, starched and stately in their Breton garb, kept the place spotless and served up their heartening soups and big meaty seafish, but woe betide the wretch who didn't scrape his boots outside the door, who dropped his paint on the floor, who cast too interested an eye on the girls. But like most sharp-tongued masterful women she had no objection to being mastered herself occasionally and after a fashion. Gauguin employed that fashion; he combined his Borgia expectation of service with a quiet deference. Coming from a man older than most of the painters, a man whose very walk had something of high dignity, who sat himself down on a chair with an impressive finality, whose slow deliberate movement of two long fingers through his moustache would silence the most persistent questioner, whose orderly room was a housewife's dream, the combination proved overwhelming. "Mère" Gloanec ordered him about as she did the other men, reprimanded, reproached, even bullied, but with a difference the subtlety of which was not lost on Gauguin. He breathed more freely. If he never earned a penny that summer he could live unmolested; no bill would be thrust at him.

But already he was talking of more than a summer. The "hole" had exposed itself as an exciting discovery, and he wrote to Mette, "Pity we didn't come here instead of Rouen. I've seen a house with studio and garden for 800 francs and I'm sure a family could live for 300 francs a month." Mette did not respond. When he next heard from her she was ill and was afraid that she might have to have an operation. "If I could be operated on for you I would do it gladly," replied Gauguin, "in spite of all the harm you've caused me and which I shan't forget."

Mette soon recovered, but there was no more talk of a home in Brittany. Nevertheless, Gauguin declared that if he began to sell his pictures regularly he would spend the whole year at Pont-Aven. Seventy years ago Brittany, like Cornwall, its fellow across the sea, was a hard, storm-beaten, infertile country, breeding a people whose struggle to live had made them dour, clannish, proud. Gauguin at once felt a bond. Everything appealed to him in his present mood—the racing river and rocky streams, the savage coast, the spare grey countryside swept by the wind, the solemn quaintly-dressed children minding geese and cattle in small sloping fields, the huddled cottages, the sudden green of the glens. Nothing pretty-pretty here. Outwardly these people with their thick clothes and heavy faces and hard lives were far from the sparrow-like natives of Lima in their sun-baked indolence, but both were alike in their concentration on essentials—the provision of food, the propitiation of a stern God. This was the simple life as it was lived. To the savage in Gauguin it appealed with the impressiveness of the primitive—the ancient, unchanging scene, the ancient unchanging behaviour of man, with clothes, customs, conventions that seemed timeless. He had been right to come; the painter would find a message there. "When my sabots echo on the granite I hear the sound, dull and strong, that I'm looking for in painting," he told Schuff.

When he arrived in Pont-Aven he found himself almost the only French painter in the village. Danes, Americans, English—these abounded. Perhaps for this reason he took up at once the attitude of contemptuous indifference to all except his hostess and the maids. He occupied a room under the roof on the second floor of the pension as far as possible from the noise below, he stalked slowly in sabots about the countryside, a green beret with a silver tassel pulled well down over one eye, in his hand a stick decorated by himself. A brightly-coloured cloak hung about his broad shoulders, his black hair covered the bull neck, a thick pipe smoked between his teeth. He would stand and stare motionless, he would paint imperturbably.

No such figure had appeared before in Pont-Aven. Anglers and painters (the only types of visitor) watched curiously. Evidently he was an important man? He did not object to the supposition, but made no concessions; he rebuffed every advance with a curt motion of the head or a forbidding glance from under his lids and, if the unhappy man persisted, with a sarcastic interrogation.

He had no objection to foreigners—far from it—but these foreigners were bizarre in the wrong way. The Danes were damned outright, but the others were little better; the strident-voiced Americans with their raw enthusiasms, the English speaking with a permanent plum in their throats, sentimental, argumentative and cocksure—he detested, despised the lot. If their nationality had not been enough to damn them, their work was and the nonsense they talked about it—for one and all painted after the academic manner. One would have thought from their conversation that they had never heard of Impressionism.

2

A change began with the arrival of French painters. Most of them were Beaux Arts men and no more acceptable to Gauguin than the foreign painters, but there were one or two exceptions. There were the great black-bearded Granchi and the heavily moustached Dupuygodeau, who dressed like a local fisherman, habitués both. There was the young Charles Laval, black-bearded too but sketchily—Laval, new to Pont-Aven, thin as a rake, pince-nez glasses clasping the narrow nose and protecting earnest brown eyes. These men, staying at the pension, were struck immediately by Gauguin and his work, the uncommon authority of the man, the daring and power of the work. They had heard echoes of the Paris exhibition. They were followed by one or two more Frenchmen, by an Irishman, O'Conor, and in a few weeks Gauguin was not only the ruling spirit of a tiny group, he was, he told Mette, "respected here as the greatest painter in Pont-Aven" and regarded as the oracle: "Everyone here wrangles to get my advice."

The "everyone" were in fact no more than five or six painters, unknown men and the butt of the foreign colony and the academic visitors from Paris; but to Gauguin who, the mediocre Schuff excepted, had known little admiration and who was conscious of his age, this sudden change from pupil to master was exhilarating. His satisfaction was limited as it was always to be—"it doesn't earn me an extra sou," he complained—but he wrote nevertheless as one who is finding his feet and is merely reminding himself (and warning his wife) that he is still hardly done by. The penniless Gauguin of Pont-Aven painting his pictures, presiding at his little court of rebels, is a very different man from the embittered, nervy, half-starved Gauguin of Paris. He now had a filled belly—a fact which can scarcely be overestimated. He was admired and he was detested—both incitements to vanity and more than vanity. For he was doing good work, and at last it was his own work. The Impressionist manner was still the basis of all that he made, but already there were pictures that no Impressionist would have painted. The attempt to follow the Impressionists by patiently building up a scene on canvas (never congenial to a self-taught painter with a limited technique) was beginning to show signs of narrowing to what his "sensation" felt that scene ought to be.

Of this he spoke briefly but impressively to his few followers when they ate together at night and sat on after the meal, smoking and drinking. He would lean back in his chair, the inevitable pipe or cigarette in his mouth, and lay down the law. Simplify: that was one command, and with it a revolutionary instruction, "Paint in your room; finish it outside." His other main concern was colour. The connection between the two was not perhaps clear to him; his was not an analytical mind, he dealt little in abstractions, he disliked theories, he preferred to stick to the practical. "I always use sables." Let them follow, keep the intensity of their colours, lost by the use of ordinary brushes, and the power of pure colours in juxtaposition.

There was some talk between the men of *synthétisme*—it was one of the catchwords of the day—but there is no sign that Gauguin realised that he was heading towards it. He thought of himself as an Impressionist and he was for ever praising, with Michael Angelo, Raphael and Ingres, Cézanne, Degas, Manet and Pissarro (before the Fall) and advising his hearers to learn from them. He would have been surprised to know that his teaching struck at the roots of

Impressionism—cleverer men than he have been unable to see where their genius is leading them.

But in a sense it would have mattered little what he said; the manner of saying it was the thing. The men sitting round the table with him felt, as the boys at school had felt, as his shipmates, as the men on the Bourse, as Mette, that his words seemed not to come from him alone; he seemed rather to be a mouthpiece for some extra-human pronouncement. They sat listening, questioning, fascinated, until Mère Gloanec bustled in, pshawing at the smoke-laden atmosphere and ordering all to their beds—for the women's beds were set up, Breton fashion, in the dining-room to save space.

Of those who listened to Gauguin the most devoted was Laval. He was a born worshipper and, being weedy and delicate, must necessarily worship the strong. Even his talent, which was considerable, had insufficient strength or personality to stand on its own feet; he had to get his inspiration through another man. At Pont-Aven that man was bound to be Gauguin. Laval clung to him, watched him paint, listened to him, laughed at his pleasantries, threw in a word when a word was in season, and painted so devotedly after him that the untrained eye cannot distinguish some unsigned canvases of his from the early Pont-Aven works of Gauguin. He also, an indispensable part of this kind of relationship, proudly shared his monetary all (which was little enough) with the great man. Gauguin accepted the mite with a careless grandeur. He was conscious of conferring a favour; Laval was conscious of accepting one.

3

Late in the summer another and even more youthful admirer appeared at the Pension Gloanec. He arrived on foot with a knapsack on his back. He was on a walking and painting tour of Normandy and Brittany. He had just come from a study of the ancient cathedral of St Brieuc on the other side of the Brittany peninsula. He was small with a pale almost beautiful face, black hair grown long to the nape of his neck and fervent, intelligent brown eyes. He wore a black velvet jacket and trousers and a wide black hat. No one could mistake his vocation.

He presented an introduction from Schuff. Perhaps he presented it with insufficient deference, at the wrong moment. Perhaps his fault was that he had the hardihood to present it. Gauguin looked him over and was not pleased. What was Schuff thinking of, to send down every rag tag and bobtail from the Paris schools? This boy could be no more than eighteen. Unfortunately he had heard about him; every painter in Paris knew of young Emile Bernard, the pet of the Ecole Cormon, painting the "prop" sail in vert veronese and vermilion stripes "because that was the way he saw it", of his dismissal and of the uproar that closed the school for months. Yes, Gauguin had heard about him, and that was annoying too. Besides, Bernard was connected with the Seurat set; his hero at Cormon's, Anquetin, had begun to dabble in pointillisme—the official name for the dot—and Bernard had promptly followed him. What a cheek, to beard one of the pillars of Impressionism proper in his Breton den! Gauguin was cold and short as only Gauguin could be.

But this girl-faced young man seemed to have a hide like a rhinoceros. He presented himself again and again, imperturbably enthusiastic, sat far from mute in the mute circle of worshippers in the dining-room after dinner. Sarcasms bounced off him, hints were not heard. He wasn't big enough to hit. Gauguin grunted and ignored him. Bernard sat on, put in his oar. He became downright talkative. Gauguin looked at him from under his lids. The boy was no fool, that was clear. Bernard did not miss that look—he was as sharp as a needle—and wrote home in triumph, "There's a big man here, an Impressionist painter of 36, called Gauguin. His work is very good." He had deducted two years from Gauguin's age, but he was edging his way into the group.

Gauguin listened unwillingly to details. It may be that he heard with approval that Bernard's father was the natural son of a nobleman. He had money—that was something. He had a charming daughter—that also was something. He lived at Asnières and was waiting for his son to choose a serious career—that so much engaged Gauguin's sympathy that he grew almost friendly for a moment. But the power in the family, it seemed, was a grandmother with whom Bernard had spent most of his youth in the north of France. She it was who had persuaded the unwilling father to build his son a wooden studio in the garden at Asnières. She was a devoted Catholic and her impressionable grandson got his first view of art from the stained-glass windows of churches, the illustrations in books of devotion and the designs on tapestries in the churches and his grandmother's house. These the small boy copied over and over again with his sister Madeleine; the common characteristics of all were simple bright colours in juxtaposition, heavy bounding lines and lack of perspective. Later, though still absurdly young, the precocious Bernard moved with extraordinary speed and ardour through the usual round of the masters until with Courbet and the Ecole Cormon he burst triumphant into the world of the Impressionists—only to shift, before being dismissed, to the "scientific Impressionism" of Seurat.

He said nothing to Gauguin about "scientific Impressionism"; that enthusiasm, it appeared, had enjoyed its brief day. He was now full of one whom he had thought—until he had had the supreme good fortune to be received by Gauguin—to be the most remarkable of the coming men. He had met him at Cormon's—a pupil too, though more than thirty at the time. His name was Vincent Van Gogh. He became Bernard's "mon copain Vincent".

Had Gauguin met Vincent—a carrotty-haired fellow with a scrubby beard? Always had a pipe in his mouth. Hissed at you in execrable French. Curious face, wide ears, wide cheekbones, deep-set glinting blue eyes, hollow cheeks, forehead perpetually furrowed. Unprepossessing. Like a convict. Horrible temper. But a good sort nevertheless, could knock back his absinthe and paint through the next day. And there was a something about his technique, it was crude but it was strong, it was. . . .

Gauguin was not greatly interested one way or the other, but the name Van Gogh was another matter. Vincent was brother of Theo, manager of Boussod and Valadon's gallery (still called Goupil) in the boulevard Montmartre. Theo had gradually come out into the open as a champion of the Impressionists and was in a fair way to rival Durand-Ruel. Already there were rumours that Monet might change from one to the other and that would say much for Theo van Gogh, for Monet was beginning to sell. Already Theo had begun to show the advanced painters. He tried to sell their canvases. He was making a name for himself as the most progressive dealer of the day.

And Vincent was his brother. And Bernard was a friend of Vincent. Gauguin unbent slightly; enough to attach the young Bernard to him. A new admirer was born, as idolatrous in his way as Laval. Yet there was a world of difference between them. Laval was content to imitate, Bernard had ideas of his own. The one was incurious, the other had a finger in every pie. The one saw perfection in Gauguin, the other wanted to put it there. Reluctantly Gauguin accepted the newcomer; he could not deny that Bernard was a bright boy. He was like a sharp-eyed terrier nosing feverishly into one hole after another and digging a hole himself when he couldn't find one. He would dig them out! But dig out what? Bernard was unprecise; he was restless, unstable, fond of novelty for novelty's sake. But he had ideas even though their lives were short; his enthusiasm was enormous, bracing, and he had talent—the drawings and watercolours he made of Breton subjects were original, audacious.

Bernard went back to Paris that autumn full of the great painter of Pont-Aven. He left the great painter in sombre state. One by one the men went off, to their homes, their studios. Gauguin had no home, no studio. Complain though he might—and as he did from time to time to Mette—of the life at Pont-Aven, it was absolute heaven to the hell of the previous winter in Paris; well fed and warmed by the sun, he worked hard, painting day after day. But autumn came down and Pont-Aven began to empty, the shadow of Paris hung over him more and more menacingly. He brooded over those months of hunger and humiliation: "I'll kill myself rather than live like a beggar as I did last winter." So he told Mette. The problem remained. He had earned nothing but praise that summer, not a penny. Was his work too advanced to sell? The answer to that would be found in Paris, not Pont-Aven; if it would not sell even there, nothing remained but the pottery that Bracquemond, Chaplet and Schuff had all praised. For that too he must go back to Paris. And there was Clovis, still in his pension, unvisited. Mette was full of fears for the boy, full of reproaches. Send him home, she demanded. Gauguin had no intention of sending him home, but he felt uneasy, he disliked being put in the wrong. It was insufferable to be unable to move him. No money, as usual. "He's the joy of the pension, but he gets no holidays." And he was fond of him: "I miss him."

All in all, Paris seemed inevitable. "I shall take that small studio near the Vaugirard church and make pots like Aubé." He bestirred himself, that is to say he commanded Schuff to find some place in which he and the boy could both live. Schuff obliged. "He has found me a little hovel in the rue Lecourbe," reported Gauguin gloomily to Mette. "Perhaps one day my work will strike the eye of the public and some enthusiast will pick me out of the gutter." But for the moment all was dark, and Gauguin was in no state to see a ray of light, not at least in a letter to Mette: the sunshine was short, the evenings were long, all about him was silence, day followed gloomy day. Gone his little group, gone the adulation, the evenings of talk round the stove. The pension dining-room was empty, cold, forsaken. He worked on—"Never have I been so active in spite of troubles"—but he was not as he pictured Mette "fat and happy". No: "When I collapse I'll do it in one go." In November he took the plunge, packed up his few belongings and, saying au revoir to Marie-Jeanne Gloanec, left the bill with her to be settled later and departed for Paris.

Chapter Eight

MARTINIQUE

1886-1887

I

THE return to Paris opened inauspiciously. First, Gauguin quarrelled with his sister. She, alarmed no doubt by the reappearance of this good-for-nothing brother, hastily thought up a plan for getting rid of him usefully. Her husband, she explained, was having trouble with the appointment of his agents. In Panama, particularly, where he then was, he could not find the right man. She thought that she might persuade Juan to take Gauguin on. Would that not be a grand opportunity to start a new and better life in a part of the world he loved? Of course he would begin with a nominal salary, knowing nothing of the business, but. . . .

Gauguin was not to be caught napping: "Marie thinks, why not get me cheap?" He knew all about the exploitation of poor relatives: "The whole thing disgusts me." He expressed his disgust by attacking her; she had not been to see Clovis for six months—that was unsisterly. Marie hit back: Wastrel! For eight years (doubling the period in her indignation) he hadn't done a stroke of work. What of his poor wife and children? The woman you love so much, sneered Gauguin, that you pester her with shrewish letters.

The argument took its usual futile course and Gauguin banged his way out to the Nouvelles Athènes. He was soothed for a moment by the friendliness of Degas, who had been impressed by the studies brought back from Pont-Aven. Then in came Seurat, Signac and Pissarro. Gauguin's bad temper exploded in a burst of rudeness; he at once got up to go, followed by Guillaumin, and ostentatiously avoided the outstretched hand of Signac. A babble of charge and counter-charge broke out—"impossible to understand a word of it" complained Pissarro—and Gauguin marched out, ignoring the farewells of Signac and Pissarro. Guillaumin, embarrassed by this treatment of Pissarro, went back for a moment to greet him, but the kindly Pissarro, who championed his new friends with enormous zeal, was more distressed than they and wrathfully denounced the "narrow-minded romantic Impressionists" with a fiery "I insist on the right to go my own way."

Gauguin's satisfaction, such as it was, did not last long. Paris that winter turned from excessive cold to excessive rain; the "hovel" was damp, he caught a chill and spent a month in hospital. "I wanted to die, but no luck—unfortunately I've come out again," he told Mette on Boxing Day. His one stroke of fortune was the sale of a small Jongkind from his collection. This paid the bill of Clovis' pension and enabled him to get the boy out; there he was, slipperless and toyless on his birthday. "Ah well, one gets used to everything," sighed Gauguin, who got used to nothing. He'd been working hard with Chaplet, but to no end; all his spare clothes had been pawned to buy food, he couldn't sell a picture, he couldn't sell a pot. Yet "ask Schuff what painters think of my painting" and "he says my pots and busts in clay are my masterpieces and the maker thinks so too". His reward—"nothing. And the man who has nothing is stunned." Mette had a home and food "a paradise—guard it", but don't let her come near her wretched husband—"I couldn't receive you politely."

He was still confiding his hopes to her as well as his complaints. Mette gave him neither sympathy nor understanding—she was far too busy feeling sorry for herself and far too sure that he was living in sin—but he persisted in his confidences. Occasionally it dawned on him that Mette and his painting were irreconcilable unless he became a successful painter in terms of hard cash, but the curious attraction persisted—he wrote on as if somehow, some day, he could persuade her to think and feel as he did.

The opening months of 1887 continued the process of disillusionment. He had friends. Félix Bracquemond, himself one of the best watercolourists of the century, thought more highly of the Pont-Aven studies than of the work he had bought at the exhibition the previous year. He did his best to help, Schuff, Jobbé-Duval and Bouillot did theirs, but nothing would sell, no Impressionist could sell except Monet and Degas. Bracquemond showed some Pont-Aven studies to his purchasers, and Pissarro, still scraping odd sous together to make the hour's trip into Paris, heard with some satisfaction that nothing could be done with them. Bracquemond, he told his son, thought them good but strange, interesting but confused: "He seemed to imply that it was the art of a sailor, a little taken from everywhere." Pissarro made no effort to contain his pleasure: "I made up my mind about him long ago, he's no artist at bottom but a maker of odds and ends." But having said as much, his spite vanished. He had heard of Gauguin's triumphs at Pont-Aven, of the "young disciples who hang on the words of the master". It was true, he admitted, that Gauguin "has finally acquired great influence". He went further: "I don't say that he won't change for the better."

This, if he heard of it (and there was little that each section did not hear about the other), gave no comfort to Gauguin. His fears had hardened to fact; Paris was repeating its terrors. His short spell of adulation at Pont-Aven, his rising reputation in the painters' world of Paris—what ironical triumphs to a man who hadn't enough to eat, who couldn't change his clothes, who was forced to send his son back to the pension once more because he could not feed him! "My fame as an artist grows every day, but I often go three days without food, I'm losing my health and energy." To a proud man conscious of great gifts the neglect was intolerable—ten times more intolerable since Pont-Aven. Not only was he denied his due, he was actually punished for daring to leave mediocrity. The world preferred him in his black suit, gambling on the Bourse, a useful citizen—it rewarded him. Now he was one of a thousand unwanted painters. If only he could die! "but this iron body of mine refuses to die".

2

By March he had had enough: "My sufferings have almost passed the limit of human endurance," he tells Mette in an affectionate letter. He had decided to leave France, had booked his passage for Panama the next month. With him would go the faithful Laval, who, one suspects, had provided the money for the fare. He would leave, Gauguin said, with a clear conscience: Paris was a desert for the poor man, he was losing strength, he had lost heart. Mette could have Clovis back. He wrote gently, as people do before taking a long and hazardous journey: "I love you and embrace you tenderly" and "I am a beast but I can also be the other thing."

Mette responded by coming to say goodbye. Where they met is not known; presumably, as Gauguin was desperately short of money, Mette travelled to St Nazaire, where he sailed from; she did not go to Paris—so much is certain. The meeting was not a success. She, he complained, had not changed; all her faults remained—the faults that in his opinion reinforced the wisdom of his flight from Copenhagen two years earlier. "Still pride put before sense, still that atmosphere of revolt, still more responsive to flattery than truth."

Mette was a practical woman and asked practical questions. Why Panama? What would he do when he got there? Would it help him to support a deserted, struggling wife and children?

Gauguin dismissed this last with "I shall always suffer from the absence of my family, but I shall have no more of that begging which disgusts me." Then he explained his plan. Near Panama he knew of a small island, Tobago; it was practically uninhabited, fertile, free. There he could live "*en sauvage*". He would take only his paints, his brushes, his canvases and, far from men and their pettiness, their pale civilised shadow of life, "live for nothing" on the fruits of the earth and the fish of the sea. Though he did not say so until later, he had even more glorious visions: "I expected to have to do nothing but dig up gold with a spade and shovel." Then what might not be done! His children about him once more, his work admired and he living at ease. It was a pretty picture. Panama was within hail of Peru one might say, stretching a point; he would be back near his origins, he could enjoy the bright colours, the rich scents, the luxuriance, the sun.

Suppose the island life didn't work out? He had thought of that —he was the businessman still. His brother-in-law, Juan Uribe, had a business at Colon in Panama: "Maybe he'll open a branch in Madagascar and put me in charge." Who dared to say that he was foolish to go? He wouldn't have a penny when he got there, but what of it—how could he be worse off? If the Madagascar branch fell through, Juan was himself at Colon at that moment. He would scarcely let his wife's brother starve.

But at this point the Gauguin with his dreams of an easy life merged into that other, admirable Gauguin. He would "live for nothing"—yes, but only so that he might "work hard and in peace". He would live "*en sauvage*" so that the savage in him, responding to familiar stimuli, would enrich and fulfil the painter. When he talked, as he talked often, of a return to nature he was not echoing the nonsense of every half-baked follower of Rousseau; he meant what he said. And when he said "hard work" in the midst of his paradise he meant that too.

His plans and dreams lasted as long as the voyage, and a few hours beyond it. He called on his brother-in-law, found him "unintelligent" but believed that "when Marie is not at his back he'll be easier to touch for loans". He even declared that "in eight days we shall be in our island where we can live like savages". Then he came to his senses. Life down that way was no longer what it had been in his days afloat. The Panama canal project had been born, gangs of men sweated and dug and died under the sun. As for the land, that land of freedom and plenty—"the fools are asking six francs a metre!" he wrote furiously to Copenhagen. Nobody, it seemed, "lived for nothing" any more; the tropical paradise had closed in; work, money, profits were the horrid catchwords of the day: "We're in the soup. Devil take the stupid asses who advised Panama."

Away, away to Tobago. But Tobago had filled up; one had to work or pay: "Life is impossible even in the most deserted spots." He could not even "build a hut and live on fruit—they fall on you and treat you like a thief". His indignation soared; the fruits of the earth denied to him! He had no money, Laval had none. He tried Urlbe once more. The business, he was told, was doing badly: nothing to spare. Why had he made the trip without warning after refusing the Panama job months earlier? It was an awkward question. "Nothing to be got out of Juan," he complained: "hasn't even forked up 100 sous". In revenge or despair or a bit of both, "I cheated him out of 35 francs for clothes worth 15."

The satisfaction was limited and would not keep life in him and Laval, far less get them to Martinique—for that was now Gauguin's objective. The ship had called at this island (a French colony) on the way down: "A marvellous country for the artist, offering a cheap and easy life among pleasant people. We ought to have stayed there." He no sooner thought of it than he was there in imagination: "What a life we could lead!" The "we" was not himself and Laval, it was the Gauguin family reunited. As at Pont-Aven, so now, without a penny to bless himself with, his mind at once soared to a home far from Denmark where he, Mette and the children could begin a new life. "If only I could sell some pictures in France we could all live in Martinique and you could give lessons."

Mette returned no direct answer—her contempt was expressed by a demand for money to send the children to school in Copenhagen—and Gauguin was too preoccupied with present difficulties to pursue the idea. He had to live, he had to find the fare. There was only one thing to do: he applied for a job as navvy on the canal diggings. This was perhaps the most appalling job in the world—the death rate scandalised the public conscience even in those days. For a European even as strong as Gauguin it was virtual suicide. He wielded a pick from half-past five in the morning until six in the evening under tropical sun and rain, then lay unsleeping "devoured by mosquitoes at night". He did not even get his full pay; he was, mercifully, turned off after fifteen days when the number of workers was suddenly reduced.

This was one of the worst moments in a life which was to have many bad moments. He had visions of himself dragging on in this feverous hell, of his strength broken, of a pauper's grave and his work undone. From these he was rescued by the devoted Laval. Laval was too "feeble" to dig on the canal, but he could paint and he didn't care what he painted if he could get them out of Panama and into Martinique. He set up as a portrait painter. There was no competition, explained Gauguin; the portraits had to be painted in a special way—very badly: "I can't do it." This was true enough; Gauguin never could and never did paint a picture to order. But the lesser artists have their uses; Laval made enough for their fare to Martinique. By June they were there.

3

At last it seemed that Gauguin had found his haven. They settled in a negro hut among the sugar plantations half an hour out of St Pierre, the little capital. The hut—part of a single village street—was perched halfway up a hill on the coast. Below Gauguin could see the blue water fringed by yellow sand and straggling cocoanut groves. Above him grew the trees with their bright fruits—oranges, lemons, guavas, mangoes, corossols—the forests of mahogany and rosewood, and above all the great volcano of Mont Pelée. "It's paradise after Panama. The negroes and negresses sing their creole songs and chatter all day. Nothing monotonous about it—the life is very varied."

At once he began to weave impossible plans—if his dreams can be given such a name: "For 30 thousand francs I could get a property here which would bring in a fine income and let us eat like gourmands"—the "us" was again Mette with the children, Gauguin refusing with touching persistence to face facts—"The only work I'd have to do would be to oversee the negroes gathering the fruit and vegetable harvest. No cultivation necessary." Where was the thirty thousand francs to come from? Where, for that matter, were the few hundred francs which he and Laval must get if they were to live at all? Even in Martinique, with its fruits free for the picking, food and tobacco cost money. Neither of them knew. But "this is the only black spot on the horizon".

It was on the horizon, no nearer; and having mentioned the point, Gauguin ignored it. What a country! And what women! "The white man has a bit of a job keeping his virtue intact, for Potiphar's wives are not lacking." So he told Mette, who had failed to send him greetings on his thirty-ninth birthday. There were women of every colour from ebony to matt white "and they do their best to enslave me by gifts of fruits". Yes, literally enslave, he assured her: "Only the day before yesterday a negress of 16—pretty, my goodness!—offered me a guava split and pressed. I took it and was going to eat it when a mulatto advocate snatched it from me and threw it away." The advocate explained that the girl had crushed the fruit against her breasts before offering it, to make sure of capturing him if he ate it. Now that he knew of the charm: "You can sleep quietly without fear for my virtue." He insisted again that he hoped one day to see them all together there. "Don't cry out," he wrote, "I mean it."

In this way he expressed his contentment. And contented he was. Here was the simplicity of living and behaviour that he wanted. Here were the colours and scents he remembered from the days of Lima, and an exuberant growth that even Lima could not match—the wild fruits, the tamarind, the bamboo thickly tangled and shining with every conceivable shade of green. Against this exciting background moved Indians, Chinese and above all the negro women with their brilliant wraps, their glistening black skins and superb carriage, their simple acceptance of life, laughing, crying, quarrelling, singing like children. To the man, Martinique seemed a paradise. To the painter it was so.

To Mette he talked of the women and the conditions of living. He said nothing of the discoveries that made the rest seem insignificant—the sky and the light. Never had a European painter worked under such skies, never had he been presented with such effects of light. No one had painted such colours, such scenes, such people. His eye responded to the challenge. Under its guidance his hand began to find itself. He painted the village, the seashore, the countryside; he painted and drew the women—women at rest, women carrying baskets and jars on their heads, women gossiping outside their huts. One drawing, *Femmes Maoris*, and one study, *Les Négresses*, though in advance of the rest were typical of all; the simplicity about him moved into his work, purged it of fussinesses which he had learned but which did not represent him. His palette brightened, his bounding lines grew bold and simple, his colours became clear, flat, powerful, he began to draw with assurance and painted more and more with stripes of flat colour instead of the delicate dashes of the Impressionists, massing and contrasting his colours rather than merging them as was the Impressionist way. Inspired by the varieties of green in the vegetation, he used brilliant greens on his canvases; and in an effort to reproduce the dense black shadows cast by the sun he used black for the first time. The Impressionists did not acknowledge the existence of black in nature, but he would still be regarded on the strength of these canvases as an Impressionist painter; he certainly did not regard himself as anything else; nevertheless, he was so no longer. He did not know precisely what he was doing or where he was going, but he felt himself to be on the right road, and that is perhaps the most satisfactory basis of happiness.

Laval painted too, delicate fanciful approximations of his friend's work. But he did not paint for long; in him the disadvantages of the simple life first showed themselves. Martinique enjoyed glorious sunshine, but paid for that sunshine with torrential downpours. The negro hut in which they lived was delightfully simple—of the cluttering, time-wasting apparatus of modern life there was nothing. They were hot, dusty, they plunged into the sea and dried in the sun. They were hungry, they plucked a cocoanut or a guava. They were thirsty, they scooped water from a pool and drank. They were virtually back to nature, sleeping under the sky. Indeed, when the heavens opened and the rain gushed down, they were to all intents and purposes under the sky; the flimsy roof of the hut gave shade but no shelter, they were quickly soaked and Laval began the next day with a fever. When the rain stopped and the sun blazed down again the island steamed, the humidity stole all energy; the well Gauguin walked listlessly and worked little; the sick Laval gasped for air, his fever mounted, malaria took a firmer hold. The delightful village street with its absence of pavement, lights, drains, the laughing, statuesque women who came to the door of their huts and threw out the refuse to lie where it might, appeared suddenly as a menace. The rotting refuse stank, and there was no escape from it for a man who could not leave his bed. Laval went from one bout of malaria to another, he grew weak and depressed, he feared that he would fall victim to the dreadful yellow fever. In a moment of despair he tried to kill himself, but Gauguin took the pistol from him.

Then Gauguin sickened and his painting came to an end. Malaria attacked him too, and dysentery. He recovered, but his great strength had gone: "I can't walk a single kilometre," he moaned to Mette. He had not had a letter from her for months, and, weak and miserable and feeling forsaken, he reproached her: this lack of love, even of interest, from her who had his furniture, his children, his precious collection of paintings, who was living in her beloved Denmark! "Of all the evils you've caused me, this silence is the worst. If I ever get back to France it will be as a man eaten up by fever and anxiety. But what's the use of telling you of my miseries? It would probably give you pleasure."

His one cry now was for deliverance from Martinique. Laval lay on his hands, coughing, emaciated, more devoted than ever since the frustrated suicide, but a heavy tie. Gauguin himself resented everything—Mette, Laval, his own feebleness, above all the attitude of the authorities in St Pierre. Repatriate me, he demanded; but they remembered his contemptuous brusquerie, his insistence on living with the coloured people. They dallied, procrastinated, kept him waiting in offices and finally advised him as an experienced ex-sailor to work his passage home. Laval they would repatriate when he was strong enough to move; Gauguin—no.

In the midst of his misery came letters from Mette; they had been delayed at Colon. They were not encouraging; she was unhappy, she was short of money, the children were growing up, how could she support and educate them? He was rising from his grave to reply, he assured her; dysentery and fever had reduced him to a skeleton, he could speak only in whispers, he had frightful stomach pains. Help her? "How can I?" he asked. "It's no use counting on me as a businessman." Help from him, unable even to return to Paris where the one immediate hope of money—his pottery—was to be found! "I'm sorry not to be dead. Your letters overwhelm me with grief. If only we detested each other! I ought to hate you... but I love you."

He appealed to Schuff: "What has happened to our friendship? Do all you can to send money. I must get out of here." Schuff sent some money, to be met with a cry of "Your letter has only one fault—it doesn't contain enough money." Gauguin went over his miseries: every evening after the delivery of the post his temperature went up through emotion; night after night he had dreadful nightmares in which Mette died and the children were kept from him. His old Paris neighbour the marine, rejecting an appeal, had shown "no delicacy of heart. He says if I drown myself it's my own fault. He never asks anything of anyone." "A lie," declared Gauguin furiously. The steamers plying between Martinique and France would not give him credit; he must pay his fare before sailing.

He was disconsolate, but the wonder is that he was not hopelessly discouraged. He was ill, weak, living comfortlessly in a shack with a nervy, coughing Laval on his hands, with a wife in Denmark who did nothing but complain, with barely enough money to exist on and no apparent hope of getting more, faced with a long exile from France and his future as painter, yet he merely grumbled; and even in the midst of grumbling he could not restrain a shout of satisfaction: "Never have my paintings been so clear and lucid. I shall bring back 12 canvases of which four have figures far better done than in any of my Pont-Aven period." Perhaps this knowledge sustained him through the next month or two; he was a strong man, as he had often said, and difficult to kill; he was also a determined man who now saw, even though dimly, a gleam of light ahead. No death for him. And so persistent was the life in him, of the painter as of the man, that he roused himself, conquered his weakness, put Laval into hospital in St Pierre and signed on as a seaman in a sailing-ship. By November he was in Paris.

Chapter Nine

DECISION

1887-1888

I

He came back to a Paris under snow and full of rumours of war. The sea air had put life into him. He was glad to be back; glad to see the snow after the fever-breeding heat of Martinique; glad even if there should be a war—so much the better for those left behind. Schuff, whose friendship sometimes exceeded his prudence and whose anxiety not to be left alone with his wife was growing, had offered him indefinite use of a bed and a place at his table. This was as well, for Paris seemed to be jammed with men producing works of art which no one wanted. Who thought of art at such a time? He and his companions at least; they thought of it, talked of it, believed in it. The time must come when they, and he specially, would win fame, make money. So he told an unimpressed Mette in Copenhagen.

He came back hoping that his pottery would bring in something to help him over the winter. But in the back of his mind, and not very far back, was a more ambitious thought. In the dark days of Martinique Schuff, no doubt hoping to lighten his misery, had written over-enthusiastic reports of a rumour that Chaplet intended to begin a pottery business on a grand scale. This was enough for Gauguin to dream of money pouring in, his family reunited in France and himself generally acknowledged as a great artist. He did in fact sell a piece of pottery for a hundred and fifty francs—a hundred of which he dispatched triumphantly to Mette—but there the sales ended. His work was admired but, as ever, by those who had no money to buy. And Chaplet, with whom he at once resumed work, was content, he commented bitterly, to live on his *rentes* and let the big pottery business await better times. Bouillot was as ever charming but unhelpful. "Friends I have, but no helpers."

This remark was less than exact. Gauguin was not an easy man to help when he was short of money and extra conscious of unacknowledged merit. It was true enough, the times were hard for artists, but Bouillot and Chaplet both seem to have done what they could for their difficult pupil. Chaplet, for instance, admired Gauguin's pottery sufficiently to smuggle a statuette into his own show-case in the Salon. This free advertisement caused him some trouble; the authorities, noticing Gauguin's signature, demanded that the statuette should be removed; Chaplet refused—if the statuette went he would withdraw the entire exhibit.

Mette was causing Gauguin some trouble; while he was in Martinique she had not only fetched Clovis from Paris, which he understood, but had ransacked his belongings at Schuff's, carrying off most of the few remaining canvases of his collection. What was she doing? he asked; they were his one hope of raising money. And this was not all; her letters always had an *arrière pensée*. "You seem to think I deliberately go out of my way not to make money." He explained once again, "The duty of an artist is to work so as to be strong. That I have done. I haven't yet reached the end of the struggle, but I have already won a great deal of admiration."

He had, indeed, come back to find himself the hero of a small but voluble circle, reminding him pleasantly of Pont-Aven days. He was the man who had really gone. He had come back, but no matter, he had made the gesture, he had gone instead of merely talking, he had painted where no man had painted before, he was creating a new kind of painting and he had suffered for it. Younger painters listened to him respectfully and regarded with admiration his Martinique canvases, which Theo had agreed to show.

The doyen of this group was Bernard, now nineteen years old. He was as eloquent and provocative as ever and resumed his rôle as Gauguin's gadfly. He had spent the Spring at St Brieuc in rooms which he had decorated with enormous murals representing the stained-glass windows of the cathedral. He also and more importantly painted a very Cézannish still-life *Pots de Grès et Pommes*, which he described as his "premier essai de Synthétisme et de Simplification"—a notable moment in the history of painting although no one suspected it, not even Bernard himself.

In Pont-Aven that summer he painted away gaily in the new manner, ignoring advice, custom and everything else except his own predilections. He presented to Mme Gloanec a picture *Les*

Blés Noirs in which reapers cut a field of corn surrounded by trees of a quite desperate sombreness. This picture was after the stained-glass manner, with heavy black circular outlines, no perspective and blobs of bright flat colour. The other painters in the pension protested. What a scandal! But Marie-Jeanne Gloanec was a woman of character, she was also susceptible. Young Bernard had charm and knew how to use it. She liked his picture and she would not be dictated to. The picture stayed where it was.

In Paris Bernard painted another startling picture, his *Maison de Mes Parents*. This he showed to Gauguin. Gauguin became thoughtful; this was the kind of thing that he was aiming at—his Martinique canvases showed as much. But Bernard was so flattering, so genuinely admiring, and his execution was plainly so far behind his ideas that Gauguin allowed himself a certain degree of graciousness. Truly the young fellow was difficult to resist; he could express clearly and vividly what one was thinking about but unable to frame in words. And he had the tact to convey gracefully that he was merely saving the master the trouble of speech.

With him was another former comrade at Cormon's, the dwarf-legged Toulouse-Lautrec, whose lewd jokes, and addiction to absinthe and brothels were received equably by Gauguin, chiefly because of his brilliant draughtsmanship, and whose noble birth won a certain condescending respect from the scion of the Borgias. Other regulars were the versatile Anquetin, a tent pole of a man, and Guillaumin (still hopefully buying lottery tickets) together with a varying company of pupils and ex-pupils of the schools who acted as Greek chorus to Gauguin's few but trenchant pronouncements.

On the fringe of the group were three men. With one, Louis Roy, Gauguin was to have little to do. Of the second, Léon Fauché, more will be heard; he was a painter and lithographer (which interested Gauguin) known to his friends as *l'homme de Nancy*, and he first attached himself to Gauguin when Bernard persuaded him to study the Martinique canvases.

The third man, Georges-Daniel de Monfreid, must have appeared rather out of place in these gatherings; indeed, he did not attend them often. He was eight years younger than Gauguin, tall with a long aristocratic face, bronzed, golden-bearded and with rather prominent blue eyes—a distinguished figure. He had the mild manner of a man who could be daring and courageous—but as the daring was not apparent in his work, he is unlikely to have been much regarded by the others. De Monfreid had met Schuff at the Collarossi Academy some years earlier, and Schuff invited him to the rue Boulard to meet Gauguin soon after the return from Martinique. The meeting was not a success: Gauguin, said De Monfreid, "was at first unsympathetic towards me"—and one can well understand it. Schuff's friends were suspect in any event; and this one appeared to Gauguin to be merely playing at painting. He had plenty of money, and until the previous year had spent most of it and his time on his yacht. He then began to paint seriously under the name Daniel George, but he continued yachting. His work was tasteful, pleasant, nothing more. To Gauguin this amateur with means would come as an insult to the great painter with nothing; and the sympathy alleged by some biographers between the ex-A.B. and the yachtsman would be less than existent. Gauguin's contempt on every score is not difficult to imagine.

However, De Monfreid had money (which Gauguin could not altogether ignore), he had a determination which was quite at variance with his manner, and as soon as he had seen Gauguin's work he became a gentle but unshakable follower. "It was a revelation to me," he said. "I understood what Gauguin was seeking and at the same moment I realised the falsity of all that I had learned about art."

2

But the man who regarded Gauguin and his works with the greatest veneration was Vincent van Gogh. He too had suffered for his art—to what extent his hollow, furrowed face ("I look like a man who has been ten years in prison") made plain. He knew what hunger was, and winters without warmth and homes without a trace of comfort. Unlike Gauguin he had for years received a small allowance (from his brother Theo) on which with care he could have lived simply. But he took no care; he was a painter; he bought canvases and frames instead of food, paints and brushes instead of lodgings, tobacco instead of fuel. He starved, his teeth rotted and fell out, his stomach grew ulcerous, his clothes hung ragged on his back, but he painted on. Vincent had then been in Paris for more than a year, but he was still reeling from shock after shock. One thing had followed another—the old masters of the Louvre and Luxembourg, Delacroix, Monticelli, the Impressionists, the "scientific Impressionists", Bernard, Anquetin and the Cormon group—with such speed that although he had mended physically since coming under his brother's eye his mind, never very stable, was chaotic and his moods frighteningly unpredictable. He lived in a state of perpetual excitement; he painted after the manner of every one of the many influences he had fallen under; he also mixed with the hard-livers, Toulouse-Lautrec chief among them, but could not take his liquor, grew muddle-headed, quarrelsome and, the next morning, savagely repentant.

Yes, Vincent was a queer bird, as Bernard had told Gauguin at Pont-Aven; he stuttered and stammered, couldn't explain himself, tied himself in knots, grew red in the face with fury, spat with rage and sudden hatreds, and yet one couldn't ignore the fellow. Gauguin regarded the unbalanced romantic with contemptuous pity, but when he discovered that the creature was not content merely to venerate but had the audacity to put forward his own crazy theories—the worship of poverty, of Millet and of a string of long-forgotten and best-forgotten Dutchmen—he stretched out his long legs shod with Breton sabots, waved his decorated stick and demolished the lot. He tore the Hague school to shreds, unmasked the sentimentality of Millet, made a public fool of the awkward, impassioned speaker.

It was exhilarating work, it gave one a sense of power, it provoked satisfactory roars of laughter from the others. And Vincent was fair game; he asked for it. But he also accepted it; he who would fight and squabble with the rest gave way with a growl; he wasn't convinced, but he was silenced, overawed by the majestic cloaked figure. He was favoured by the criticisms of a great artist—that was his attitude. Had not Gauguin also entered late into art, was he not the senior of all? Vincent had found his last and greatest hero—the born leader of an Impressionism that must develop if it were not to die. This attitude fell soothingly on the susceptibilities of a Gauguin still conscious of a vast public disregard. He could enjoy sport and homage at one blow.

But that was not all. Vincent would come in with a canvas under his arm, prop it against the wall away from the arguing group and stare at it with a frown until someone pityingly threw him a word.

Gauguin, though ostensibly ignoring him, did not in fact overlook him or his latest study. Vincent did right to frown, the work was a mess, a hashbash of half a dozen styles and attitudes. But Vincent was the brother of Theo. Gauguin was after all a businessman, an ambitious man, a penniless man. He occasionally noticed Vincent; and if to notice meant to single him out for punishment and ridicule, it was nevertheless notice of a kind and in his view a concession.

And to be just, there was a something about one or two of Vincent's canvases that justified Bernard's praise. His emotionalism was frightful, his execution uneven—in a sense the man scarcely knew how to paint—but he was an original, no one else had painted pictures like these. What attracted Gauguin above all was his colouring, the bright, gay childlike colours. Where had the fellow got them from? Not from his dark Dutchmen, with their dirty yellows and browns, not from the delicate shades of the Impressionists. Where then? The matter was soon explained. Just before coming to Paris Vincent had discovered some Japanese prints in a dealer's. He reacted violently away from his Dutch manner to this new and delightful approach to life, covered the walls of his room with prints, changed his palette to include the bright colours, the scarlet, the emerald beloved of the Japanese. In Paris he ransacked the attic of Bing's shop in the rue Provence, unearthed "millions" of Japanese prints and gave Bernard and Anquetin no rest until they too were spreading the news. At the Café du Tambourin, then their nightly haunt, Vincent organised an exhibition of the prints and decorated every corner of the café with Japanese motifs. He painted a portrait of Père Tanguy against a background of studies after the Japanese. The gay, flat, contrasting colours, the lack of perspective, above all the strong decorative element of the Japanese pictures began to appear in the work of all.

The Japanese manner reinforced Gauguin's own inclinations. In some such way he had begun tentatively to paint at Pont-Aven and had continued with more assurance at Martinique. In the Japanese prints he saw justification and example. He inclined always to the ancients; now his resolve was strengthened. In so far as use of colour and simplicity of design and execution were concerned, the new influence was altogether good; it merely brought out what was inherent in him. But the decorative element was another matter.

This too appealed to Gauguin, but to the commercial artist in him. A commercial artist he could never be, but he tended at times to concern himself with decoration to the detriment of true vision; he was drawn to it by the cheap streak in his nature and by his technical shortcomings; it was a simple way out and superficially an effective one.

3

By this winter of 1887 the days of the Café du Tambourin were over. Vincent quarrelled with the voluptuous manageress, Segatori, was thrown out by her latest admirer after a scuffle, and never showed his face there again. The meetings and free exhibitions came to an end. Bernard, Vincent, Anquetin, Toulouse-Lautrec still showed a picture or two at Père Tanguy's, where they bought their colours, but their main meeting-place, where Gauguin came into his own once more, was the Goupil gallery in the boulevard Montmartre.

Goupil, Gauguin told Mette, was now the centre of the Impressionists. He meant the advanced Impressionists led by himself. This was entirely the work of Theo van Gogh; fighting every inch of the way—almost to the point of suicide—he had at last established his right to show the moderns in the entresol apart from the main gallery. From that moment the entresol was a permanent exhibition for all interested in advanced painting and a kind of club for the painters themselves. It was open every afternoon for two hours, and there Gauguin, Vincent, Bernard and the rest would settle round the stove smoking hard and—Gauguin excepted—talking even harder. Gauguin presided, godlike, penniless, immensely proud; he asked nothing, accepted anything if offered in the right spirit—even, on the rare occasions when one of the others was in funds, a loan. He sat there, the huge beak of a nose jutting away from the beret, eyes hooded, pipe puffing, lazy voice cutting in to confound the speaker or end an argument. The work of all was in a state of flux; theories sprang up daily.

Of these, one of the most persistent was advanced by Vincent. With a series of hisses between his teeth, clenched as always on his pipe, slewing round his eyes with a characteristic sidelong glance, he elaborated his plan of an Impressionist studio in the south. He was sick of Paris; he was drinking too much, spending too much, he had quarrelled with almost everyone, had been taken up by the police; incessant arguments and the shock of one excitement after another had overstrained his nerves. He was afraid of a seizure, he longed for the peace of the country. Fired by Gauguin's stories of Martinique, his mind turned to the tropics—what colour, what subjects! The tropics were unattainable but the south of France, within reach yet with clear skies, a brilliant sun, and an atmosphere as different from Paris as Paris was from the Netherlands had long attracted him. He had a passion for the colours of the south used by Delacroix in North Africa and Monticelli about Marseilles. Someone should carry on the work of these magnificent colourists, and that someone should be a man with the vision to see that if Impressionism was to survive it must go forward, and that if it were to go forward it must use the pure strong colours that painters could find only in the south. Would he not justify his life and save his sanity by pointing the way? Theo, with whom he lived and whose life he was making an absolute hell, would certainly help him to go.

But that was not enough; he might be able to found a studio, but how could he, unworthy he, produce work that would attract painters there? He could not. But Gauguin could. With Gauguin in the south the studio would become famous, Impressionism would be saved, would lead the world. He worshipped Gauguin as a painter, but he also yearned after him as a man; he, Vincent, the lonely, the misunderstood, the vulnerable needed the independence, the calm confidence of this man who knew what he wanted and would get it. He believed that in Gauguin too, deeply hidden, was a wish for love and understanding. Working together, what could they not do—for each other and for painting?

At last he broke through his own diffidence and Gauguin's inaccessibility to hint at an offer. He said nothing about personal reasons. Let Gauguin come; there was nothing to keep him in Paris, he was for ever talking of the joys of painting in Martinique. The south of France was not Martinique, but the light and colours were almost tropical and the fare could be raised; Theo might send them both there, might buy their pictures. Gauguin would of course be undisputed head of the studio, his work would bring him the fame and the money he deserved.

The plan stammered itself out in hoarse bursts. But if Vincent made his meaning clear, Gauguin, taking the compliment as no more than his due, brushed the offer aside curtly; there was, to be sure, some attraction in that picture of the colourful south, but to expect him—Gauguin—to shut himself up away from his friends with a half-daft Dutchman—no. Besides, the man could scarcely paint.

4

No, he had other ideas. At last affairs were improving. He told Mette in February of the new year, 1888, that Goupil (meaning Theo van Gogh) had bought some pictures for nine hundred and fifty francs. He was triumphant but apologetic. He could send her nothing; his debts, including the last months of Clovis at the pension, swallowed up almost everything. But the triumph was not in the money, it was in this first acknowledgment by a famous dealer that his work was or would be saleable. The purchase sent his spirits up with a bound.

These spirits had fallen somewhat. His stay with the Schuffeneckers had come to an abrupt end. He had, as his manner was, taken over the Schuffenecker house in the rue Boulard the moment he entered it. It was not that he was untidy or dirty; on the contrary, unlike the popular conception of the painter, he was meticulously clean and neat. But this was poor consolation to Madame Schuffenecker for the disruption of a household by a man who insisted coldly that the children be kept quiet so that he could work, who expected meals to be served at hours convenient to himself and the friends he brought back with him.

Many rumours have been handed down of the guest's behaviour. As all were recorded by one man they must be treated with care—Gauguin's eccentricities were a standing temptation, which few resisted, to exaggerate. Nevertheless, some incidents are acceptable, and sufficient to account for his departure as soon as he had a few francs of his own. At least two of these Schuff brought on his own head.

Gauguin invited Theo van Gogh to inspect his Martinique work. Schuff, anxious to help his friend and plagued by his wife to get rid of him, began to praise the canvases. Praise—from Schuff, who could neither paint nor understand nor explain in anything but clichés! Gauguin, not unexpectedly blind to the kind thought, flew into a rage, bundled his host out of his own studio and shut the door in his face.

If rumour is correct (and it may well be, for Schuff was exceptionally obtuse), Schuff did not learn his lesson; Gauguin one day found him "explaining" the Martinique pictures to a possible buyer; he threw the visitor out of the house and locked himself in the studio until his anger had cooled.

Perhaps it was after this affair that he, having sold a piece of pottery through Theo, set up in a cheap studio in the impasse du Saint-Gothard off the avenue de Montsouris.

By some miracle the friendship held—Schuff was a faithful and deeply admiring man—but Gauguin was out. Gone the good meals, the soft bed, the regular shelter; the studio was uncomfortable, too far from the centre of Paris; he had little money for food; he feared a return to the hunger and cold of previous winters in Paris. He must get away—but where and how?

Then came the Goupil purchase, and his mind was made up: "I must make a supreme effort to get launched in painting. I'm going to Pont-Aven for six months, possibly eight. I must get under the skins of the people and the country—that's essential in painting." There was no easy way out, he told Mette, and she must have patience: "Don't give up hope for another year." She had made no effort to hide her hatred of his work. "My interests are yours," he replied. "Painting doesn't consist of the Ecole des Beaux Arts. I know you don't believe in me as a painter, and won't believe till I sell. I know painting is your bane, but you'll have to accept it and try to profit by it in the future."

Mette disagreed; his duty was to be with her and the children, to keep them. Why waste more money returning to Brittany? The first visit had done nothing for him or for her; he would be better off in Copenhagen, and would be doing the correct thing. He complained that his bowels were still horribly wrong; he would not make them better by drinking, smoking and painting at all hours. Why not try a few months sea bathing in Denmark?

Gauguin received this letter just before he left for Pont-Aven. He was at once faced with a decision—perhaps the most fateful decision of his life. Mette had at last made a definite gesture: forget all that has passed, she implied, let us live together again; let us at least try it.

Most of Mette's letters to Gauguin have been lost; they have usually to be deduced from his replies. They can be deduced with fair accuracy. It is quite plain, for instance, that affection for her husband was not the main motive or even a leading one in this suggestion that he should come to Denmark—indeed, had she loved him and cared for his self-respect she could never have made the suggestion. Her thought as ever was first and foremost for her children, secondly for herself *vis-à-vis* her family. Let the children have their father, but a respectable one earning a salary and her family's respect—this was her main thought. No doubt she wanted her husband back, but on such terms that appearances clearly went a long way before affection. She was perhaps slightly impressed by the Goupil purchase—her offer followed it closely—but her attitude to painting had not moved an inch.

As much was plain to Gauguin. But he was troubled as she was not by affection, and strange though the word sounds, by loyalty. He still wanted a home, a wife and children—and despite his occasional threats of finding others he made clear by his actions that it was no more than pique and a childish attempt to force her to leave Denmark and join him through jealousy. He did not then or ever want anyone but Mette.

The temptations to give way were many. He wanted to see Mette and the children. He wanted to end the state of self-reproach in which he lived and to stifle the surprise of others. The knowledge that he could not support his family, and that everyone knew it, was hard for a proud man to bear. The question "Where is your wife?" whether put into words or not had affronted his pride for years. He overrode all with a haughty disdain, but even a man of strong character suffers under undeserved imputations.

The problem was a real one to him—and not the less real because there could be only one answer. To expect him to return to Denmark! But he replied seriously and with care. "There is still a wall between us—the wall of your bourgeois mentality. The difference between us is the difference between the rentier and the man who lives on his work, between the mediocre and the creative. You don't love art, you love money. When the artist makes money you're an artist too, but that's not good enough, you've no right to share the joy of art if you've shirked its pains."

That was one reason why he refused to join her. There were others. He couldn't afford the journey. He hadn't the clothes: "My appearance in that bourgeois country of yours would dishonour you." If he returned to Denmark she might have another child by him—"Do you want that?" And he feared the effect of the five present children on his art; he couldn't trust himself to live with them for a few months and then leave them—a feeling on which Mette counted.

All these reasons were sound, unanswerable. But he went on, driven by a feeling of guilt—a feeling which did him credit—to give additional reasons which were most unsound. "We get on well enough when we live apart, but the moment we tried to live together the same old troubles would crop up again." That was true as a fact but was not true as a reason for his keeping away from Denmark; in his heart he always hoped that he could change Mette so that she would love him and his work.

But still he went on. Did she understand him? he wondered. "There are two natures in me, the Indian and the sensitive. I have suppressed the sensitive. The Indian in me enables me to press straight ahead." For the sake of his work the Indian must remain supreme.

"I have suppressed the sensitive". That, unfortunately for his peace of mind, fortunately for those who were to come after him, he could not do. He had made his choice; the artist equally with the Indian (the savage as he usually called it) drove him for the second time to Pont-Aven.

Chapter Ten

ECOLE DE PONT-AVEN

1888

I

THERE is a period in the lives of most men which gives particular pleasure to those who try to recreate it. Such a period Gauguin had now reached. His second and third visits to Brittany, broken only by a winter in Arles and Paris, formed without doubt the most contented and most productive time of his life.

Gauguin is popularly known as the man who went to Tahiti and painted picture after picture of the islanders. But dramatic though this venture was, it was at Pont-Aven that he first found himself as a great artist, and it was at Pont-Aven that, in the opinion of many, he painted most of his greatest pictures. From Tahiti he wrote (sandwiched between others quite the reverse) lyrical letters about the country and the people; he even wrote a book extolling the beauty of both. But he wrote: that is the operative word; he wrote because he was alone, because if he wished to express his thoughts he had to write. He wrote little from or about Brittany because there was no time for writing and no need of it; he could say all he wanted to say to the men grouped about him. Gauguin, though he sought solitude, though he often needed solitude, was not a solitary; he needed praise, he needed disciples, he needed the sense of progress. At Tahiti this sense became increasingly intermittent because he had always to awake it in himself; in Brittany in 1888 and the following years he never lost it—it was kept alive by discussion, example and the responsibilities of leadership.

Once more he was the leader, no longer the accidental leader of half a dozen rebels but a man accepted by the world of advanced painters in Paris whose reputation attracted the young, curious and ambitious painters anxious to escape from the dead hand of the Ecole des Beaux Arts. These men believed that they lived in a world where everything was interesting and could be beautiful, where laws were made to be broken and the truth of the painter's vision alone was all-important. One after another made the long journey, came to the Pension Gloanec, heard Gauguin, saw the work he was doing and stayed on.

Based on a village where the tiny *Place*, the solitary street were natural debating grounds, surrounded by a people and a countryside that had not visibly changed for centuries, the group soon acquired a homogeneity impossible in a city. And not only in painting. Gauguin and his followers bathed, fished and walked together, fenced in the school that he had persuaded the harbour master to open and, after Gauguin had been taught to box by one of the painters, all boxed too. In these sports, which helped to mould the men into a community, Gauguin's great strength and surprising agility kept him head and shoulders above his companions, reinforcing his authority as a painter.

A school was being born at Pont-Aven which, though not long-lived, was to influence profoundly the future of painting. Yet those who looked on could scarcely be blamed for blindness; all they saw were men who dressed weirdly, talked loudly, behaved like children and painted pictures which matched their behaviour. Even the men themselves were hazy about the future; they lived from day to day happily enough, working hard, playing hard and talking incessantly. They repeated the dicta of their master: simplify, paint away from the scene, use sables, use pure colours in juxtaposition. It was exciting work, as their canvases showed, and their conversation; heard in the darkness they could be identified by their fervent and frequent exaltation of the virtues of "vert véronèse et du jaune de chrome employés purs". Indeed, their high spirits were the most obvious thing about them—these and their faith in Gauguin, the great man who could do no wrong.

He was surely the proudest and the most satisfied of all. No one would think so to look at him; he was neither gregarious nor talkative; he covered his feelings as cautiously as any Englishman though with less care for the conventions; to the outsider he remained haughty and arrogant, his sharp tongue a scourge to the philistines. He had moments of moodiness and doubt even with his intimates; but as a rule, surrounded by his group, he was another man—genial, helpful, with a childlike pleasure in fun and, when serious, possessed by the irresistible urge of the man with a mission. He could justly be described as a silent man, but when he discussed painting in the right company he became transformed. Several of his disciples have left impressions of him at such moments and all concur: his eyes, those lazy, dull, half-hidden eyes, opened wide, shone a brilliant blue-green, were fanatical, as inspiring as his words.

In February, when he arrived at the pension, all Gauguin's satisfaction was to come; only a stray painter or two was about; the welcome of Marie-Jeanne Gloanec was his one obvious gain. She in her rather severe fashion was clearly glad to see him and so, less restrainedly, were Louise and Marie le Pape—at least until he tried to make them pose in the nude. Between them they made him feel at home, fed him, built up the stoves so that they crackled and spat with heat, slid the long glowing pan into his bed before he trod heavily upstairs, and in other feminine ways gave him that reassuring sense of a return home. To a homeless man this is bliss even in a stone pension in bleak Brittany, and Gauguin relaxed—but mainly in his bed. The effect of Martinique had still not worn off completely—he was troubled by dysentery—and he replied bitterly to Mette, who had complained of feeling lonely: "You have the children, your Danes, your sisters and brothers, your house, but what about me? I'm alone in my room in the pension from morning till night, I never speak to a soul, there's no one to exchange an idea with."

He was not a good patient, that was clear, and by no means a stickler for accuracy; and he did not tell Mette of the one immediate joy that Pont-Aven had given him. He had seen Brittany for the first time under snow. He never forgot that sight, and he painted it again and again, and when, in March, the rains came, he wrote in a very bad temper to Schuff, who had obligingly sent a spare fifty francs: "My God, how sad everything is just now! No snow, lots of rain and hail, impossible to work out of doors, and inside I can't get models."

His letters, as spring changed to summer, bore less and less relation to the life he was living. This was not deliberate deception; he was a man of moods—a rainy day, the refusal of the scandalised Marie le Pape to pose, the discovery of an empty tobacco jar plunged him into melancholy; he was occasionally a sick man when all the world looked black; and he had lived so long with misfortune that he had difficulty in realising that for the moment he was not actually suffering it. When he was not painting, when he sat down to write a letter, for instance, or could not sleep, he was the genius denied all material reward. His memories of the hell of the Panama canal workings at Colon, of his helplessness in Martinique, swept him into bitterness every time his body reminded him of them. His pride, enormous, insatiable, rose up into hatred when he thought of those winters in Paris, a beggar, a supplicant. Even at this moment he was fed and housed by the kindness—charity he would call it at such times—of a woman who understood nothing of his art, and he had no guarantee that it would continue. Next month, next year, where would he be and how? How he had suffered! And for what? For an art for which the world cared nothing. And to him Mette, the philistine, typified the world.

He had long since grown into the habit of stressing the contrast between their situations. He did this partly to anticipate reproaches and to soothe his conscience, but he also genuinely felt aggrieved by the comfort of her suburban existence and the uncertainty of his own. When she complained in early summer that she had heard nothing of him for weeks, he burst out angrily: what was the use of writing? "Our letters aren't an exchange of thoughts and feelings." A friend to whom he had shown one of her letters was amazed; they were like business letters, cold and unloving, dealing always with money.

"You do nothing to give me courage," she said; and he, taking her up, asked what need she had of courage—was she living in an inn "without a mother, without children"? And "If you had a regular income you'd be the luckiest of women." Like so many French people, he placed great store on birthday greetings. He reminded her that he would be forty in a few days. "Some people of consequence have written me letters of sympathy and admiration. I haven't had one-tenth of it from my own family."

Mette sent the birthday greetings—"you will see that we are thinking of you"—but accompanied them with the usual self-pitying complaint: the children were at the sea, "I shall pass the summer it doesn't matter how or where providing I don't spend anything." She didn't want to whimper, but "You give the impression of caring so little what becomes of us." Again she pulls herself up—no recriminations—"the aim of this letter is simply to tell you that I'm far from forgetting you which is probably all the same to you. Perhaps you don't care anyway. Write soon. I torment myself much for you."

The general tone of this letter did not please him, and he evidently took Mette's protestations with a grain of salt, remembering that she had written only after repeated requests. He replied curtly, "Thanks, I'm well enough. I'm here till I let you know. Can't move at present because I owe two months' pension."

But that was not the only reason why he stayed, and when Schuff soon afterwards offered to buy his last Cézanne he declined to be rescued: "It's a rare pearl and I shan't sell it while I have a shirt on my back." This showed his strong feeling for Cézanne—an influence seen plainly in his work, and particularly in his still lives—and indicated that life at Pont-Aven was not wholly displeasing; if he were a prisoner—and in a sense he was—he was a fairly unreluctant one.

2

By this time Pont-Aven had filled up, the Pension Gloanec was stuffed with painters and Gauguin was no longer solitary unless he chose to be. Not that all the painters were acknowledged by him as fit to bear the name of painter or even of human being. But there is a comfort in opposition, and Gauguin flourished on it. Of the many painters strolling the street, sitting by the river, comparing canvases in the pension, only a few had been admitted to his confidence. But his small group was the talk of every painter in that part of Brittany. This was not surprising; like yeast, the Gauguin group—the Ecole de Pont-Aven as it came to be known—was alive; the rest, although they moved and talked and painted, were so many dead men. These consisted mostly of Americans and members of the Ecole Julian, then solidly devoted to the principles of the Beaux Arts—that the art of the painter must be divorced from common life and based on the classical style. These men looked with astonishment and indignation on the work of Gauguin and his followers; they saw them as disciples, though outrageous ones, of the still abhorred Impressionists. They nicknamed them the "pestifères" and the group, not backward, retaliated with the epithet of "pompiers". The small dining-room in which Gauguin and his men took their meals was called by the crowd in the big room the "Succursale de Charenton" after the notorious lunatic asylum at that place. One evening the Americans went to the point of invading this room. Gauguin, boxing, fencing, swimming and eating good food, was fitter than he had been for years. He threatened shortly to throw them out of the room and the Americans realised with a shock that he meant business.

Thereafter the "pestifères" were left alone, proud of their isolation; they painted together, played together and argued together, deferring always to the great man. It was a good life for all; they felt, as men feel at such times, that the future of painting rested with them, but, being French most of them and profiting by the example of their leader, they did not march about with long faces, they enjoyed life, painted with ardour and talked thirteen to the dozen—nonsense, much of it, but with sense too when they were in the mood. And when Gauguin intervened, and his eyes shone and his sarcasms changed into inspiring affirmations, then the men about him knew that they were privileged.

There were times of course when all was not well. Wrangling could usually be cured by a sharp word from Gauguin, who had the art of making a man look foolish. But when Gauguin himself succumbed to melancholy the group was in a poor way indeed, and no one could feel easy until his humour was restored. The cause was usually simple; the story of the tobacco jar will do as well as any other. One day Gauguin appeared, to the general consternation, morose, silent, unapproachable. He strode heavily about, his sabots clinking ominously on the granite, the beret pulled far down over one forbidding eye, the pipe clenched between teeth that did not open to say one word—a study in massive dissatisfaction. The group conferred anxiously: What had they said or done? They examined their canvases—no answer there. They examined their conversation the previous evening—that too appeared blameless. An uneasy cloud hung over the day. Then one, brighter than the rest, noticed that no smoke was curling from the pipe in Gauguin's mouth. He hurried into the pension. There was Gauguin's tobacco jar—empty. He rushed round to the Tabac, bought tobacco and filled the jar. That evening Gauguin stalked as usual to the jar, took off the lid, filled his pipe, held out a hand for a match, lit it. The heavy frown left his face, he began to talk and all breathed again—they were forgiven.

He was, in fact, entirely dependent on his followers. He had no money, nothing. Tobacco, brushes, paints, canvases—all had to be furnished by them or by Schuff in Paris, and furnished without the asking. On no account would he ask a favour, but woe betide the man who did not regard it as a privilege.

These little clouds apart, the group flourished, differing in many things but united in admiration of Gauguin's work. He too thought well of it. He painted two or three seascapes—one *La Falaise* a dramatic subject matched by violent colours and bold forms—but as summer came on he at last went back to the nude; he made studies of Breton boys and girls bathing in a glen, and drying themselves after a bathe, of boys fighting near the river. "You'll be pleased," he told Schuff, who had urged him to paint the nude ever since the triumph of the *Etude de Nu*; now he had free models in the children whenever he cared to walk to the water, and he made the most of it. "They are quite Japanese by a savage from Peru—not at all Degas," he assured Schuff.

They were not like Degas; and if they are compared with Degas' early Spartan boys and girls these studies show despite their roughness ("très peu exécuté", he tells Schuff) a feeling for the nude and for children that the older man did not possess. Gauguin had no intention of denying his debt to Degas; he revered the superb draughtsmanship of the master and knew that he lacked it; and not only had the *Femmes à Toilette* given him the idea for his first nude, he had also absorbed the attitude of Degas towards the subject. Of all the Impressionists Degas was the least interested in landscape, the most interested in the figure. These figures—jockeys, ballet girls, laundry women—were painted at their work in unstudied attitudes. Gauguin learned the lesson. He demonstrated it first in his *Etude de Nu* and now, seven years later, in these child studies. With these he showed that he had not only a genius for the nude, he had a genius for putting children on to canvas. That summer he made many studies of them—they were the obvious models for a penniless man—bathing, dancing, tending animals—and he also painted their portraits. In all he broke new ground; his are not the idealised little girls of Renoir, the sentimental little boys of Murillo, they are real children represented with understanding and compassion. The trio of dancers, uncouth, angular in their stiff Breton clothes and formal round game; the faces, with the strange mingling of youth and age

—all are real children with their innocence, awkwardness, appeal. He had not the technical skill with the brush of Renoir and Murillo, but his children are nevertheless living as theirs are not.

His admirers claimed that no other man had recreated the child as he did; the scoffers, missing the daintiness, the hint of the celestial, the curls, the cream and satin cheeks, rejected the travesty—this womaniser, this hard-drinking, foul-mouthed, vanity-ridden heathen, to paint the innocent, the pure in heart! But the scoffers were mistaken; Gauguin often said about himself: "I am a savage. I am a child." Because he was so much savage and child he understood children; he had a feeling for them and they for him—not the patronising feeling of the adult but a fellow-feeling.

Regarding these child studies, seascapes, Breton women in a field and half a dozen more canvases, Gauguin might well feel satisfied, but satisfied he was not, and not all the homage lavished on him could make him so. By and large he remained restless—he had sold nothing, he could not pay his way—and in mid-summer, in the midst of his triumphs, he tells Schuff (after a caustic comment on the current price of three thousand francs for a Monet compared with—if he could get it—the four hundred francs Theo van Gogh was asking for a Gauguin) that he has accepted the offer of Vincent van Gogh and is only waiting for money to be off.

3

This offer of Vincent's was substantially as before. When Gauguin left for Pont-Aven Vincent went off abruptly to Arles. There he took a house, painted furiously, but was soon desperate for company, and in particular the company of Gauguin. A desultory three-cornered correspondence began between himself, Gauguin and Bernard. Gauguin, when he wrote, complained of his lot, without money, without friends, without a home, wife or children: "My God! how terrible these money questions are for an artist!" This more or less automatic grouse appeared to Vincent almost as a divine interposition. All was not lost; and when he heard that Gauguin had asked Theo for help he appealed again to him to share his home, to be master, to paint in the poor man's tropics; he was sure that Theo would pay Gauguin's keep in return for one canvas a month.

Gauguin said yes, he would come; all he needed was money for the fare and the pension bill—at any rate, for the fare. He had hopes of getting the money; Schuff was teaching a business friend to paint and at the same time strongly recommending the purchase of a Gauguin or two.

Why should Gauguin accept what he had rejected months earlier? There was certainly the important addition—Vincent's promise of Theo's help, but this seems scarcely enough to make Gauguin abandon all that he had gained at Pont-Aven. Unhappily no man is able to see one period of his life in relation to the rest of it, and few men are able to make the most of the present without longing for the future or lamenting the past. Gauguin did not know when he was well off. He enjoyed much of the Pont-Aven life and he was conscious of progress, but he was not free; he had no money and could not move without it. This state drove him again and again to escapes which were no escape. Logically he would be no more free at Arles than at Pont-Aven, but logic does not rule at such moments; he was at Pont-Aven, not at Arles—one was the prison, the other the momentary goal.

But this was not sufficient reason for him to leave a place where he had good friends, was well fed and housed and was working better than ever before—and to leave it to join a man for whom he felt no more than contemptuous pity. There were further influences. There was his unfortunate assumption that he was a good business-man, which is not at all the same thing as a successful gambler on the stock exchange. This assumption led him into one fix after another; it now persuaded him that by deigning to live for a time with the difficult Vincent he would please Theo, always worried about his brother's friendlessness, and that this pleasure would be expressed in a special effort to sell his work and make him famous. But Gauguin, as so often, was being too smart. He could earn Theo's gratitude; but to do so he would not only have to go to Arles, he might have to stay there. And what possibility was there that he and Vincent could live together? This he never even considered.

Finally, there was that in Gauguin which time after time made nonsense of all calculation. He called himself a savage and he was visited by imperative longings for a life away from modern civilisation. It was not a pose nor was it mere escapism. He welcomed his

Mme. A. Joly-Segalen

GAUGUIN IN 1888

Former coll. A. Vollard *Photo: Vizzavona*

LA RONDE DES TROIS BRETONNES. 1888

affinity with the simple and the savage, he boasted of it; he was tired of talking about it, he wanted to live it, to put it on to canvas. Arles, it was true, was a far cry from the tropics, there would be no unspoiled children of nature, but there would be sun, a clear atmosphere and, if the enraptured Vincent were to be believed, a gaiety, a freedom and a blaze of colour sufficient to make the sombre Pont-Aven with its starched and coiffed women, its bleakly sounding sabots, its fogs and storms, appear temporarily unendurable.

So the savage, the businessman, the prisoner and the discontented joined to accept Vincent's offer, but the gods looked kindly on the truant busily turning his back on his destiny. Schuff's friend hesitated, decided not to buy the pictures. Before Gauguin could make other plans for raising the fare Laval arrived at Pont-Aven from Martinique (recovered in health, so it seemed, and repatriated at last), followed by Bernard from St Brieuc. Vincent, Arles, the south rushed from Gauguin's mind; he had something else to think about.

Chapter Eleven

EMILE BERNARD

1888

I

This time Bernard brought with him his mother and sister. Madeleine Bernard was seventeen, delicate, intense, intelligent, a devoted Catholic and, with her large, burning black eyes, her white oval face and massed dark hair, something of a beauty. She looked with compassion on the gaunt bearded Laval, whose melancholy cough, courage in Martinique and adoration of Gauguin gave him a romantic prestige. She too had weak lungs, she too loved poetry and painting. Were they not made for each other? Laval began to think so. Gauguin thought otherwise; the arrival of this ethereal young creature in a backwater like Pont-Aven was little short of a miracle. He took her under his wing—not, however, the wing he usually extended. He took her for long walks, listened to her pathetic stories of parents who wished to stifle all her artistic impulses, told her of his own troubles, taught her to paint, made her portrait, asked her to sign a still life on the the Pont-Aven fête-day. He behaved like a lover with the love left out; she must be always with him, she must have eyes and ears only for him, but he gave her, instead of caresses, good advice. He appeared to regard her as a substitute for his adored daughter, Aline, now much of an age with Madeleine. He grew amiable and was once seen to nod to an American.

He spoke to Madeleine of her brother, of his brilliant promise. This was not said merely to please; he had studied Bernard's gift to Mère Gloanec, hung in the small dining-room, and saw in it, even more than in *Maison de Mes Parents*, a daring but justifiable advance on Impressionism as well as an exaggerated echo of his own unrealised visions. What with the picture and Madeleine, Bernard found himself fully accepted at last; so much so that Gauguin within a few days, in mid-August, is writing hopefully to Schuff: "The group grows. Little Bernard is here and has brought from St Brieuc some interesting things. There's one who fears nothing!" As for himself: "My latest work is going on well. I'm beginning to strike a new note, or rather my previous researches are at last beginning to show themselves in a synthesis of form and colour." He adds a word of advice in terms which must have astonished Schuff: "Don't paint too much after nature—remember, art is an abstraction. Dream in front of nature, draw from it the essence of what you see, but think more of the final aim on your canvas. That's the only way to lift yourself towards God, the only way of being a true creator like our divine master."

What had happened? Bernard had happened—Bernard full of his latest discovery, a Bernard to whom Gauguin now listened. Earlier that year Bernard had thrashed out the matter with his particular friend, Anquetin. "When you study a scene," he said, "and recall it later in the studio, you will paint not that scene but its essence. The imagination simplifies what the eye sees, rejecting unessential detail. The forms become the clear lines of geometrical architecture, the tones reduce themselves to the seven colours comprising white light." There was no original thought here: Pissarro had advised his son Lucien to draw in just such a manner as the only means of expressing his own vision; Gauguin had discussed the question at Pont-Aven two summers earlier and had fumbled his way towards it as far back as the beginning of 1885 when, searching vaguely for his true "sensation", he announced that pure nature was not enough, that the intelligence of the artist must take from nature only what his "sensation" demanded. But it was left to Bernard, overflowing with words, young, eager, and confident that he would overturn the world, to state simply the idea behind the synthetic school of painting.

There was nothing new in this idea; Bernard's originality consisted in his application of it to painting and his choice of the one man who could develop it. He hastened the break with Impressionism by condemning the division of tones—the essence of Impressionist painting—as causing the colours to lose intensity and appear dirty. He extolled once more the beauties of the stained-glass windows, the frescoes and the stone carving at St Brieuc—synthetic art. He flourished Japanese prints at the group—synthetic art. And to work off some of his exuberance he gave practical demonstrations; he made sketches of Breton girls at the fête, then painted a study of the girls in a meadow; he brought the painting home one afternoon and showed it to Gauguin in triumph—synthetic art.

Bretonnes dans la Prairie is almost covered by a field of brilliant yellow green. On this field the Breton women stand and sit in their black dresses and huge white coifs. The composition is elementary, or, more exactly, there is no attempt at composition. The only suggestion of perspective is conveyed crudely by the relative size of the figures. The whole canvas is reminiscent of the work of a highly talented child—an effect intended by Bernard, who was soon writing delightedly to Vincent, "Gauguin and I are painting as children paint."

For Gauguin responded immediately. He was struck by Bernard's daring and effective use of black and bright colour, the bold forms, the obliteration of detail, but his chief thought was that he could do this kind of thing and do it better. He wasted no time; he borrowed from Bernard some of his more vivid colours, including the Prussian blue ostentatiously left off the Impressionist palette, he accepted Bernard's tip for the making of a dense black, and that same evening he painted his *Vision Après le Sermon*, the picture from which modern painting may be said to have sprung.

The charge has often been made that this picture is a blatant copy of the Bernard: there are the figures dominating the foreground, the Breton women with their coifs; there is the ground of vivid colour—the famous Gauguin red instead of Bernard's yellow-green. But this is to take a shortsighted view; the *Vision* is a perfect demonstration of Gauguin as artist, his strength and his weakness. Unable by himself to discover his true "sensation", he had the insight to recognise it when shown to him. He used the Bernard canvas rather as springboard than model; he transformed an ambitious shot in the dark to a work of art. He kept the simplicity of form and pure bright colour, he restored perspective by a device of genius, he added strong and satisfactory figure work, he gave his women expressive features and he bound the whole with a double unity, of composition and of story.

Gauguin had never before painted a picture like the *Vision*; yet in one important characteristic it resembled all the good work that he had made before it and all that he was to make after it; it possessed, as they possessed, a classical calm, difficult at first to associate with the painter. Here was a man publicly removing himself from the so-called classical school of the day, glorying in his reputation as arch-rebel, treading where none had trod before, producing work from which all but a handful of painters would shrink, to say nothing of the public. Yet the chief quality of the *Vision*, as of the *Etude de Nu* and all the great canvases following it, is a monumental peacefulness. It may appear an enigma that the sensual, the bitter, the discontented, should convey not these things in his work but spiritual certainty and calm. Gauguin gave the answer: "Those who condemn me don't know all there is in an artist's nature. The artist is not born in one piece." Gauguin was a man of many faults, but in essence he was not the man he has been thought to be, he was not as he took some pains to represent himself; fundamentally he was a man of an assured and noble faith.

With the *Vision* Gauguin achieved mastery of his art at a bound —so Bernard claimed; Gauguin declared that the bound was made up of immeasurable small steps self-taken, with at most a small final push from behind. In this divergence lay the seed of future trouble, but for the moment both were too full of their discovery to quarrel about the relative merits of their contributions to Post-Impressionism. The group admired, copied. All felt a sense of great happenings in the air, and they were not mistaken. A movement had begun whose ends are not yet seen and a great painter had established his right to the name.

It would be convenient to be able to say that from this moment Gauguin never turned back, but in truth he never ceased to turn back to the very year of his death. He was to renounce Impressionism, to renounce the Pont-Aven school that he founded, but he still from time to time painted after both schools and he remained, one might think, at his greatest when he remembered Brittany.

2

Up to this point the contribution of Bernard was wholly good, but unhappily the boy (he was only twenty) did not stop there; he had many bees in his bonnet and they buzzed busily about Gauguin in the next few weeks. Synthetism was not enough, declared Bernard; to make the great picture Symbolism must be added. Again there was no novelty in Symbolism; Bernard knew his Rimbaud, Verlaine, Baudelaire; he appreciated the symbolism in Baudelaire particularly; he had joined with the young poets (for he wrote verses too) who scribbled Baudelairean stanzas on tambourine skins in the Café du Tambourin. Had Gauguin read him? Gauguin produced a copy of *Curiosités Esthétiques* published a few years earlier. Bernard responded with *Fleurs du Mal* and read from the *Rêve Parisien* a description of a countryside—red fields, yellow rivers, blue trees—which Baudelaire declared was inevitably more satisfactory than nature because "Nature has no imagination." The artificial—the contribution of the artist to nature—must necesarily prove superior to the real.

It was plain that Synthetism should add to itself Symbolism. They had agreed to paint as children paint; children were not realistic; they always rendered what they had seen in terms of expressive symbols. The whole mission of the painter, Bernard insisted, was to express his idea by the forms ("the idea is the form of things regathered by the imagination"). Consider what could be expressed if one manipulated those forms freely—if, in fact, one became a synthetic-symbolist! Baudelaire, Verlaine, Rimbaud were tied to words, Debussy and his followers to notes of music; the painters had resources besides which those of poet, musician, actor were poor indeed: "In the artist's imagination the emotions or mental state provoked by a visual image take the form of signs and plastic equivalents which reproduce the emotions or mental state without copying the visual image."

Gauguin perhaps remained a little cloudy about this complication of the obvious and natural synthetism; he was a plain man and disliked pretension. But "signs and plastic equivalents" struck a chord; he had a weakness for decoration, and if, as Bernard would have it, these decorations were more than decorations, were symbols, significant of much, he would not say no—he had a weakness for symbols too. But symbolise his idea? Bernard was ready for everything; he motioned to Madeleine. There was a divine purpose in the world, Madeleine, earnest, devout, young and beautiful, insisted. Gauguin listened to the prolific Bernard, looked into the soulful eyes of his sister, considered: one can imagine him nodding the great head slowly, the pipe smoking, blue-green slits of eyes regarding boy and girl.

He was under a too congenial influence. While Bernard was painting *Madeleine Au Bois d'Amour*, in which his sister filled a pastoral rôle, Gauguin was to produce his *Christ Jaune*—Christ crucified against a Breton background—*Le Calvaire* and companion pieces, powerful works all of them carrying forward the new principles with boldness and brutality. But he was not at ease, as Vincent van Gogh was to see even through his worship. "I'm not an admirer of Gauguin's *Le Christ du Jardin d'Oliviers.* As for Bernard's, he has probably never seen an olive tree, he fails to get hold of such a thing, either its reality or its potentiality. No, I don't place any store by their biblical interpretations."

When Gauguin paints a self-portrait with a yellow crucifix and follows it with another self-portrait in which even the crucifix is banished and he alone appears dressed in the Christ-robes awaiting the sacrifice with a holy calm—then certainty takes the place of suspicion, he is leaving his rightful path. Religious in the broad sense he was, but mysticism sits on him uneasily. At such moments he saw himself the Christ-type, sufferer, martyr, crucified by a world which rejected the one who came to lead them to true art.

He had suffered for his art, he was a martyr to it, but this was not the way to show it; it was cheap and it was false to Gauguin's "sensation". His agonised or, perhaps even more embarrassingly, his saint-like face was to mar several pictures. Nor did the mark of distinction he began to besprinkle liberally on himself and others improve his canvases—for Cézanne's faint blue surround became in the hands of a Bernard infatuated by mediaeval windows a pronounced blue halo. *Cloissonisme* took its place (mercifully only for a while) beside synthetism and symbolism. It had a value in emphasising the forms, it had a decorative charm, but for Gauguin it was not good, encouraging the "flashy" element in him.

But Bernard had not finished with Gauguin. Considering perhaps that Madeleine's religious influence was stealing too much of his thunder, he proceeded to interest his friend in the ancient civilisation of Egypt. Strange beliefs there, fascinating rites, and all preserved for posterity in those relics thoughtfully brought to France by Napoleon, and in the monuments abounding still in the valley of the Nile, an area that Bernard intended to explore as soon as his father would put up the money. Let Gauguin consider the Egyptian workers in stone, a lesson was to be learned from them—the primitive powerful treatment, the mystic meaning hidden by that deceptive simplicity. The artist was nothing if not a man with a message; from the Egyptians to the Gothic cathedrals all great art had a message for the world. Let them carry that message further, in their own way.

Gauguin remembered the Inca memorials, the buried cities he had heard of when a child; scarcely a rich house in Lima was without Indian sculpture, Inca vase or figurine. He remembered the effigies set up by the coloured people in Martinique. He was impressed; he sought the simple people and the simple life so that he could produce an art with all the strength of an unspoilt tradition behind it; he was surely right to learn from their own art as well as from themselves. Idols, ugly, mysterious, began to appear in his paintings and wood carvings; they lurk and squat in corners, they grin or scowl incomprehensibly, they come forward, malevolently beaming, to share the honours with a self-portrait, they are set side by side with a devout Breton. For good measure he once at least throws on to a single canvas a crucifix, an idol and himself, the haunted man of sorrows.

What were these idols symbolic of—what connection have they with the main body of the picture? There have been many guesses, some elaborate, some learned, some highly mystical. Another explanation, more simple, is that they mean nothing whatsoever and that they merely hinder a good work from being a great one. Certainly the decorative element in Gauguin's work becomes increasingly obvious; this same summer he paints a couple of *Paysage Decoratif* which, though skilfully designed and showing a masterly colour sense, are nevertheless no more than excellent railway station posters.

3

Bernard released much of the trivial in Gauguin, but did him more good than harm. What Gauguin would have done without Bernard can only be a matter for conjecture—most probably he would have arrived at the same point later on—but at the very least Bernard hastened the process. Yet another man was to make Gauguin's work known; and to him more than any other must go the credit of setting Post-Impressionism on its way. Bernard provided the link by persuading this man to meet Gauguin.

Paul Sérusier was one of the leading lights of the Ecole Julian. He was a "massier"—that is, the man responsible for collecting the monthly subscriptions of the pupils. He was a highly educated young man, ambitious, passionately interested in painting. He painted, but not well; his genius was for instruction. He had gathered round him at the Ecole a group of men, better painters than he, but who in general tended to follow his enthusiasms. The group was known as the Nabis—the Hebrew prophets—because most of them were Jews and many wore beards, strangely enough almost all red ones. But the reddest of all was Sérusier's, who was popularly known as *le-Nabi-la-barbe-rutilante*. He spent the summer of 1888 at Pont-Aven, keeping naturally enough to the anti-pestifères crowd, including other men from Julian's, and listened with amusement to their diatribes against the abominations of Gauguin and Bernard. When he caught sight of the *Vision*, however, he was startled by its originality and power. He might have approached Gauguin then and there, but was repelled by his reputation for hauteur. Sérusier, who at twenty-three considered himself something of a great man, declined to risk a snub.

But Bernard, who knew everyone and to whom snubs were nothing, saw in Sérusier a disciple of incalculable worth; he must meet Gauguin. Sérusier needed a great deal of persuading; not until the end of September did the persevering Bernard, using every ounce of his charm, get him into the little dining-room. The meeting was momentous: both men were striking to look at, Sérusier with his red hair, bushy red beard and fiery eyes, Gauguin black, heavy, bold. The group must have wondered what dramatic scene would break out; Gauguin had a short way with the schools, Sérusier was excitable and could give a good account of himself. But the onlookers were disappointed or pleased as the case may be; Gauguin, worked on no doubt by Madeleine and her brother, took his visitor aside with an air. The two men talked together for a long time.

The effect of their talk was seen as early as the next day, when Sérusier went out painting with Bernard and Laval in the Bois d'Amour—the romantic little wood where Bernard had painted the mystic study of his sister. Sérusier was holding his brush in one hand, in the other a small panel of wood on which he was painting what he afterwards called *The Talisman*. He had paused to study the trees and the shadows they were making when Gauguin walked heavily through the falling leaves to join the party. He watched

Sérusier for a moment, then spoke to him as he was accustomed to speak to all his disciples, in the pontifical manner which gave his words the property of mystical truth.

"Comment voyez-vous ces arbres?" he asked. "Ils sont jaunes. Eh bien, mettez du jaune; cette ombre plutot bleue, peignez-la avec de l'outremer pur; ces feuilles rouges, mettez du vermillion."

It was an historic moment, but only one of the four men had an inkling of it. Laval and Bernard had heard many similar commands; Gauguin was accustomed to making them; neither they nor he gave the matter a second thought. But to Sérusier the words came as a revelation; he saw that in a sentence Gauguin had conveyed the essence of a new approach to painting, and had conveyed it with a certainty of tone that defied question. Gauguin had in fact struck a death-blow at Impressionism, but Sérusier, startled though he was, could not be expected to see as far; and, not knowing much about Impressionism at that time, would perhaps have accepted the fact calmly. He was thinking of the standards of the Ecole Julian being uprooted, and that was sensation enough. The one thing that mattered at that moment was his perception, dimly but with great excitement, of a new movement in painting. He was destined to spread this movement and so to become a man of importance—more so, indeed, than even he could imagine. He was soon on his way back to Paris to show *The Talisman* and to repeat Gauguin's words to his comrades at Julian's.

At Pont-Aven Gauguin's work went from strength to strength; by the beginning of October he was telling Bernard, who having finally torn himself from Pont-Aven was writing ecstatic letters about their joint future, that Degas wanted to buy one of his latest canvases, of two Breton girls in a meadow. "This is the greatest compliment—I have the utmost confidence in Degas' judgment." A rosy prospect opened out in his mind. "Degas' friends all believe in him"; they also would buy his Pont-Aven work; Theo van Gogh was hoping to sell the rest. He would have money, he could go where he wished.

4

This would not be to Arles if he could avoid it—that much he made clear. The correspondence with Vincent continued. Bernard sent heartrending reports to Arles of the genius unable to buy paints or canvases; Theo praised his pictures although he had not yet sold more. At Vincent's request, Bernard and Gauguin painted self-portraits with each other's canvas as background and exchanged them for a self-portrait of Vincent, strongly influenced by the Japanese—"a portrait, not of any one painter in particular but of an Impressionist in general" he explained. He was working like a madman under the sun of the Midi, excited by the colours, the exotic growth, his nerves strung up by the mistral, the loneliness ("for days I don't speak to a soul"), the lack of food ("I've lived for 4 days on 23 cups of coffee with bread"). He felt an hysterical need of the strong silent Gauguin; felt, too, indignation and pity for the great artist persecuted, fettered, his genius stunted. He looked long at the Gauguin self-portrait proudly hung on a wall of the yellow house: what a master! Ah, but the sadness of that face! "He looks like a prisoner ill and tormented." Vincent knew all about that—he had suffered for years at the hands of men and his face showed it. He was nothing, but Gauguin "must not go on like this". He entreated him to come to Arles, he pestered Theo to promise to support him, he began in a frenzy of love to decorate the yellow house in Gauguin's honour; he would scarcely eat or sleep until huge sunflowers, blazing with his beloved yellow, lined the walls.

Gauguin remained a businessman, he prided himself on that. Such an offer could not be turned down flat; Arles, all food found, was preferable to a winter of solitude in Pont-Aven, his admirers far away in their snug Paris studios. Theo, the one dealer who showed the slightest interest in him, must not be offended. But if he followed his inclinations he would be going to a very different place: "I'm rather of Vincent's opinion that the future will rest with the painters of the tropics—countries which have not yet been painted. The public will buy these pictures, I'm sure of it."

For months Laval had been at his side again, Laval back from Martinique, his sufferings forgotten, whispering husky lyrical praise of the island, its people, its possibilities. The gaudy colours of Martinique, its strapping women and free and easy life, a paradise for the painter, chased away memories of the fevers, nightmares, hunger, despair. "If Theo sells my pictures and Degas' friends do their part I shall go to Martinique again, will do good work this time." His imagination raced on; he was back and not alone: "I hope to buy a house there and found a studio where my friends can find everything they need." The autumnal chill of Pont-Aven, the cloaked and bundled figures, the bare trees, the whistling wind tearing straight across the Atlantic, the sullen sound of the sabots became intolerable. He huddled by the pension stove, silent, sulky. Martinique!

But he hadn't a sou, he couldn't move a step, he must be patient. He wrote off to Vincent: he longed to be in Arles, but he was ill, he dreaded the thought of the journey. That would keep him quiet, he thought. And, not wishing to have all his eggs in one basket, he launched an ambitious and, if the truth be told, nonsensical plan, to raise six hundred thousand francs to back a dealer in Impressionist pictures. He received instead three hundred francs from Theo, who, pressed on all sides, from Vincent, from Bernard, from Gauguin, had managed to sell some of his pottery. Three hundred francs would not get him to Martinique. It would settle some of his bills—not all—and get him to Arles, but he could not bring himself to go to Arles; he talked about it and wrote about it, but he did not go.

He said afterwards that he had an intimation of disaster. Undoubtedly his resistance to a ménage with Vincent remained strong, and Vincent's hysterical letters did nothing to diminish it. He made one more effort to compromise: "I've now organised life here so that three of us could live together cheaply," he told Bernard; and he suggested to Theo that Vincent might do better to give up Arles and try Pont-Aven. The fact was, that in spite of the three hundred francs "every day I'm slipping deeper into debt and the journey to Arles grows more and more out of the question". If Vincent couldn't be persuaded to try Pont-Aven, it looked as though he would be forced to ask Theo for the fare. To Vincent he sent reassurances in what he imagined to be the appropriate language. Vincent's suggestions that he didn't want to come to Arles were "so many knives twisted in my heart". He would come the moment he sold a picture. It wouldn't be easy; Mère Gloanec had been so good that for him to leave would give the appearance of outrageous ingratitude. But even this he would do—let that be a sign of his anxiety to join his friend.

The suggestion pleased no one. Bernard, close to his army service, hankered after Paris for his last free months and was in any case powerless to move—his father, taking a poor view of the company he was keeping, cut short supplies. From Arles came cry after cry of angry protest.

Theo, to save his brother from a disappointment which he would feel, as he felt everything, with desperate intensity, had warned him again and again that Gauguin might not come to Arles and if he did come might not prove the perfect bedfellow. His warnings were received with hurt dignity. What did Vincent care whether Gauguin came or not? "Let him go on fooling away in the north with his friends, arguing and fighting with the English." He knew what had been going on: "The moment Laval turned up at Pont-Aven there was no more talk of Arles, and if Laval had had more money Gauguin would have left us in the lurch altogether. If he sells a picture or two I suspect he'll have other ideas than coming down here. He's after success—I don't care a jot about success or happiness, only in making this new Impressionist movement a permanent one and in giving food and shelter to all who take part in it. But Gauguin, if all goes well, will probably take up with his wife and children again."

This should have been conclusive, yet here was Theo acting as devil's advocate. "I'm not going to Pont-Aven to stay at the inn with the English and the Beaux Arts people and argue every evening," Vincent shouted. "That would be living in hell. I'd rather shut myself up in a cloister like the monks, free to go to the brothel or the café as I please."

That too sounded final enough, but was not so. Vincent had set his heart on Gauguin. Theo had scarcely read one letter, adamant, defiant, than another turned up: Gauguin must come, would come, Vincent was working like a demon at the yellow house, he was now decorating Gauguin's bedroom with his *Poet's Garden* sequence, he wanted to make it "as much as possible like the boudoir of an artistic woman", he must ask Theo for more money to buy an armchair he had seen which would exactly suit Gauguin. "It would make an enormous difference to me if Gauguin comes here." He wanted the studio to be absolutely ready: "a setting worthy of the Gauguin who is to be its head". He was taking a vast joy in the home and the work: "And I dare to hope that the joy will be shared. . . . If we make up our minds not to quarrel we shall help each other to increase our reputations."

The letters poured out; and to Theo two facts became clear—

Vincent would not leave Arles or desert his studio of the south, and he would have Gauguin. Theo told Gauguin so, offered to keep him at Arles for one canvas a month. Gauguin, cornered, threw up his hands and thought hard of the sun of the south; he was ill, miserable, he feared the worst, but . . .

He wrote off to Mette and to Schuff; he was going to Arles. "I expect to stay for some time because I shall be able to work there without worrying about money." He was going, but only if Theo supplied the fare; Schuff must ask him to wire the money.

Schuff obliged as usual, Theo sent the money, Gauguin packed gloomily.

Theo did more, rather more perhaps than he would have wished to do at that particular moment; he sold a Gauguin picture, *Les Bretonnes*, for five hundred francs and hurriedly warned Vincent, "He'll be solvent for the moment, but will he come to you? Don't lose heart if he doesn't."

But Gauguin was on his way at last after a gesture in keeping with the situation; he wrote to Madeleine Bernard. Now that he was in a manner martyring himself, he felt himself to have a right, a positive duty. He didn't pretend to be a great letter writer, but he sat down heavily, took a pen and laboriously composed in his beautiful handwriting a self-portrait which most readers may find unrecognisable, yet which is as true to the man as his other, more obvious ones. His general attitude should be familiar to the Englishman, who will go to lengths of the most desperate frivolity to disguise his deepest feelings. But Gauguin was not English, he distracted attention from his virtues by most un-English expedients. He succeeded too well, for he was essentially serious, he was a religious man in the best sense of that word. Madeleine, the shadow of the daughter he could never see, was one of the few before whom he did not assume a mask. Anxious to influence her for good, he leaned back too far; but his letters to her, despite sanctimonious touches and unintended humour, reveal a side of himself that cannot be disregarded if the man and his work are to be understood. "Dear Sister," he wrote, "don't read this if you are satisfied to go through life like most young girls, without aim or reason, a prey to every whim." And having obtained his audience, he launched his craft. First, he insisted, Madeleine must consider herself sexless: "the soul and heart, the divine, must not be the slave of matter, that is the body". What then must she do? She must know that the virtues of men and women alike should be the Christian virtues, to be good and self-sacrificing and to do their duty to the like-minded. "Judge everything by conscience. Set up an altar to your dignity and intelligence and those only. Lying and venality are crimes." It was to ignore or misunderstand the divine laws to act as a slave. "Do all you can to earn your own living. But suppress *vanity*. Fear not. If you need help appeal to me—brother, sustain me. We artists also have need of you."

As a reminder that he was taking his own advice he added a postscript: "2 place Lamartine, Arles, from October 22." Soon afterwards he climbed despondently into the train and was trundled slowly southwards.

And in Arles, Vincent, disregarding Theo's warnings, sent up a great shout: "My whole mind is set on Gauguin now!"

Chapter Twelve

VINCENT VAN GOGH

1888

I

GAUGUIN arrived at Arles in the early morning. He went to the only place that was open, the all-night café. He knew all about this café; Vincent had spent three days and nights there making a study of the hell he believed it to represent, with its down-and-outs, its billiard table shining a ghastly green under the lamps, its cards and dice and white-coated *patron*. This man now came forward to welcome the visitor: oh, yes he was expecting M. Gauguin. He explained: Vincent had hurried in a few days earlier clutching a photograph; he had thrust it at him excitedly—"That's my pal: he's coming to live with me, look out for him." Gauguin remembered the photograph, "taken by an admirer"; he had sent copies right and left from Pont-Aven and had commanded Mette, "show it to the children so they shan't quite forget their father".

Gauguin did not care much for the company he found himself in, and as soon as the sun was up he walked round to the *Place* Lamartine on the edge of the town. There was the yellow house at the corner beyond the Café de la Gare where Vincent drank his cognac and absinthe with his friend, Roulin the postman. Across the *Place* were the gardens in which Vincent had painted his studies to decorate Gauguin's room. All was much as expected. Gauguin thumped the yellow door, Vincent opened it, stammering a welcome. He looked ill. Up the little stairs was the guest room, the best in the house; Vincent threw open the door with a mixture of pride and humility; he had tried to make it fit for the modern Petrarch, as he had christened Gauguin. Gauguin said nothing—"I don't yet know what Gauguin thinks of my decorations," Vincent was writing a day or so later—but he would scarcely appreciate the feminine note, nor would he understand the reason for it. Nevertheless, he was a practical man; he had known worse; there was

National Galleries of Scotland

LA VISION APRES LE SERMON. 1888

Des vignes pourpres
forment triangles sur
le haut jaune de chrome
à gauche bretonne du
Pouldu noir tablier
gris. Deux bretonnes
baissées à robes bleu
vert clair et corsage noir
au premier plan terrain
rose et pauvresse
aux cheveux orange
chemise blanche et
jupe (terre verte avec
du blanc –) Le tout
fait au gros trait
rempli de tons presque
unis avec le couteau
très épais sur de la
grosse toile à sac.

C'est un effet de vignes
que j'ai vu à Arles.
J'y ai mis des bretonnes –
tant pis pour l'exactitude

M. Roland de Margerie

(two-thirds original size)

LETTER TO EMILE BERNARD Dec. 1888

something unsound about Vincent's ideas, but he had a gift, no doubt about it. Next door, a step away, was Vincent's room with its plain white wood bed, chairs and dresser. He would decorate the bed, Vincent explained, with a nude or a child in its cradle; but not yet; he had no time. He never had time; the blossom rushed out and fell, the trees bent under the weight of fruit, the vines thickened overnight and were cut, the reaper followed the sower, and how should he, the painter, get on to canvas all his studies of Provence—Provence in winter, spring, summer, autumn? But do it he must if he had to paint day and night and miss every meal; these Provençal studies might establish him as a painter, they might even sell (he had not sold one picture so far), they would surely attract worthwhile artists to the south.

Gauguin was summing him up from under the heavy lids: pretty far gone; he needed pulling together. Diffidently, Vincent took him downstairs to the studio. The state of the room shocked every ounce of the bourgeois in Gauguin: "Everything was in the most appalling disorder. His box of paints was crammed with tubes and the lid could never be closed." The colour box was a fair example of the chaos on every side. All Gauguin's forebodings at Pont-Aven returned; how right he had been to procrastinate, how wrong ever to come.

But when he turned from the mess to what Vincent had made out of the mess, he was surprised. How the man managed to paint at all in such conditions was a mystery, but somehow the canvases got themselves covered. Gauguin disentangled them and spread them out. The faults were obvious—the overloaded brushstrokes, the sentimentality, above all the emotionalism—and didn't surprise him. He was not prepared for the virtues and must have had hard work to conceal his astonishment at the sunflowers, the peach tree, the study of the bedroom, the still lives. This man was worth helping, he had something to say; if only the clutter of Dutch rubbish could be cleared out of his crazy brain, he could perhaps be turned into a good synthetist-symbolist. He said an approving word or two and Vincent was beside himself with pleasure.

A sight of the kitchen shook his good resolutions: ghastly; unbelievable; Vincent lived like a pig. However, he would change all that. "I find your brother somewhat nervy," he told Theo, "but I hope to calm him down." The house must be cleaned and tidied from top to bottom, everything put where it could be found (Vincent, he discovered, had starved to buy colours and brushes which he already possessed but could not find), the day-long, night-long bouts of painting must be abandoned, regular meals eaten, regular times kept, the money pooled. "We kept a box—so much for hygienic excursions at night, so much for tobacco, so much for incidentals, so much for rent. On top of the box we kept a pencil and piece of paper so that each could write down what he had taken out of it. In another box we kept the rest of the money to buy our food; we divided it into four parts, one for each week."

Gauguin cleared up the mess, took the radiant Vincent out shopping, bought a wardrobe, food, kitchen utensils and "heaps of things we need". Suddenly the yellow house became a home. Soon they were sitting down to meals cooked by Gauguin. "He cooks *perfectly*," cried Vincent, scarcely able to believe in his luck. He was one of the loneliest men who has ever lived; he yearned for a companion; he felt, he often said, that his heart would burst with longing for love; and this cant phrase was for once used exactly. But everyone found him impossible. In Arles it was the same story; people avoided him, stared uneasily at him—he was mad, they said. A word or two with the Ginoux husband and wife at the Café de la Gare and an occasional evening drink with Roulin were his only human contacts. He worked furiously—it was second best, he knew, but at least it prevented him from brooding. But even he had to rest, and his rest was no rest; half-starved, he slept abominably. His loneliness overwhelmed him. There was Theo; but Theo was not an artist, Theo was not in Arles, letters were not flesh and blood, they could not break the silence in the house. Now here was Gauguin, the great Gauguin, living side by side with him, looking after him. Vincent confessed to Theo that he had been "horribly worried"; if Gauguin had not been satisfied, still more of Theo's money would have been spent for nothing. But Gauguin, incredibly, seemed to be satisfied. Two days passed and he was still there. A miracle! "Gauguin is an astonishing man, he's not packing, he's waiting here very calmly and working hard for the right moment to take an immense step forward." Even his manner, only a shade away from outright contempt, seemed to Vincent in those first weeks as no more than just; to be ordered about, directed, his life taken up and reshaped was absolute bliss; let Gauguin frown, close his eyes, nod or shake his head instead of speaking, criticise his work—no matter, he was taking an interest. "I felt I was going to be ill," he told Theo, "but Gauguin's turning up has so much taken my mind off it that I'm sure it won't come to anything. . . . He's a very, very interesting man and I'm sure that with him about we shall do heaps of good things."

He followed Gauguin, did his bidding, began to echo his words. Bernard and Laval had been discussing the treatment of shadows; they sought Gauguin's advice. "I would avoid as much as possible anything conveying the illusion of an object," he replied, "and as shadow is the *trompe l'oeil* of the sun I'm inclined to suppress it." A few days later Vincent was telling Theo: "The shadows on objects and figures and projected by them are quite different under the stronger sun of these luminous countries and contain so much colour that one is tempted to suppress them."

When Gauguin put his foot down about *plein air* painting, he listened. Why spend the whole day outside, baked by the sun, battered by the mistral? asked Gauguin. He explained the synthetic principle; avoid photographic realism; use the imagination in the studio. Vincent protested at first, "I can't work without models. . . . I'm afraid of losing accuracy of form." But he was soon obeying, overcome still by the marvellous novelty of a companion who took the trouble to direct him. "Gauguin has brought me to see that it's about time I varied my work."

When the weather made *plein air* painting impossible, he no longer fretted himself into a nervous wreck: "I'm thankful not to be alone. Now I work from memory. Gauguin gives me courage to use my imagination, and it's true enough that paintings of this kind have something mysterious about them. . . . Gauguin and Bernard don't ask what the exact shape of a tree is, but they do insist that one should be clear whether the shape is round or square, and they're right. They are fed up with the photographic but absolutely empty perfection of certain painters. They don't ask what the exact shade of the mountains is—what they say is 'By God the mountains were blue, were they? All right, then chuck on some blue and don't bother to tell me that the blue was rather like this or that. Make the mountains blue and that's enough.' When he's explaining this kind of thing Gauguin is often like a genius, but he's afraid of showing his genius. It's touching to see how he takes the trouble to say things that will really help the young painters. What a queer creature he is!"

Vincent was not in fact temperamentally suited to this kind of work, but it kept him quiet, and that was one of his greatest needs. "It does me an enormous amount of good to have a companion as intelligent as Gauguin and to watch him at work." When he did work after his own heart Gauguin's influence showed itself at once. Don't overload your brushes, said Gauguin; cut out inessentials. Vincent painted portraits of Gauguin's chair and his own. He had never painted finer pictures; portraits in a double sense, of the chairs and of the men who used them. The precepts of Gauguin are plain to see in these canvases, yet only Vincent could have painted them; it was a true collaboration. He painted at Gauguin's special request more sunflowers—"better than Monet," said the great man briefly, at which Vincent, incredulous but happy, painted at great speed portraits of Roulin and every member of his family down to the most recent baby. "If by the time I'm forty I can make a picture with figures as good as the flowers Gauguin has spoken about, I shall have an artistic standing worthy of comparison with anyone. So let us persevere."

He watched Gauguin paint a landscape near Les Alyscamps, the main walk of the town, and marvelled. He watched him make quick studies of washerwomen down by the river, of women gathering grapes in the vineyard, of loungers sleeping on the tables in the night café, of a reclining nude with pigs in the hay. "Very original," he declared of this last: "oh, very fine, of enormous distinction." And of their maker: "He is a very great artist and a friend in a million."

But oh, that nude in the hay! Vincent could never paint from the nude, and except for the Roulins and Madame Ginoux he could not even do figure work—no woman would pose for him. For months he had been searching for his Arlésienne, the typical girl of the town; they were all about him, but not one would have anything to do with him, they looked at him with aversion and fear. But Gauguin—"Gauguin has practically found his Arlésienne already," wrote Vincent after they had taken a walk or two about the town. He saw how Gauguin looked at the women and how they looked at him; no trouble there. In two days—and he had been in Arles for six months: "I wish I had got as far." In despair he painted the portrait of Madame Ginoux, while Gauguin sketched her at the same time, painted it in three-quarters of an hour. There was his Arlésienne, a nervous middle-aged woman at the café cash-desk. It was a great picture, but he was more concerned with Gauguin's sketch—"A synthesis of the Arlésiennes"—and praised "the sober character and style of the drawing".

Gauguin took him in hand in this matter too. The Zouaves were stationed in the town and as a result brothels had sprung up everywhere—models by the dozen. They could combine business and pleasure, he explained. "We are going the rounds of the brothels pretty often," Vincent was soon telling Theo, "so as to study them."

They went the round of the brothels. Gauguin was popular, Vincent made a solitary friend, a girl who pitied him. "Gauguin is having lots of luck with the Arlésiennes." So Vincent, not free from envy but still the admirer before the envious; Gauguin was wonderful and he was the luckiest of men: "I dare to predict," he wrote to Theo, "that in six months Gauguin and you and I will see that a studio has been founded that will last."

Gauguin was well contented for the moment: "I find everything cheap here, and everything pretty, the country as well as the people." He had had his usual struggle to settle down, but he had done it: "I'm working fit to burst myself." He thought well enough of the country to invite Bernard if he escaped Army service: "Life won't be too difficult, I've examined the money question and we can manage all right." The Arlésiennes offered the kind of challenge he liked. "Here they are with their elegant coiffure, their Grecian beauty, their shawls falling into folds that remind me of the primitives. Ah, I think, the Greeks walk again, the girl who passes me in the street is as much a lady as any other and looks as virginal as Juno. Well, we shall see. In any case, I can see here the basis of a fine *modern style*." His *amour propre* was being less outraged than usual; with the money from the sale of *Les Bretonnes* he had paid his debts in Pont-Aven and had sent two hundred francs to Mette. That left him with nothing but Theo's allowance—and the unspeakable relief of being able to show the people at Copenhagen that the waster was making money from his despised painting. In the near future loomed the promise of recognition; he had been invited by the Vingtistes to exhibit at Brussels, hitherto the stronghold of the Neo-Impressionists: "It's probable," he tells Mette, "that I shall be able to send you more money this winter if the exhibition goes well. My affairs are looking up at last, slowly." He enclosed another letter from Schuff so that Mette could see "what is thought of my work in Paris and Brussels". He was sending gentle reminders to Madeleine Bernard of their unique friendship, asking her brother to give her a pot he had made, with a "Silence is the order of the day, but I hope when she puts flowers into it she'll think of her elder brother. It's a wild thing, but it expresses me." ("Magnificent!" cried the admiring Vincent.) And in Arles he was living well, exhilarated by the clear atmosphere, the brilliant colours: Vincent was right, the place was the next best thing to the tropics. His work was going well; already he had painted "my best canvas of the year"—a Provençal landscape into which he had put Breton women cutting grapes—"Tant pis pour *l'exactitude*!"

But his biggest surprise was Vincent himself; he was unexpectedly amenable, he really gave very little trouble. Gauguin was used to adulation, but he had no objection to more; he basked under it, worked, played, and his common sense was lulled into a short sleep. He had tamed the untamable—was that so remarkable? On reflection he could not think so. What exactly he thought of Vincent he nowhere makes clear; all his remarks are so tied up with his awareness of Vincent's relationship to the best art dealer of the day that his true opinion cannot be disentangled. Uneasy pity was perhaps the dominant note; but Gauguin knew goodness when he saw it. Vincent was a good man. He had, said Gauguin ,"a noble nature". He also had great talent; it was obscured, he thought, by mannerisms, technical weaknesses and a mistaken attitude towards painting, but it was there and must be respected. He expressed this respect in practical fashion. The Pont-Aven school, he decided, must have an exhibition; Synthetic-Symbolism must be put on the map . He wrote to Schuff and to Bernard commanding them to do all they could to arrange such a show "for a little group of pals". He made out a list of those who should and should not be invited: "I refuse to exhibit with *les autres*—Pissarro, Seurat, Signac, etc. This is our group!" Who then should come in? Bernard, of course, Schuff, Laval, Guillaumin, himself and one or two more. Vincent was one of these; Gauguin officially invited him. Vincent looked out six canvases. That, early in December, was perhaps the happiest moment of his life.

2

But neither this nor Vincent's worship could for long hide the fact that two more unsuitable companions never lived under the same roof. Admirers of each have sought to show that the other was responsible for the final disaster. The truth is simpler; they were incompatible; the wonder is that they stayed together ten days, let alone ten weeks. From the sorry business only one certainty emerges—that Gauguin's instinct was wiser than Vincent's when he resisted the entreaties to go to Arles.

Beyond this all is conjecture, but an effort must be made to seek a beginning of the trouble. "Our days pass in working, working," wrote Vincent. "In the evenings we are dead beat, go off to the café for a bit, then early to bed." There was one activity he failed to mention: they talked. Antipathies appeared almost at once. At first Gauguin wrote good-humouredly, "It's a bit of a joke, he sees this place as pure Daumier. To my mind it's Puvis as plain as a pikestaff with a bit of Japan thrown in." This was in the middle of November, three weeks after his arrival. He had no wish to provoke trouble then, Arles was showing its best side, and he did not wish to be uprooted again so soon. Besides, there was a "something that shone out of" Vincent's talk; "Daudet, Goncourt and the Bible inspired his Dutch brain." For a time Gauguin respected this something.

Three weeks later he again mentioned their conversations, this time with a distinct note of irritation: "Vincent and I don't see eye to eye very often about anything and still less about painting. He admires Daumier, Daubigny, Ziem and the great Rousseau, all people I can't stand. He dislikes Ingres, Raphael, Degas, whom I admire. He's a romantic, I'm a primitive. He's always raving about Monticelli's colour, I detest it. But to keep the peace I say, All right Brigadier, have it your own way."

But Gauguin did not always say "have it your own way"; or if he did he qualified it with remarks that Vincent found alarming. Reports of these remarks, with comments, begin to appear in Vincent's letters to his brother. "Gauguin, though he works hard here, is still longing for the tropics"—in other words Arles, or

Arles plus an argumentative Vincent, was beginning to lose its charm. Gauguin talked idly no doubt, but to Vincent this meant one thing only: Gauguin was thinking of leaving him.

Then came the invitation to Gauguin to exhibit at Brussels. "His imagination," says Vincent, "already begins to draw a picture of himself settling in Brussels." Another threat to leave Arles! But that was not the worst of it. Brussels was horribly near to Copenhagen. "That would probably lead to a meeting with his Danish wife." In Vincent's imagination threat followed threat, there was no end to them. Gauguin in Copenhagen might be fatal to his hopes. "I couldn't believe that such a meeting would be without consequences from the moment when, waiting here, he was successful with the Arlésiennes." True, "he and she don't get on . . . but he naturally cares for his children who, to judge by the photographs he has shown me, are very pretty." How could Gauguin resist such children? What was he, Vincent, beside them? To this worst threat of all he reacted with an ominous "We aren't so dangerous in that department."

Thought of the children led directly to the brothels. Gauguin's nightly triumph began to appear offensive. Vincent was not merely unattractive to women, he was impotent too; the years of starvation and wretchedness and the excesses in Paris had done their work. He was only thirty-three, but "I begin to resemble in physique the man in Maupassant who was so exhausted by hunting that when he married he found himself useless." He added, "if a man robbed of the power to create physically tries to create thoughts in place of children he's still a part of humanity," but this was poor consolation in the brothel watching Gauguin carrying everything before him. The contrast became unbearable the moment his fear of losing Gauguin overbalanced his worship: "No one would think him a married man the way he goes on." The suffering behind the words is unmistakable.

Gauguin for very different reasons was feeling dissatisfied. For one thing, he found Vincent's choice of companions distasteful; he seemed to go out of his way to mingle with the scum of the town. The wasters who hung about the all-night café, for instance, were the salt of the earth according to Vincent, rejected and persecuted as he had been. To Gauguin they were just down-and-outs, and their haunt "a café that Vincent loves much and which I love less. At bottom this kind of place is not for me, and the type of local *canaille* in it doesn't attract me. I like some of these places well enough, but here I always feel a sort of apprehension. It's a matter of education, and one can't change." He had found other, more serious flaws in his companion. "When I arrived," he says, "I found Vincent absorbed by the theories of the Neo-Impressionist school, floundering about and suffering, not because the school was bad in itself but because his nature was antipathetic to its patient teaching and technique. His work was a mess, he achieved only the mildest of incomplete and monotonous harmonies, the sound of the trumpet was missing. I enlightened him—an easy job because like all original natures Vincent had no fear of another man. From that day he made astonishing progress and without losing a scrap of his originality he learned a useful lesson from me." Elsewhere and at greater length he claimed to the end of his life that Vincent's use of colour and his method of drawing improved vastly under his tuition.

The exact truth of these claims is not of great importance here; there is little sign that Gauguin exercised a permanent influence on Vincent's work and no sign at all that Vincent influenced Gauguin. But it was a fact that Vincent, though he had thrown off the technique of the Neo-Impressionists, kept his admiration for the theories of their leader, Seurat. He talked and wrote enthusiastically of Seurat's plan to form painters into a kind of guild sharing a common pool of materials and working together, as the builders of the Gothic cathedrals had worked, to decorate public buildings and private houses with a series of large canvases or wall paintings; his series of Provençal studies, his *Poet's Garden* sequence, even his sunflowers, were all attempts to follow Seurat's lead.

Gauguin could endure neither Seurat nor his work nor his theories; he was for ever making sarcastic references to the "damned dot" of the Neo-Impressionists, and at Pont-Aven had enjoyed ridiculing them with Bernard, christening one of his still lives *Le Ripipoint*, while Bernard, who fancied himself as a poet, wrote mock verses *Au Petit Point*. To Gauguin, Vincent's admiration for a man whose technique he had rejected was madly irrational, and if there was one thing that he could not abide it was the irrational—physical disorder, mental disorder, both were alike to him, faults to be eradicated, even diseases to be cured. He had cleared up the physical mess in Vincent's life, he had persuaded him to clear up some technical disorder in his painting. Now, with a blend of irritation and genuine concern that defy separation, he decided to clear up the mess in his mind, "to disentangle from his disordered brain a reasoned logic in his critical opinions".

It is difficult not to sympathise with Gauguin's perplexity: "I couldn't explain to myself the complete contradiction between his painting and his opinions." For Gauguin to be unable to explain anything meant that he would not rest until he had let in the light of day. It was not only the matter of Seurat; Vincent "had a boundless admiration for Meissonier and a profound hatred of Ingres, Degas was his *bête noire* and Cézanne he thought nothing but a faker. When he spoke of Monticelli he burst into tears."

Gauguin probed the discrepancy with sharp questions, ridiculed the answers; he realised that Vincent had not discarded a single enthusiasm but had merely added others; he heard him hysterically defend the Hague school, prostrate himself before Millet. When he looked at his paintings and could see no relation between them and these enthusiasms he passed quickly from bewilderment to anger; this was nonsense and must be knocked out of him.

But at last Gauguin had struck hard rock—and a rock, if the metaphor may be humanised for a moment, that had become resentful, fearful, suspicious. The lot of a hero is never a happy one, and Gauguin was no exception; he could not live up to the ecstatic imagination of the worshipping Vincent. The hero became a man who sat bulkily in his chair puffing at his pipe and ejaculating wounding remarks about Vincent's gods—a man, moreover (and this was the heart of the matter), who having done his worst to tear away those props on which Vincent's reason was supported, might at any moment withdraw the most vital prop of all—himself.

As soon as such ideas began to rush through Vincent's brain he was a lost man; all the peace that Gauguin had given him, all the illusion of stability, slipped away and he was left worse than before, a bundle of nerves, his terrible temper flaring up, unable to sleep, to work, to do anything but brood: "We talk until our nerves are so stretched that we can scarcely raise a spark."

Gauguin girded himself for trouble. He had become a stranger to opposition; he was not to be defied, browbeaten by this stammering fanatic with his sentimental prejudices who actually dared to criticise; "he loves my paintings, but when I've done them he always finds something wrong". Vincent even questioned Gauguin's ability to discuss the matter rationally—a cruel cut, this—on the grounds that a narrow forehead betrayed lack of intelligence. No, it would not do: "Between the two of us, he like a volcano, I boiling inwardly, a struggle of some sort was inevitable."

The struggle was an unequal one—a fact which has brought much censure on Gauguin's head. Why didn't he leave Vincent alone? But the question, often asked in indignation, is not so simple. Vincent was a good man but he was also an impossible one. The pattern of his life was merely being repeated; the first short period of bliss over, nothing remained but flight or a fight, the one as cruel and disastrous as the other. "There's something about Vincent," said Theo, the only person who ever truly loved him, "something in the very way he speaks that forces people either to like or dislike him violently. And even when people like him it's the most difficult thing in the world to stay on good terms with him. He can't be indifferent—it's love or hate all the time. When he sees anything he thinks is wrong he says so, he spares no one's feelings, and that causes trouble." Theo knew the truth, but even Theo had not aroused the feelings that now raged in Vincent, his love turning to hatred through fear of losing Gauguin, his mind tortured by suspicions, by the dreadful knowledge that he was his own worst enemy and was driving the loved one away. He began to spend whole days in an ominous silence followed by periods when he banged angrily about the house. He scribbled strange texts on the walls. At night Gauguin would awake suddenly to find him coming towards the bed; he would say loudly, "What's the matter Vincent?" and Vincent would go away without a word. It was unnerving. Gauguin was no coward, but something had to be done; Vincent was obviously losing control of himself. He wrote to Theo asking him to send the fare to Paris: "I respect your brother's intelligence, but our temperaments don't mix, we can't live here together in peace."

This letter brought Vincent to his senses; he begged Gauguin not to leave Arles; he would control himself, they would work together as before, all would be well. Gauguin hesitated; he shrank from another poverty-stricken winter in Paris; Vincent's distress was difficult to resist. He wrote again to Theo: take no notice of the letter.

To celebrate the new accord they went over to Montpellier to see the Fabre collection. At first Vincent was taken out of himself by this rare excursion. In the gallery were canvases by Delacroix, Courbet, Giotto, Botticelli, Th. Rousseau. Gauguin copied a mulatto woman by Delacroix, Vincent cried in an ecstasy over some Courbets and saw in the Delacroix portrait of Brias another brother—"just like us" he told Theo. "We talked a lot about Delacroix and Rembrandt." One of the Rembrandt portraits, Vincent declared, reminded him of Delacroix and of Gauguin—all three had a manner in common. Gauguin, pleased, admitted that "I feel myself returning to my old nature". All seemed well.

But a picture gallery was an unhappy choice nevertheless. The conversations did not stop at Delacroix and Rembrandt. All their differences came into the open again; Gauguin couldn't endure Vincent's passion for Th. Rousseau, to mention only one of the disputed subjects, Vincent couldn't endure Gauguin's gibes at his heroes. Soon after they returned they were back in every sense where they had begun, and Vincent was once more strung up, dangerous. "Our discussions become *excessively electric*. We come out of them with heads as exhausted as used-up batteries." He was beside himself; the slightest provocation would send him over the edge.

Gauguin provided the provocation. As usual he remained outwardly calm, but he too was angry—angry with himself for changing his mind, even more angry with Vincent for breaking his promise of good behaviour; he must be taught a lesson. Gauguin's anger found its way into his hand. For some time he had been making a study of Vincent at work on the sunflowers he had asked for. At first Vincent was delighted: "I don't consider it likely to be thought one of his less successful projects," he announced proudly to Theo. Then he became perplexed as the portrait neared its end. "At times I look like that," he told Bernard, "absolutely exhausted yet charged with electricity." Yes, he looked like that at times, he felt like it at that moment, after the return from Montpellier, but why did his friend emphasise what he wanted to forget?

Then Gauguin finished the picture. His anger guided his hand only too well. Vincent looked at it. "Yes, it's me all right, but me mad."

That evening at the café, Vincent suddenly flung his glass of absinthe at Gauguin. Gauguin got up, took him in his arms, walked home and laid him on the bed. Vincent at once seemed to go into a kind of coma.

The next morning he apologised. He could not remember exactly what had happened, but he believed he had been offensive: would Gauguin forgive him and forget? Gauguin accepted the apology. As for forgetting, that was another matter; the next time the glass might hit him, then there would be real trouble. He had better leave Arles, it would be for the good of both. Vincent begged him not to go; Gauguin shook his head.

That day—two days before Christmas—Vincent wrote to Theo: "I'm afraid Gauguin is a bit tired of the good town of Arles, of the little yellow house and particularly of me. Both of us have serious problems to settle, it's true, but the problems come more from ourselves than outside. I believe he'll either make a clean break or an equally definite decision to stay. I've urged him to think again and consider his own best interests before acting. He is very strong, very creative, but precisely because of that he must have peace. Will he find it anywhere else if he can't find it here? I wait with absolute serenity for him to make up his mind."

Poor Vincent, there was little serenity for him that day or any other day of his short life. Since Gauguin's arrival at Arles, his need of him had grown beyond all bounds. In Paris Theo had fallen in love. Had Vincent remained alone and unhappy at Arles Theo would have said nothing to him about his intentions; indeed, so great were his love for Vincent and his unselfishness that he might have postponed his marriage indefinitely. But reading Vincent's ecstatic letters during the early weeks of Gauguin's stay he felt with surprise but enormous relief that his forebodings had been mistaken—Gauguin had not only gone to Arles, he really appeared to be settling down there; Vincent at last had found a companion. He broke the news. Vincent received it with equanimity; he no longer expected to come first with Theo, for thirty years his only support, but what a compensation he had been given!

Now Gauguin talked of going and he would have nothing, no one. And Gauguin really was going; as the day wore on there could be no mistaking his intentions; the heavy steps up and down the stairs as he collected his belongings were more decisive than any words. Yes, he was really going.

Did Gauguin realise what was passing in Vincent's tormented mind? Like most people, he disliked and despised the dependent. Vincent was quarrelsome, violent, aggressive through fear of losing him, no doubt, but what right had one man to lean on another?

Methodically, he began to pack. Vincent watched the precious canvases rolled up, stacked together, stowed away, the tubes of colour neatly arranged in their box. He saw the bedroom, the room he had decorated with such loving care, slowly stripped. The measured tread sounded pitiless.

By the evening the atmosphere in the yellow house had become suffocating. Gauguin went out for a breath of air. He had not gone far when he heard hurried footsteps behind him. He knew those steps well—short, quick, uneven. He turned. Vincent was coming for him with an open razor in one hand.

Gauguin looked at him; he was appalled, but he looked at him sternly. That look had never failed to pull Vincent up short. Vincent hesitated, Gauguin held his breath. Vincent bent his head, turned and ran back towards the yellow house.

Gauguin hurried on to a hotel, took a room and tried to sleep. Early the next morning he went back to the house. A large crowd pressed round the door. He pushed his way through. Inside, the floor was covered with bloodstains and towels and sheets soaked with blood.

Two policemen were in the room. His friend was dead, they said; what did he know about it? Nothing, he protested. Then he heard the story. Vincent had come back to the house the previous evening and had hacked off one ear with the razor. In doing so he had cut an artery and lost much blood before he managed to tie a towel round his head. He wrapped the ear in paper and staggered round to their usual brothel. He gave the package to the girl who was kind to him. She opened it and fainted; in a moment the brothel was in an uproar and soon the entire street. Roulin the postman heard the noise. Vincent's behaviour had worried him for weeks past, and he had kept a concerned eye on him. He ran round to the brothel; there was Vincent swaying on his feet, silent. Roulin led him home and got him on to the bed before the police arrived.

Gauguin and the policemen went upstairs where Vincent lay on his bed unconscious, a rough bandage wrapped round his head. He was not dead, as Gauguin demonstrated. He also satisfied the police that he had been nowhere near the house for the past twelve hours. He was freed and immediately wired to Theo: come at once.

Theo was just about to go to the Netherlands with his fiancée. He crossed Paris and caught the train south, travelling through the night. When he arrived at Arles the next day, Vincent had been taken to hospital. He had lost much blood and his condition was critical. He was sane, but tortured by remorse and by fear that he was going mad; he could not express himself, the words would not come—all the suffering was in his face. Theo could scarcely bear to look at him; he would not be comforted.

Vincent made one request: send Gauguin to him. He had asked repeatedly for him ever since he became conscious, but Gauguin would not go near him. He continued to refuse: "I should excite him again; the sight of me might prove fatal."

When, the Christmas holidays over, Theo had to go back to Paris, leaving Vincent still very ill, Gauguin went with him; he had not seen Vincent.

Vincent recovered strength and in the first days of the new year, 1889, was able to write letters. Why had Gauguin not come to see him? he asked Theo: was he afraid? And he asked Gauguin, "My friend, was it really necessary to bring my brother down from Paris?" But that was his only reproach, and one that he was to regret. He begged him "not to say anything bad about our poor little yellow house". He wished him well. He could not believe that all was over: "I still hope and believe that we shall both have a happier future together in the South."

Gauguin was widely blamed for his behaviour at Arles and has been blamed ever since, but all his critics have one thing in common; they have never tried to live with Vincent. The two men most concerned did not share this attitude. Vincent, after that single reproach, apologised for causing Gauguin so much trouble; and for the rest of his life his one overwhelming wish was to be with Gauguin again—Gauguin was his master, the hope of modern painting, he was a good man and "like me you are the unhappy kind".

Theo, with every apparent cause for anger, showed none. He

had lived with Vincent for the best part of two years. The experience had made him ill, had practically driven him mad. He knew Vincent; he agreed with him that Gauguin was an unhappy man and a great artist. He tried to help Gauguin in every way—more, in fact, after the tragedy at Arles than before it.

It was a tragedy, but not as commonly interpreted. Vincent would almost certainly have lost his reason whether Gauguin had come to Arles or not. Gauguin may have hastened the inevitable, that is all. If so, he gave Vincent what no one else had given him, a whole month of happiness, the only truly happy period in his life. It is no wonder that he afterwards continued to worship Gauguin and, regardless of the result of their companionship, yearn for it again. He considered—and who will say that he was wrong?—that to risk madness for happiness and good work was worthwhile. Each man had much to give the other. Both lived for their art, had abandoned everything for it and had suffered for it as few men have suffered. Both were great artists; both wished their work to advance the cause of art. Together what might they not have done? The true tragedy of Arles was that they could not live and work together.

LE FAUTEUIL
DE GAUGUIN
Dec. 1888
Van Gogh

Coll. V. W. van Gogh

GAUGUIN PAINTING
IN SCHUFF'S GARDEN
IN 1889.

M. Maurice Malingue

Národní Galerie, Prague

BONJOUR MONSIEUR GAUGUIN. 1889

(Showing the beret, MacFarlane and sabots)

Chapter Thirteen

THE VOLPINI EXHIBITION

1888-1889

I

SCHUFF had already proved himself a good friend to Gauguin and he did so now, once more taking in the homeless, penniless man. This courageous act met with a better reward than it had done hitherto or was to do in the future. Gauguin repaid the hospitality by making a portrait group of the Schuffenecker family—a work which kept him busy and gave pleasure to his host. Presumably Madame Schuffenecker was appeased by the thought that he was earning his keep; she could scarcely have been flattered by her own likeness. The portraits, like all those painted by Gauguin, made no concessions to the sitters; the two children are children, not dolls, the wife is an elegant, faded woman, not a beautiful stick, and Schuff himself is an anxious, eager little man bending forward with the characteristic soap-washing movement of the hands. Exactly how much this family group differs from those of contemporary painters, even the great ones, may be seen by comparing it with, say, the much-praised *Le Premier Pas*, *Mesdemoiselles Cohen d'Anvers* and *Madame Dauberville et Son Fils* of Renoir.

Gauguin had suggested to Mette that he should come up to Copenhagen to see the children—"I haven't seen them for five years," he complained. He also had faint hopes of arranging a show of his work there. But the suggestion had a stony reception, perhaps because Mette suspected that he would almost certainly need help with his fare, to say nothing of his keep. No, she replied: too expensive; let him make some money first, then pay for himself; she had all she could do to keep herself and the children.

This offer rejected (which he was to remember bitterly), Gauguin, when not at work on the Schuffenecker group, spent his time in the rue Boissonade on the far side of the Cimetière Montparnasse. There Léon Fauché had his studio and, more to the point, his workshop—for it was now Gauguin's intention to learn the art of the lithographer. He was led to it by the restless Bernard panting after new worlds to conquer. Bernard had seen some lithographs by his friend Toulouse-Lautrec; the new enthusiasm had to be shared, and who better to share it with than Gauguin, welcomed back rapturously from Arles as from the tomb. They worked in hard spurts in the Fauché studio. Bernard proved to be unhappy in the medium—it seemed to him too finicky for his large notions and demanded a discipline he didn't possess—but Gauguin took to it at once. Perhaps this was only to be expected in the grandson of a lithographer, but Gauguin's versatility is none the less remarkable.

In the first burst of enthusiasm Bernard had suggested that they make an album for display at the exhibition Schuff was trying to arrange. After he had made a couple of lithographs his ardour slackened, but Gauguin plodded on and made thirteen that he thought fit for showing—of Martinique, Pont-Aven and Arles—delicate, distinctive, good works every one of them.

The album was made ready, fifteen prints in all, and so was the exhibition. The faithful Schuff had proved himself not only the good friend but the skilful negotiator; great painter Schuff might not be, but genius of a kind he undoubtedly had; if he did not beget ideas he knew one when he saw it. On the esplanade du Champ de Mars the great Exposition Universelle was soon to be opened. The academic painters would be represented in the Palais des Beaux Arts, the unacademic painters not at all. Yet this world fair would attract large crowds, it would provide precisely the publicity needed by Gauguin and his group. At this point the ubiquitous Bernard noticed that a certain M. Volpini had obtained a concession for a restaurant and café at the entrance to the Exposition, and that shortly before the Exposition was to open the café was still without windows. He spoke to M. Volpini who explained that the plate-glass manufacturers had failed to deliver. Why go to the expense of plate-glass windows? said Bernard. Be original, save money, attract custom and open in time for the first great rush. I have friends who wish to exhibit their pictures; put the large ones in the windows, decorate your walls with the rest. You will scarcely be able to find room for the crowd.

The bargain was struck, Gauguin and his friends swarmed into the building, decorated it, hung their pictures and fixed some in the window spaces. Gauguin illustrated a catalogue (part of the cover design later became the famous *Femme à la Vague*), and *L'Exposition de Peinture du Groupe Impressioniste et Synthétique* opened to the minute right inside the enemy's camp.

Eight painters took part—Gauguin, Bernard, Schuff, Laval, Anquetin (now entirely weaned from pointillisme), Fauché, Louis Roy and De Monfreid. Guillaumin had dropped out and Vincent, by that time in the mental hospital at St Remy, was not in a fit state to decide whether or not to exhibit. Theo decided that he should not, and Vincent approved, although he did not agree with his brother's criticism of exhibiting in cafés: "You cause a stir, and if it's bad taste then I'm guilty too."

Gauguin showed seventeen canvases from Pont-Aven, Arles and Martinique—all the best of his work—Bernard showed twenty-three and the rest about sixty between them. There were also two "peintures pétrole" exhibited by a certain Ludovic Nemo. The mystery man was, need one say, the insatiable Bernard who, growing slightly bored with the recognised methods of painting, used paraffin instead of the customary turps. The joint album of lithographs completed the show.

The exhibition was a success—a *succès de scandale*. The public swarmed in to drink their coffee and enjoy their pipe and cigarette and, through the haze of tobacco and the clouds of steam perpetually rising from a vast kettle, contemplated the host of strange canvases. They were lulled or distracted by the music of a small orchestra thoughtfully provided by the astute Volpini, an orchestra "dominated by the strident bow of 'Princess Dolgoronka'"—a picture that needs no elaboration. It was the popular café-chantant.

The public needed "the rhythmic snoring" of this orchestra. There, in the blue and white banner across the café, were the words *Groupe Impressioniste et Synthétique*, but where was the *Impressioniste*? The café customers, leaning back in their seats and joining in the choruses of the popular songs ground out by the orchestra, gazed bewildered at pictures that had absolutely nothing in common with the Impressionists they were, after a struggle, beginning to get accustomed to—Monet, Renoir and Degas. In place of subtle tones spread over the canvas in tiny dots and dashes they saw large patches of strong colours contrasting violently; in place of delicate gradations of contour they saw heavy outlines; instead of feeling a sense of depth in the canvases they were presented with a surface almost flat and without any of the recognised conventions of perspective; for atmosphere they were offered colour and design —a design which bore little relation to the world they knew, with forms deliberately distorted to convey an individual expression. It was all reminiscent more than anything else of talented children cutting a dash. But at least it provided something to talk about—and talk they did.

The painters from the Palais des Beaux Arts—the Meissoniers, the Carolus-Durans—strolled across to inspect the absurdities of "les incompréhensibles", to inspect and to mock. Why, if one looked no further than the frames, all the signs of the crank were immediately apparent: strips of white wood instead of the gorgeous gilt recognised for centuries. There was in fact nothing to look at but the pictures.

Their supporters the conventional critics expressed their thoughts admirably. Gauguin, they said, seemed to be sinking into his second childhood. Look at his horses, for instance, and then look at the horses of Meissonier which, thanks to photography, presented one with the true aspect of a horse, every curve, every hair of it. Why, one could scarcely tell the difference.

Exactly, replied Gauguin with one of his rare profundities; he had gone back, but not as they understood that term: "Quant à moi, je me suis reculé bien loin, plus loin que les chevaux du Parthénon, jusqu'au dada de mon enfance, le bon cheval de bois."

The public, the academicians, the academic critics complained, abused. That was only to be expected. The great point was that Gauguin and his group had made themselves seen. Thereafter they must trust to the influence of time and of the far-sighted. There were not many of these, but they were the coming men. Of the critics, three, Felix Fénéon, Albert Aurier and Maurice Denis, were all young, brilliant and with a gift for words. Like Huysmans years earlier they saw at once the great artist in Gauguin—saw and proclaimed it to a small but influential audience. Denis, indeed, fired by Gauguin's work, was soon to write an essay on painting that remains a landmark to this day; the essay beginning with the famous "Se rappeler qu'un tableau avant d'être un cheval de bataille, une femme nue ou une quelconque anecdote—est essentiellement une surface plane, recouverte de couleurs en un certain ordre assemblées."

Denis was not only in embryo a critic of distinction, he was beginning to paint and he was one of the most notable Nabis. Since the previous autumn Sérusier had struggled to impose his *volte face* on his fellow Nabis. He had had hard work, his manner being partly to blame. When he came back from Pont-Aven he repeated the words of Gauguin and "not without mystery" showed the band of students *The Talisman* and an even more precious relic—the lid of a cigar box which Gauguin as a practical demonstration had covered with pure colours side by side.

The first reaction of the Nabis—most of them still in their teens—was to laugh at the rather pompous prophet and his colourful relic, and they made no effort to restrain themselves. But "as they were fundamentally sensible and not children they began to reflect". So said Denis, who was far too intelligent to laugh for long at novelty; he came round to Sérusier's way of thinking; and being in his quieter fashion a much more dependable young man, he brought with him the bulk of the Nabis and their friends. At least they ought to explore the matter—that was his feeling. And so it was that Gauguin's cigar-box lid, studied by Denis seriously and flourished dramatically by Sérusier, eventually led the students into a new world: "We began to frequent places ostentatiously ignored by our Patron, Jules Lefèvre—the entresol of the Goupil gallery in the boulevard Montmartre where Van Gogh, brother of the painter, showed us not only Gauguins from Martinique but some of Vincent's work, of Monet and Degas; and the shop of Père Tanguy in the rue Clauzel where we discovered with enormous emotion the work of Paul Cézanne." Soon afterwards the Volpini exhibition opened and the Nabis trooped over in a red-bearded body—chief among them after Sérusier and Denis being Edouard Vuillard, K.-X. Roussel and the beardless "le Nabi-très-Japonard" Pierre Bonnard.

Within a month or two, then, these brilliant young men from the Ecole Julian were faced with examples of some of the best work of men whom, after the manner of students, they had derided without knowing more about them than their names—Impressionists and (though the term had still to be coined) Post-Impressionists. Denis, rallying from the stupefaction common to all but Sérusier, made his choice. The teaching at Julian's was, of course, outmoded from that moment, and to Denis so also was Impressionism "because it involved submission to nature and abandonment to pure sensation". This he could not accept after seeing the Gauguins at Theo's gallery and the Volpini, which "showed me the way, or rather, since Gauguin was not a logical theorist, a group of ideas and solutions of an extremely simple kind which brought me back, brutally but surely, to the fundamentals of painting—drawing, colour, composition".

One would have expected to find Gauguin in the thick of the fumes of the Café Volpini, his bulky shoulders and tall narrow head standing out among the throng, laying down the law in measured tones. But having seen the exhibition launched, he lost interest, or rather he found stronger ones. One thing led to another. In the Exposition grounds the replica of a Javanese village had been built and the life of the village was reproduced with reasonable accuracy. Gauguin had talked much to Vincent about Java, which he had seen in the much-praised photographs of the time. There was the place in which to live and to paint, he had insisted, with Vincent uneasily agreeing. Now here were the photographs "come to life". He was at once enthralled, and wrote off to Bernard: "You must see it. There are Hindu dances and all the Indian art can be seen."

Bernard proved strangely unmoved, even though Gauguin more than once offered him a dinner at Schuff's before they explored the village. Bernard was preoccupied for a fleeting moment or two by the prospects of industrial art as a means of escaping from his father's leading reins. No, said Gauguin, "you haven't enough bad taste. I don't want to live by commerce even if I could." And then, getting back to the business of the moment, he made a gesture of friendship. The next time he went to the village, "I have a rendezvous with a mulatto woman," but nevertheless "come, and dine first with Schuff."

The enthusiasm for Java and the Javanese led understandably to a return of the passion for the tropics; Java itself seemed out of the question, but Martinique was another matter; Laval was always talking about it, talking a shade too knowingly for Gauguin's liking—he had, after all, spent a full year there. Then he fell in with another authority. One Sunday he, Schuff and Bernard went to a

Concert Colonne at the Châtelet; leaning against the entrance to the third amphitheatre where they sat was a man of about fifty unconcernedly eating an orange. Schuff knew him—he was on nodding terms with most artists—and introduced him as Odilon Redon. Redon haunted the place, he explained, he came of a musical family and "was born on a wave of sound". More to the point, he was an unsuccessful and adventurous painter, the creator of "fevered nightmares", a "designer of the invisible, of myths of woe, anguish, condemnation and spiritual suffering". This was enough to engage the lively sympathy of Bernard. Gauguin was relieved to meet a struggling painter older than himself—he was becoming increasingly aware of the youth of all who surrounded him—and was soon flattered by the adherence of Redon to his group. Redon's birthplace at Bordeaux was another link of a kind, and his friendship with Huysmans, the sculptor Rodin and the poet Mallarmé brought Gauguin occasionally into the company of the cultured and witty that except for Degas he had not known.

But what at once struck his imagination was the discovery that Redon's wife knew Madagascar well; not only knew it but encouraged him to go there. All his old plans flared up again, the venue only was changed. "A light has appeared on the horizon," he told Bernard, "I'm on the eve of selling some canvases for 5000 francs. Madame Redon says one can live for 30 years in Madagascar on 5000 francs. It costs nothing to live there. If I sell the pictures I'm going irrevocably to Madagascar to buy a house, enlarge it and found the studio of the tropics, to live freely and simply and paint. I invite all the men who can't work here in Europe. You will find *without money* an assured existence in a better world."

Bernard, faced with this drastic decision, shilly-shallied, but Gauguin, anxious for company, took a kindly view of it. "You're over-excited and nervous. The life of an artist without money or support is difficult and sad." But, he reminded Bernard, "I've had ten times more trouble on my shoulders. You're lucky to have found a friend like me—something I haven't found yet. At 22 life can be grand and beautiful. At 42, with little time ahead of me, I'm trying to forget the past and family responsibilities!"

There only remained, it seemed, the composition of the party. "I'm not going to try living in Madagascar as I did with Laval in Martinique—once is enough, it cost me dearly." Laval had "a fine and noble nature despite his transcendent faults", but he was not to come to Madagascar. Had the news of the secret engagement of Laval and Madeleine Bernard reached his ears? Who can say? Be that as it may, Laval was now *persona non grata*. "You'd think it was he who was sacrificed there, the way he talks." And he talked too much. So: "Don't tell Laval. I don't like gossips, misunderstandings, bickering. I shall move heaven and earth to get us there. Keep calm until I give the sign."

Bernard, one may be sure, did nothing of the kind, which was as well, for the sign never came. The five thousand francs sale receded into the vague, and Madame Schuffenecker became restive at, among other things, Gauguin's free use of her dinner table for his friends. The next thing she knew he would be bringing home the mulatto woman. What Gauguin thought of her was seen in his remark to Mette: "Schuff thinks very highly of you when he compares you with his bore. There's yet another weighed down by a marriage."

In March, as the atmosphere in the Schuffenecker house was becoming too uncomfortable, Gauguin postponed Madagascar, shook the dust of Paris off his feet once more and retired abruptly to Pont-Aven with a valedictory note to Bernard. The munificent offers had shrunk: "The most beautiful tart in the world can only give you what she has—me likewise. If you're unhappy my only consolation is—the half of my overcoat."

Chapter Fourteen

LE POULDU

1889-1890

I

At Pont-Aven Gauguin began work as soon as he had settled into the pension. The weather was poor, so he turned to portraiture. He was introduced to a Madame Satre, who agreed to sit to him in her Breton costume. She was a young woman of parts, later to become mayoress, but her judgment of painting not surprisingly lagged behind the times. Her suspicions were first aroused when Gauguin refused to let her look at the portrait while he worked on it. Then came alarming rumours from the pension; Gauguin had shown the portrait to other painters; they declared that it would make her a laughingstock in the district; there had been violent arguments, and would have been a fight if Mère Gloanec had not intervened. When Gauguin finally allowed her to see it, remarking that it was one of his best works, her worst fears were exceeded. While he walked about the room looking for the most suitable place in which to hang his gift, she stared appalled. There she was, hands folded, rather prim, on the right hand of the picture. Gauguin had not only made no effort to lend her the beauty she lacked, he had given her two brick red patches on her cheeks and a bulbous discoloured nose. This was insulting enough; but on the left of the picture a hideous unclothed idol squatted malevolently on a shelf. Was it a mock of the cross on her own breasts? Delicate flowers floated in space above the idol and over her head—they were absurd enough in stormy Brittany, but Madame Satre was preoccupied by the presence of that creature by her side, and by the words *La Belle Angèle* printed at the bottom of the canvas. A jest? She waved the picture away—"What a horror!"—and refused to have it in the house. Two years later Degas, who knew great work when he saw it, bought *La Belle Angèle*; today it is one of the most cherished possessions of the Jeu de Paume.

After-fame, however, was no consolation to Gauguin. This was the second time that his pride had been savagely wounded at Pont-Aven. The previous summer, spurred by Madeleine and Bernard, he had offered his precious *Vision* to the church. The curé, nervous of his parishioners' comments, refused it. Gauguin and Bernard then carried the large picture across the river to the church there. Again it was refused. Now a little villager had insulted him by rejecting an even greater work.

Fortunately he was no longer alone at the pension; one or two of his followers had joined him, with a new one on whom he could unload his wrath. Meyer de Haan had been introduced to him by Theo van Gogh; he was a Dutchman, once a flourishing manufacturer of biscuits, who had given up his business to paint, accepting only a small pension. This provided a bond between the two men except, as Gauguin remarked, that he had no pension. All that he had was at Gauguin's disposal, De Haan quickly explained, and was forgiven. Indeed, Gauguin quite took to him. He had an uncommon flair for downing spirits and remaining on his feet: that won approval. His devotion, for he was Gauguin's slave from the moment of meeting, and his ability, for he was a fair artist, qualified him further. But the strongest bond, one suspects, was the Dutchman's appearance; he was one of the ugliest of men, with a face more like a gargoyle than a human being and a body that was undersized and misshapen. Debauchery had made him an even more repulsive sight, but this only appealed to Gauguin's love of the bizarre. De Haan began to appear in many of his canvases—*Contes Maoris* and *Nirvana* for instance—leering, his famous reddish lock of hair falling between the crooked eyes. Gauguin also made a bust of him in oak, and used him as model for his idols. Usually he is contrasted with a well-formed, pleasant-faced girl; for Gauguin, as Madame Satre had discovered, had a weakness for contrasts. That was why he relished the walk down the street, the dwarf-like De Haan shambling crookedly beside his large upright companion.

Although in unhappy moments he complained about his age, Gauguin had changed little; he was described early that summer as "tall with a brown face, black hair worn rather long, an aquiline nose, big green eyes, a slight horseshoe beard and short moustache. He looked grave and imposing. He gave the impression of calmness and of acting only after consideration, but he sometimes grew sarcastic in the presence of the philistines. He had great physical strength but was reluctant to use it, and his powerful bearing, his slow rather sluggish walk, his severe look combined with this general impression of sobriety and earnestness to give him a natural dignity which kept strangers at a distance. But under the mask of cold aloofness were hidden senses responsive to every impression."

Of his rapidly re-forming group, one was at first rather less than a disciple. Sérusier was a highly analytical young man, and emotional too—a difficult combination. He lived in a state of almost perpetual terror that his enthusiasms would prove hollow and worthless, but he was driven on, nevertheless, to enthuse and to probe the reasons for it. So, having preached Gauguin through the winter at the Ecole Julian, he hastened down anxiously to join him in the summer—would his god prove to have feet of clay? And sure enough, "I realised as soon as I got here," he told Denis, "that Gauguin is not the artist of my dreams."

That seemed definite enough, yet Sérusier stayed on. Gauguin's strong personality began to assert itself, but the decisive agent was his work. The return to Brittany brought out all the best in him; in these early summer months he painted one canvas after another of an excellence that he never afterwards surpassed: *La Gardienne de Porcs*, *La Barrière*, *La Gardienne de Vaches*, three more studies of children, *Petit Breton* and *Jeunes Bretons Debout*, *Petit Breton à l'Oie*, the curious painting *Bonjour Monsieur Gauguin*, after the Courbet he had seen at Montpellier, a striking nude and seascape *Femme à la Vague*—all these convinced even the sceptical Sérusier that he had not chosen wrongly, and perhaps especially *Environs du Pouldu*.

Le Pouldu, not Pont-Aven, because Pouldu was now Gauguin's home. In June he left Pont-Aven and moved to this tiny fisherman's hamlet on the coast a few miles away. Pont-Aven, he said, was becoming too crowded, too touristy—a state which he, curiously enough, had done something to bring about—and there may have been another reason for the move in the scandal following the elopement of the pretty Louise with one of his group. However that may be, at the end of June Gauguin breaks a long silence to tell Mette, "I'm on the sea coast in a fisherman's inn near a village of 150 people. I live like a peasant and have the name of a savage and I work every day in canvas trousers, all I have left. I spend 1 franc a day for food and 2 sous for tobacco so I can't be reproached for enjoying myself. I don't talk with anyone."

A sombre picture, as it was meant to be, and like so many of his defensive remarks to Mette it was and was not true. The wildness of the coast, the sense of solitude in a place where one could walk all day and see only an occasional Breton fisherman—this harmonised with his mood and the work he was doing. Yet he need be alone only when he chose. The owner of the inn, Mlle Marie Henry, fat and comfortable, was as kind to him as Marie-Jeanne Gloanec. De Haan, who footed the bills, was with him almost all the time, and five others for much of it, and all were ready and flattered to join him for the day if he permitted them.

Of these five who elected to leave Pont-Aven and rough it with him, Sérusier and Laval are known. Of the others Armand Séguin was the most interesting. He had been a barrister at Concarneau, close to Pont-Aven, until he met Gauguin. He threw up the Bar at once, but his painting, like Laval's, never became more than a pale shadow of his adored master's. This abandonment of career, money, comfort, was the one bold act of a timid, deeply religious and in every way conventional man. It must have been difficult to imagine the thin, nervous, precise Séguin keeping on terms with such company, yet he was—shocks apart—happy enough; Gauguin laughed at him, teased him, but accepted him. Another barrister, the young Ernest de Chamaillard, from the nearby town of Quimper, was also introduced to Gauguin at Pont-Aven, promptly stopped practising, and took up painting for good. Charles Filiger, a Swiss who had first known Gauguin at the Collarossi, became interested after the Volpini show, came down to Pouldu for his holiday and never left Brittany again. He was of a mystical turn of mind and his gouaches were to earn him faint praise. All three were to end their days destitute in Brittany after lives of struggle and sacrifice.

But at this moment, in the summer of 1889, there was no thought of failure in the minds of any who filled Marie Henry's little inn. They lived a hard and frugal life, they followed Gauguin in a mood of austere self-denial, but certainly they and he too were far from discontented. They bathed, enjoyed music (Gauguin played the guitar well, the piano badly), talked endlessly, drank and smoked heavily, and copied their leader by decorating everything they could lay hands on, from sticks to sabots, plates to chairs. Above all they worked at their painting from early morning until the game of draughts or loto just before bedtime, worked at painting, drawing, woodcarving, lithography, modelling—there was no end to it.

Gauguin was an inspiring leader, hardworking, plain speaking and inventive; "I have seen him," wrote one friend, "make jewels with iron stove-piping, all without apparent trouble or hesitation. Everything in his hands was transformed into a work of art." He was never fully satisfied in his life, and one cannot expect it of a man so proud and ambitious, yet in all his years as a painter these months gave him most pleasure. He was surrounded by disciples; he had left behind at Pont-Aven the older group of admirers who were busy propagating his principles; he was painting excellent seascapes, landscapes, the witty, economical *Baigneur* which, showing only the back and profile of the red-faced customs officer, conveyed the whole man, and still lives displaying the prominent influence of Cézanne; and he had begun work on a large sculpture in wood of which one panel, the famous *Soyez Amoureuses Vous Serez Heureuses*, expressed "synthetically and symbolically" his ideas on love and man. In all: "I'm one of the artists whose work causes the greatest astonishment," he tells Mette, sending his usual bunch of press cuttings in an effort to convince the unconvinceable. As for the work in wood, he was almost certain to sell it; then "I'll send you 300 francs—you can count on it."

He had even begun to write. Bernard, whose father had forbidden him to join Gauguin, was preparing in his hours of captivity a spectacular entry into the world of letters. Why didn't Gauguin do the same? Well, why not? Gauguin cleared a table and sat down to hammer out "an article about the purchase of pictures for the Louvre and attacking present-day art critics". The article was disconnected but pungent. A few extracts will give the sense of it.

"Painting is the most beautiful of all arts. Like music it acts on the soul through the senses, the harmonious tones corresponding to the harmony of sounds, but a unity is possible in painting which one cannot obtain in music. The ear can grasp only one note at a time, the eye takes in everything and simplifies as it does so. Like Literature the art of painting says what it wants but says it all at once. An effort of hearing is needed to appreciate literature or music; sight alone produces an immediate and comprehensive reaction. When you listen to music or look at a painting you are free to dream. When you read a book you are the slave of the author's mind. Yet art critics are always men of letters, who spend their time defending their own work—as if a truly good work does not defend itself. These gentlemen flutter about like bats who beat their wings in the twilight—restless animals whose awkward bodies prevent them from ascending. 'This work pleases me—it is done just as I should have done it if I had been a painter'—all art criticism is like that. But to judge painting and music one must be a born artist. . . . These critics reprove us for putting our colours side by side, unmixed. Does nature do otherwise? A single colour is crude and doesn't exist in nature, but look at the rainbow—there nature places her colours side by side in an unalterable order as if each colour was born from the other. . . . We are told 'Sir, you must draw properly before you can paint'—and told as a Professor tells his students—the greatest stupidities are always announced with the greatest pomposity. But do you really expect to convince me that drawing does not derive from colour, and vice versa? Try to draw a head of Rembrandt, then apply the colours of Rubens and see what a monstrosity results, and with unharmonious colours into the bargain. Vast sums of money have been spent on the teaching of drawing for centuries past, and what is the result?—more people are painting without showing any sign of improvement. Look at the painters we admire today. They all rejected the schools and triumphed by personal observation."

He finished the article, one may assume, with relief. He had castigated the critics, tried to explain his own beliefs, but he was not a writer—of that he was convinced. He must have enjoyed taking a brush in his hand again, or even a hammer—for one of the first jobs awaiting him was to provide a studio that all could use.

Le Pouldu became a true back-to-nature life, as much so in its way as the hut in Martinique, when he and his group fitted up first an attic then a hut next to the inn. What more could he want, except that it was a studio of the north instead of the tropics? He began to have the sense of a home by the time he had done with the sitting-room; Mlle Henry had given him *carte blanche* and the windows facing the street were soon covered with studies of Breton life, the ceiling with a fresco by Gauguin showing his favourite emblem, the swan, and his favoured woman of the time, the walls with canvases, drawings, lithographs, mottoes and comments. Under a still life including onions someone had scribbled, "I like onions fried in oil." On the plaster below the window was a quotation from Wagner condemning the artist who worked for money. On the mantelpiece Gauguin put a large coloured bust of De Haan carved from oak, flanked by pots decorated with fantastic designs, and on shelves to each side of the mantelpiece statuettes of a Javanese dancer and a negress. The top half of the door was covered by his *Bonjour Monsieur Gauguin*, and on the bottom half he had painted directly on to the wood the portrait of a coloured woman. The doors of a cupboard carried a self-portrait and a portrait of De Haan painted on to the wood. In the place of honour, in the centre of the wall facing the door, they hung a large portrait of Mlle Henry by De Haan with a broad painted frame by Gauguin. Filiger filled the only undecorated inches by painting a gouache of the Virgin Mary on the pier-glass. Outside, above the taproom door, was a painting with a title scribbled boldly underneath "The Terrestrial Paradise". On the walls of his bedroom, which he shared with Sérusier, Gauguin fixed Japanese prints—a habit he had learned from Vincent—some of Puvis de Chavannes' "decorations" and photographs of paintings he particularly admired, including Manet's *Olympia*, Degas' *Arlequin*, Botticelli's *Triumph of Venus* and a Fra Angelico *Annunciation*. These photographs he carried with him whenever he moved house. There was a busy traffic between Pont-Aven and Pouldu, disciples crowding over to see the inn which had become the talk of that part of Brittany. One at least of these men—Moret—stayed on.

2

In one sense Gauguin's life appears idyllic, but there was another side to it. He accepted De Haan's money, or what it gave him, because he could do nothing else, but he grew bitter when he compared the lot of the painter with the stock exchange gambler. His work aroused the greatest astonishment, but the feeling is double-edged. As he told Schuff, "My paintings and sculpture terrify everyone, to crown my misfortunes," and he had to confess to Mette that they "make a great sensation but are terribly difficult to sell".

This was hard to say to a woman whose letters were mostly complaints and calls for money—and to a woman whose husband had said time and again, wait, be patient and I shall be famous. Gauguin chose to concentrate on the perpetual demands for money. Six months earlier, he reminded her, she had refused his proposed visit to Copenhagen because it would cost money. "Always money, never the heart." Once again he demanded: "What do you want from me? Above all what did you want? In the Indies or anywhere else I'm a *beast of burden* and for whom? for the wife and children *I must not see*. In exchange for this sacrifice of an existence without anything whatever, I am *loved if I love*, I am *written to if I write*, and so on. You know me. Either I calculate (and I calculate well) or *I don't calculate*. Hand on the heart, eyes front and I fight openly. Your powerful sister has not abandoned her authority over you, but where is her protection in exchange? Oh well, I accept the rôle I am given and I must calculate—not abandon the substance for the shadow—and the shadow is the rôle of an employee."

He remained adamant; he would not give up his art, he would not rejoin her on her terms. His conscience not being quite easy, he had consulted men whose opinions he respected. "All are of my mind—that my business is art, my capital the future of my children. The honour of the name I've given them will be of enormous value to them one day. So I work only at my art, which is nothing (in money) at present (times being difficult) but will stand out eventually. A long time, you say, but what can I do? I'm the first to suffer." Was not the labourer worthy of his hire? Apparently not.

To those who have seen the work of Matisse and Picasso derided (two of the many who were influenced profoundly by Gauguin's work in Tahiti), the plight of their forerunner will not cause much surprise. Gauguin was too far ahead of his time to hope for practical success. But what comfort was that to him? He said it, he even believed it, but hope remained. Never had he worked so hard, never given so much of himself. His reward was "howls" in Paris, a primitive inn for a home, and a stubborn pride forced to bow perpetually to charity.

Poverty, like starvation, has to be experienced to be known. Its effect on the mind is incalculable, but certain symptoms are common to all—suspicion, envy, shame, intolerance. Poverty, said Shaw, is a crime; certainly the poor feel themselves to be as criminals, an embarrassment to their friends, avoided by all but the poor. They are a race apart, tolerated but without the rights of the well-to-do to enjoy pleasures or even comforts. Mette in her snug Copenhagen home was not an unkind woman, merely unimaginative. If her husband had no money, whose fault was it? The daily humiliations of grinding poverty escaped her because she had never known them, and when she ever thought on the matter she managed to persuade herself, like all who take for granted certain civilised amenities—carpets on the floor, food on the table, a maid to put it there, a woman to wash the linen—that the poor, being unable to afford them, in some providential fashion cease to want them. Of course, they do nothing of the kind. If anything, they long increasingly for the comforts they are denied. Gauguin was an easy-going man unless roused, but years of dependence on others—from the Gad family to De Haan—had hopelessly embittered him. Who worked harder than he and offered the world as much? But he had to wait until someone filled his tobacco jar, called him to a meal that he could not pay for, threw him a pair of trousers they had done with. He grew savage, unapproachable. At Pouldu he was with men who were struggling too, but De Chamaillard and Séguin had local friends, Laval and Sérusier had enough to keep themselves, and De Haan had his pension. He alone had nothing.

In such moods—and they were frequent—he felt "a dreadful apathy of sadness". He even lost confidence: "I grope," he told Bernard. "My studies are very maladroit. I hope you'll see an almost new Gauguin by the winter—almost, because I haven't the pretension of inventing something new. What I seek is a still unknown part of myself."

These outbursts were partly due to the dissatisfaction that every true artist must feel, but even Vincent at St Remy, struggling to work in periods of sanity, read between the lines of Gauguin's letters—for they still corresponded desultorily. He offered Gauguin all his furniture from the yellow house to make a home of his own, and declared, "I still believe that Gauguin and I may work together again. But how to make him comfortable!" The question was, whether they could make common cause in Brittany if he ever managed to escape from St Remy. Vincent believed that they could; he could see that Gauguin was not "comfortable" at the moment: "He writes animatedly about De Haan and their rough life, but I can see clearly that something is wrong with him. And I know quite well what the trouble is—they're too hard up to get models and they can't last out even though they try to live cheaply. That's the terrible thing about the Impressionists, the movement hangs fire, they are held back for years."

Vincent knew all about it—look what poverty had done to him—and was not at all surprised when he heard that Gauguin was talking of an administrative post at Tonkin. The idea was, Gauguin explained to Schuff, that he might earn a salary for a year or two and help his family until the Impressionists (amongst whom he still included himself) were selling. He had another reason: "I can then go off and study the Annamites near Tonkin," he told Bernard. He had said at the very moment of arriving in Pouldu, "I go to gather strength for the voyage"—the voyage then being to Madagascar. Tonkin, Madagascar, Martinique—it mattered little which it was to be; he was concerned chiefly with getting away; the savage in him could not remain easily in civilisation, even the bare Breton version of it. As it happened, delivered from the "abominable foreigners" crowding into Pont-Aven, his life at Pouldu appeared better than he had thought likely. Even so, the moods of restlessness persisted, allying themselves inextricably with the dissatisfaction of the penniless genius. He explained this exactly in a letter to Bernard: "I have a terrible itch for the unknown which makes me do mad things."

By *force majeure* he did nothing madder than return to Paris. But the return was a long business this time, fought every inch of the way. September, October, part of November passed and he was still at Pouldu. Theo van Gogh had sold a little piece of pottery for him, he had got lithographic materials into the top floor of a big empty house by the sea, he was working hard with them and was finishing *Soyez Amoureuses*, looking out on stormy seas—"superb". The backsliding of disciples was mentioned in passing: "Laval hasn't touched a brush for six months, Moret has done nothing much," only De Chamaillard pleased with "an excellent portrait of his wife".

By October all but Gauguin and De Haan had gone off for the winter. For a time Gauguin, greatly encouraged by his sculpture in wood, not only kept up his spirits but tried to cheer Bernard, who wrote dolefully from his "prison"—that is, apart from Gauguin.

His work had been criticised harshly—Schuff's "beautiful mysticism" seemed to be his only consolation and he remained unconsoled. "We're both in the same boat," wrote Gauguin, "doubts of ourselves, results always below expectation." But painting, he reminded Bernard, was like men, always fighting against the material. "If I thought of the absolute I should stop living. Try to live and paint in hope."

He showed how far he had progressed towards the absolute when he dealt with Degas. Degas had criticised his figure work, criticised his detail or lack of it. Draw every finger five times, he said, draw, draw, draw, be satisfied with nothing short of perfection. "Can't be done," commented Gauguin, "with food the price it is." But he went further, much further: there was something more important than draughtsmanship: "You know how I esteem Degas, but I sometimes think his work lacks heart, lacks a sense of something beyond reality." It was true. His own painting was without the technical mastery of Degas, it had not the finish, the brilliance, the close observation, the humour, but one thing it had that Degas had not: "There is a resigned suffering in my work which all with a heart can see. And suffering brings its own poetry."

As for Bernard, "You've seen too much in too short a time. Take a rest." Why did he not come down for the winter with Laval and Moret, live simply, get new strength from the simple life?

The suggestion did not appeal. No one joined the hardy pair. By the end of November the plan to winter by the sea had collapsed, the big house was freezing, there was no money to heat it and they were driven back to the inn and the shed next door. Nor was that the worst of it; De Haan's money was running out. "I'm nailed to Pouldu by debts," Gauguin cried. Troubles gathered thick and fast. He had heard nothing from Theo. Why? He knew: Theo had married. "That's just about the bottom; the only man who has ever interested himself in me is forced to drop me." Theo's wife would not want to help a man who had left his wife and children—how could she know his true feelings? "I take this old body of mine along the shore in the north wind, I can see my family destitute, I've no one to confide in, the soul has gone out of my work, I scarcely dare take up a brush." Isolation, he now saw, "and concentration on oneself is a trap, an intolerable trap unless one is made of ice". He was not made of ice: "Since January I've sold for a total of 925 francs. At 42 to live on that, buy colours, etc.! One can't live even humbly. And I can't work for money, some elevated sense in me seems to prevent it. I've been conquered by events, time, family, but not by opinions. And I seem cut out for the rôle of the heartless, the wicked, the grouser. Ah well."

Bernard knew better; he felt the heart and the sorrow in his work. Madeleine too; she wrote to him sympathetically and he revived sufficiently to follow the cry "my horizon is black and I can't see a break of fine weather" with a letter that the most conscientious headmistress could not have bettered and the offer of another pot—"rude but the work of Gauguin the savage". He roused himself to give Bernard a final heartening message before misery submerged him. "One has a duty even when feeling powerless. Courage! The money changers may one day be chased from the temple."

This was the last piece of optimism to come out of Pouldu that year. The weeks passed, the inn grew cheerless in winter storm and fog, the studio uninhabitable, painting out of doors impossible, De Haan was poor company; the Tonkin post came no nearer ("I'm not stupid enough"); the five thousand francs' sale which would take him to Madagascar still hovered in the wind. The cold persisted, his discomfort became insupportable. "Gauguin is suffering very much" De Haan told Theo. "It is so sad that he can't sell anything—he is a very great painter. If I hadn't supported him during the last three months he would have starved . . . Don't you think it miraculous that a man living in such circumstances makes such fine things? If he had the means he would show us still better. My God, can't we do something for him?" In the first days of the new year a final calamity fell on them. All money had gone, they were living on credit, and thinly: "I have given up smoking and I suffer. By stealth I wash part of my linen. Except for food I have nothing. Never have I been so discouraged as now. Nothing to do but to wait like a rat on a barrel in the sea."

The thought of Gauguin without tobacco was too much for Schuff. He offered him the fare to Paris. Gauguin accepted with dignity: "In Paris I shall sell and repay." A few days later he was there.

Chapter Fifteen

THE SYMBOLISTS

1890

I

SCHUFF not only sent him the fare, he once again took him into his house—this time the house he had bought in the rue Durand-Claye in the suburb of Plaisance. The stay was a short one; in a week or two Gauguin was put out by Madame Schuffenecker. There could be only one master in a house, and she was determined that it should be herself.

It may even be that Gauguin was bored by the journey into Paris; in any event he took a studio for three months in the avenue Montsouris just below Denfert-Rochereau and within striking distance of Fauché's workshop. How he paid the rent or whether he paid it is not known. It is possible that Theo van Gogh (whose marriage had not changed his attitude) kept him afloat; Theo was a kindly and generous man, he believed in Gauguin as the man of the future and was always trying to push his work. It is also possible that the friendship with De Monfreid, who was slowly taking the place of Schuff, had already progressed sufficiently for money to change hands or—for Gauguin disliked the obvious—for the rent to be settled without fuss.

There is a third possibility. Gauguin now had the entrée to an influential circle—the Symbolists. In the boulevard Montmartre, a step from Theo's gallery, was the Café des Variétiés, where the *patron*, Bauchy, would provide meals in exchange for a poem or a picture by men who had managed to win his confidence. Gauguin knew the place well—Bauchy had several of his canvases—and poor Séguin, coming up to see more of his hero, practically lived there. And Séguin it was who one day brought up to his master a young man whom he introduced as Charles Morice. Gauguin knew Morice by name and had seen him eating there often enough; his was not a figure one could overlook—tall, slender, with long black hair framing a white face, broad high forehead balanced by the dark Imperial, a brown eye, liquid and fiery, on each side of the strong nose. It is likely that he had avoided him—for Morice was a little too beautiful, his gestures too mannered, his immaculate frock-coat worn with too careless a grace.

However, Morice had charm, he was all things to a number of men, and the music of his sonorous voice sounding the praise of Gauguin's work conveyed a fervour and an admiration that only the churlish or suspicious would question. Gauguin was neither churlish nor suspicious; he was a simple man and vain; he accepted the compliment; and when he saw that the frock-coat, though immaculate, was almost threadbare, when he discovered that Morice had starved like himself and had stuck it out with, in his case, a dandified front (*joie amère de la privation!*), he accepted the love that was soon and enthusiastically offered. He began to eat often at Morice's table. Here he met poets, critics and journalists like Morice, and sculptors; he heard much congenial talk of the greatness of Verlaine (for Morice had made his name with a first study of the poet); above all, he heard of the Symbolist movement. This group, with Stéphane Mallarmé as patron, Charles Morice as leader, and Aurier as spokesman, was chiefly concerned with literature—it stood for revolt against the academic tradition and expressed its theories in the work of Mallarmé and Verlaine. But as these theories were applicable to every form of art, musicians, sculptors and painters were also to be found at the Café Voltaire, where the Symbolists met every Monday evening. In Rodin, already known to Gauguin, they had a great sculptor, but they still lacked a great painter. Who greater—potentially at least—than Gauguin, the admitted leader of the Volpini exhibition and whose work since then on canvas and in wood now to be seen in Theo's gallery confirmed his importance? Did it not conform exactly to Mallarmé's dictum "suggest, don't state"? If Gauguin had doubts (and he did not say one way or the other), Aurier and Morice had none.

Synthetism, said Morice, must lead the painter to Symbolism. He should "eliminate any suggestion of direct observation and retain only those aspects of nature relating to his ideas. He will then reunite all aspects in some great image that is at once profoundly true and freed from probability. This image is Symbolism." Aurier's version did not differ radically: "The work of art will be idealistic since his unique ideal will be the expression of the Idea; it will be symbolist since he expresses this Idea by the forms; synthetic because he draws these forms, these signs, in a manner that is generally understood; subjective because the Idea will never be considered so much as the object, as the sign of the Idea perceived by the subject. And it is in consequence decorative because the decorative picture is nothing but a manifestation of an art at once subjective, synthetic, symbolist and idealistic. The picture of a wooden horse is illogical; the duty of the painter is to decorate his thoughts, dreams, ideas, the walls of the building. But an element of this work of art is still missing—the feelings, not the feelings of makers of chromos but the feelings of the soul which shudders before the flowing drama of the abstractions."

What did Gauguin think of all this? His view of the art critic's incomprehensibilities and pretensions was curt except when the critic happened to be praising his work. His later comments on Symbolism were blistering. A guess may be hazarded that he ignored the verbiage and fastened on the one thought of Aurier's that was clear and congenial to him—hence the famous "Des murs, des murs, donnez-lui des murs!"

For the rest, he was a practical man, and whenever he dabbled in abstractions his work suffered. But he was practical in every sense. Morice and Aurier proclaimed in his work a demonstration and proof of their theories. He may have felt that the demonstration was of more moment than the theories; but why should he complain if his work introduced him to congenial and influential company and procured him the loan of a studio? He said nothing, began to frequent the Café Voltaire, attended the Tuesday soirées of Mallarmé, and produced a tribute in his etching of the poet, a profile showing the sharp nose and famous drooping moustache.

The company he was keeping, though it had not enriched him materially, gave him a comfortable sense of consequence—a sense that he at once expressed in a burst of feeling for Mette who had not written to him since his rebuke from Pouldu: "Your silence has made me more unhappy than all my money worries. I have self-respect if not money, but I don't want to be isolated, without wife or children." He was magnanimous about Fritz Thaulow. This erstwhile model husband had run off with another woman and had been divorced by Mette's sister. Gauguin met him and his new wife in Paris. What a temptation! But no: "His wife is much below Ingeborg, she's the fleshly type." And, almost as though he were writing to Madeleine Bernard, "Well, perhaps some people need that kind of thing."

He greeted enthusiastically the latest photograph of his children, he once again invited himself to Copenhagen, and to enhance his value he went into a combined rhapsody and threat about the future life he was contemplating: "The day may come, perhaps soon, when I shall run off into the woods of an island in Oceania to live in an ecstasy of peace and art in the bosom of a new family far from this European struggle for money. There at Tahiti I shall be able to enjoy the silence of the beautiful tropic nights, listen to the sweet murmuring movements of my heart in loving harmony with the mysterious beings surrounding me—free at last from fear of money, able to love, sing and die."

Mette remained unmoved. She responded affectionately but with caution: "Don't come before April 15. Think well before coming. You may meet my brothers." Also, Emile must soon take his first communion—could Gauguin send money for the new clothes?

Gauguin turned from the letter disgusted and perplexed. "You write in adoration, but your contradictory nature comes out too. I can't reconcile your remarks, they don't seem to make sense." As for his journey to Denmark, "Forget it." Mette obviously preferred to spend the cost of his fare on first communion clothes for Emile. Very well: "If it's really necessary I'll try to send it."

The Tahiti daydream shows, not only that the travelled Madame Redon had been reminiscing again, but that Gauguin, remembering the last months at Pouldu, was desperate to get away. Tahiti, except for this outburst, was very much in the back of his mind. The Tonkin appointment was a dying hope, the Madagascar plan had shot up into first place. In Père Tanguy's shop he and Bernard (whenever he could escape his father's eye) talked with such confidence that Tanguy told Theo that they were leaving for Madagascar at once. The very tones of Gauguin's voice had no doubt made elementary difficulties seem so absurd that Bernard had not the heart to raise them. To get straight on to a ship—"We can always get a job as steward, one can't afford to be fussy"—seemed the most obvious thing as one short sentence, lazy but decisive, followed another. Bernard was prepared (while he listened to Gauguin) to try anything.

The plan had widened. Gauguin's hope of a five thousand franc mass purchase of pictures lived on, but he now had a sheet anchor. In Brittany he had "seduced" a countess from academic painting, she had promised to speak to a friend, a Minister: something might come of that. He had also decided that Schuff must be brought in. Schuff was doing well: he was coining money on the Bourse; he was Professor of Drawing at the Lycée of Vanves; he was getting together at bargain prices a collection of canvases by Vincent, Cézanne and Gauguin (these last usually for nothing, being Gauguin's only method of paying for Schuff hospitality); he owned two houses and was about to buy land on the flourishing rue de Vaugirard; he had even sold some of his own pictures. Yes, he must certainly come into the scheme. Schuff in Madagascar was not imaginable, but why come, why not simply finance the venture? He was, it is true, a businessman, but so was Gauguin; let him put up the money for a piece of land, merely that, and in due course, without lifting a finger, the profits would roll in from the crops raised by Gauguin, Bernard and De Haan and from the pictures they would paint.

Gauguin put the matter to him. Schuff had never been known to say No in so many words, and he would never say Yes if he could help it. He usually rubbed his hands together, smiled amiably, screwed up his eyes behind their glasses and left the seeker to make what he could of it. Gauguin couldn't make much, familiar though he was with Schuff's tactics, but he persisted. When, in early summer, with nothing decided, his studio taken over by its owner and his pocket empty, he was obliged to go back to Brittany, he continued to write exhortatory letters in which the success of the scheme was taken for granted. Bernard, he told Schuff, would soon be free to do what he liked; let him at once buy a dictionary of the Madagascar dialect and send it down to Pouldu. As for himself, "My age there would be almost nothing. That's a thought if you like!"

To Bernard, raising objections at a distance, he outlined the essentials of the simple life, simplifying as he wrote: "We could buy a hut like the one we saw in the Java village—wood covered by a thatched roof. We buy a cow, hens and fruit trees, then live for nothing." There was no future in Madagascar as Europeans thought of it, no big business profits, "only the free life. . . . I shall live there as a man retired from the so-called civilised world so that I can be only with so-called savages. Of my daily bread exactly half will be at your disposal." There was another inducement. "It is practically obligatory there to take a woman. That will give us a free model every day. And the Madagascar woman hasn't the calculating nature of the French woman, she has a heart." Did Bernard perhaps think that such things no longer interested him, "that I'm incapable of loving, that my 42 years are an obstacle to youthful impulses?" Not a bit of it!

This was a change indeed from the Gauguin of the previous winter "dragging his old body" along the seashore. As he wrote, in June, he was entering his forty-third year, he was far from forgetting it, but he remained confident: he had shared his studio in Paris with a model, Juliette, whose portrait adorned the sitting-room ceiling of the inn, and he was not averse to the maid of all work who, when the inn was crowded, slept in the taproom a bare step from his bed. And the inn was crowded all through the summer. The very look of him in the Latin Quarter had been an advertisement for Brittany; he strode slowly and with a noticeable roll along the streets in sabots of light coloured wood carved into fantastic patterns and painted in vermilion, bright blue and gold; he wore a seaman's jersey decorated across the chest with bold Breton designs, a rough jacket splashed with paint of every colour; his trousers were blue, coarse and of an extraordinary width; a faded leather MacFarlane cloak swung from his shoulders and the tasselled beret was pulled down over one scornful green eye. In his hand he carried a large and daringly decorated stick. His was not the only colourful figure in the Quarter, but it began to be whispered in the cafés that that stick and those sabots had not been bought in the pawnshop round the corner, the man had decorated them himself; the paint on his jacket had come from his own palette; he really had led the rough life and intended to lead it again; he had actually painted pictures in that Breton hut next to the inn, and good ones too, perhaps even great; and, most astonishing of all, that aloof stare was not a secret appeal for notice, but a warning—he could and would box, fence, shoot! The name of le Pouldu was repeated with respect.

2

It often happens that as the mind plans a desirable future, the present begins to assume undreamt-of charms. The more Gauguin wrote about the perfect life in the tropics the more life at Pouldu opened out, until during these summer months at least his references to the joys of the tropics became almost mechanical. Filiger, Séguin, Sérusier, De Haan, were back again, followed by Laval and, most notably, by Moret, O'Conor, Denis and the engraver Paul-Emile Colin, to say nothing of the curious and the admiring painters coming over from Pont-Aven. Whatever he might say of schools in general—and his comments were unprintable—his own was flourishing and its master working better than ever. His *Les Meules, Cour de Feme au Pouldu*, his self-portraits, portraits of children and of Mlle Henry, his flower studies, showed a serene confidence.

All accounts at this time reveal how his companions admired and respected him. Colin, like Sérusier, arrived a sceptic and left a believer, though not an idolater. "I can still see Gauguin bathing, with his beak of a nose, his clear seaman's eyes, his black hair worn a little long under the beret. Normally he had the air of a conquistador, but in his bathing-slips he looked like a pirate gone wrong—a pirate with the paunch of a businessman." Gauguin could be a troubadour too, Colin thought, when "he took his guitar, Filiger his mandoline and we walked over the sands to a corner by the rocks."

Gauguin admired Balzac's Vautrin, "and I felt that in other times and under other circumstances and without his love of art he could have been his brother. He seemed to produce an enormous amount of work, he had read a great deal, with the Bible, Shakespeare and Balzac holding first place, he liked to speak of the things he admired, his comments on nature were piquant and sound, and from this point of view all his friends have rightly called themselves his pupils." He had a profound admiration for Gauguin's character, Colin summed up, because he "sacrificed everything to art with the half-certainty that he would never profit from it".

Colin and Sérusier both commented on Gauguin's gentleness. His humour was often broad but not cruel; this is seen in his treatment of Séguin: "When Séguin placed complementary colours next to each other Gauguin quietly took his revolver from his pocket, ostentatiously loaded it and put it on the table beside the canvas. Séguin never put complementary colours together again."

The summer and autumn of 1890 passed quickly for them all. Gauguin worked hard, reserving his words of praise or blame for the evenings. On occasion he gave Pouldu, and Pont-Aven when he visited it, a foretaste of the finery that was to burst on this part of Brittany a few years later. His idea seemed to be, Breton wear in Paris and in Brittany a dreadful version of the American clothes in vogue in certain parts of Paris. He was observed by astonished fisherfolk and peasants to walk heavily through the lanes and by the shore in long, pointed bright yellow shoes with an enormous Buffalo Bill hat on his head.

On the day before the national fête, for example, a painter, Maxime Maufra, was standing outside the Pension Gloanec when a ramshackle cart trundled into the *Place* and stopped before the inn. Four men "not less bizarre than the cart" got out. The first was powerfully built and was dressed in an appalling blend of American and Breton clothes. He had, Maufra thought, the face of a South American Indian, swarthy and impassive. He said nothing, regarding with magisterial contempt the crowd that had collected.

The second man looked like Jesus, with long red hair and beard. He seemed to Maufra to be modelling himself, not with entire success, on Jesus, wearing a gentle half smile that was evidently intended to indicate the wisdom of a philosopher put down amidst barbarians. The third man was smiling too; he was short and rather stout and the beatific expression on his plump face suggested a little incongruously but unmistakably the mystic.

A small red-haired hunchback climbed out last, but with a comical air of importance. This man, Maufra realised, had taken upon himself the function of watchdog to the big man; he bustled about crookedly, keeping back the curious, introducing the favoured and clearing a path to the pension. He also made clear, by his reverent attitude, his rapturous pronouncement of the big man's name and repetition of the few words he deigned to utter, that "he was carrying out with fervour his rôle of Greek chorus".

Most of the men in the crowd were from the Ecole Julian; their attitude to the newcomers was hostile but timid. But there were others who welcomed them enthusiastically—Laval, O'Conor, Moret and many more Gauguin disciples, including the Dane Willemsen, Verkade, Loiseau and Desnaunay. There was even a friend of Maufra, a man from his birthplace, Nantes. "Bon! voilà les Impressionistes!" Maufra heard on all sides—for the visitors from Pouldu were reckoned by the villagers too to be one of the sights of the year. Their names were familiar to him—Gauguin, Sérusier, Filiger and De Haan.

Maufra, bored already with the Julian men (he had been in Pont-Aven only a day or two) and intrigued by the sight and reputation of Gauguin, asked his friend to introduce him. This was a ticklish business, he was given to understand; his reputation was against him, for he was a painter of exemplary seascapes and he had exhibited in the Salon only four years earlier. He could go into the small dining-room, he was told, "providing that he listened to the words of the master". Maufra agreed, and did not regret it. He was a small man with pince-nez, a receding chin and black receding hair brushed into a defiant quiff as was the manner of so many Frenchmen of that time. He looked up at the great man and listened, wisely discounting first impressions. Gauguin, he found, had a "rare loyalty and a singular sensibility which he hid under bitter and eccentric manners and, to make sure that his disguise was complete, by actions of particular insensibility". Like so many before him, Maufra admired Gauguin and his work at once. Gauguin relaxed his guard, overlooked the Salon exhibits, and "treated him with a benevolence that, not being seen often, was regarded by all about him as a high favour".

Another admirer was won. And Maufra, who was a perceptive man, did not change his opinion of Gauguin's greatness, still less his goodness, when at the village ball the next evening (for which the Pouldu party had come) he saw the master dancing heavily but with tremendous gusto in every dance "like a very big child".

There remained only the clothes. Gauguin's exhibitionism, which burst out from time to time, may have been intended to shock the philistines—particularly the foreign painters and the Julian men. As an attitude of defiant independence it is common to many extraordinary men. He may also have felt—since his followers followed him in everything—that his Breton costume was becoming too ordinary. But whatever the reason, his exhibitionism was foolish; it smacked of the naughty boy and the tasteless man, and it cheapened what was far from cheap. Everyone is familiar with frustrations caused by the faults of others. One wishes to love or admire wholeheartedly, but something in the other person is constantly and maddeningly preventing it. Even more so is it with the great man.

But faults must be weighed against virtues. Inside the auberge Gauguin abandoned finery and even footwear. A young man of twenty, who had just decided to devote himself to literature, walking round the coast to collect his thoughts stumbled on Le Pouldu. "This village consisted of four houses, two of them inns; the smallest appeared the most pleasant. . . . A servant showed me into a room with whitewashed roughcast walls where she left me with a glass of cider. The scarcity of furniture and the absence of curtains allowed me to see all the better on the floor a great many canvases turned to the wall. I was no sooner alone than I began to look at these canvases, turning over one after another with increasing stupefaction; it seemed to me that they were no more than a collection of infantile efforts, but the tones were so alive, so individual and so gay that I thought no more of leaving. I wanted to know the artists capable of making such amusing freaks; I gave up my idea of pushing on that evening, took a room and asked what time dinner was. 'Where do you want to have it? By yourself? Or in the same room as the gentlemen?' asked the maid. 'The gentlemen' were the makers of the canvases; there were three of them, who soon came in with easels and boxes of colours. It goes without saying that I had asked to be served with them if it did not put them out. They soon showed that I did not bother them—or rather, they did not bother themselves about me. All three had bare feet, were superbly untidy and spoke sonorously. For the entire meal I sat with my heart beating, drinking in their conversation, tormented by the desire to speak to them, to make myself known, to know them, and to say to the big one, the one with the bright eyes, that the tune he was singing at the top of his voice and which the others took up in chorus, was not by Massenet as he believed, but by Bizet."

But the young André Gide could not pluck up courage to talk to "the gentlemen"—Gauguin, Sérusier, Filiger; he had to wait until later, at one of Mallarmé's soirées, where he found and spoke to "the big one with the bright eyes" who sang at the top of his voice.

Gauguin sang, but was he happy? One man did not think so. In the south Vincent, struggling against one attack of madness after another, used his faith in Gauguin as a hold on sanity. When Aurier devoted an entire article in the *Mercure de France* to Vincent's work, he, though overcome by pleasure at the first public notice he had received, qualified his thanks by a regret that justice had not been done "to Gauguin and Monticelli before speaking of me." He consoled himself in his wretchedness by thoughts of the day when he and Gauguin, together once more, would achieve great things for the new Impressionism. He spent a month making a study of Gauguin's Arlésienne sketch because the doing of it seemed to bring them closer; and when he heard that Gauguin had seen and approved: "I feel enormous pleasure that it pleases you. It is a synthesis of the Arlésiennes if you choose. Take it as a joint work, a summary of our months with each other. The doing of it cost me a month of illness, but I knew that you would understand."

Vincent had only one reservation about his master (for so he called him). "The future of painting," he told Theo, "is in the tropics, in Java, Martinique, Brazil or Australia, but I can't feel convinced that either Gauguin or I or you is the man of that future." When Gauguin wrote about his latest plan "he writes vaguely of having quite decided on Madagascar, but so vaguely that I can see he's only thinking of it because he doesn't know what else to think of". He found the letter "gloomy". What he needed, he felt, was like-minded company. And when at last, in May 1890, he escaped from the horrors of St Remy and settled in Auvers-sur-Oise, he was soon suggesting that "if you allow me, I shall come to Brittany for a month. Then we can try to make serious, decisive things—the kind of things we should probably have done if we'd been able to stay together in the south." He had taken up etching, had seen some of Gauguin's work, and was full of plans for a joint volume of southern subjects.

The suggestion was not appreciated. Gauguin was glad enough to write to Vincent, he felt sorry for him—he was a serious painter and he had suffered for his art, suffered horribly—but to have his "assassin", as he spoke of him in playful moments, at close quarters again was another matter.

A few weeks later, at the end of July, Vincent shot himself. His suicide was not unconnected with Gauguin, but the thought of such a thing never entered Gauguin's head; he couldn't afford the journey to the funeral, but he wrote a kind of epitaph to Bernard, who attended: "It doesn't sadden me much because I foresaw it and I knew how the poor fellow suffered in the struggle with his madness. Death at this moment is a great happiness for him, it puts an end to his sufferings and he'll reap the reward of his fine behaviour in another life (according to the law of Buddha). And he carried with him the consolation of never having been abandoned by his brother and of having had his work understood by several artists."

Chapter Sixteen

THE DROUOT SALE

1890-1891

I

THE death of Vincent did not appear to have any serious consequences for Gauguin, or any consequence at all for that matter. In the event it led directly to his abandonment of France. Vincent had not been far wrong when he spoke of the Madagascar plan as made by a man who "doesn't know what else to think of". The "dreadful itch for the unknown" was enough to unsettle anybody, let alone a good painter who could not sell his pictures and a proud man who lived most of the year on charity.

Yet Gauguin had not gone; he had been talking about it for years, but he still oscillated between Paris and Brittany. He was not given to empty words. The Martinique expedition had given him a shock, but he was no coward, and if he couldn't take precautions would try again without them. He wanted company, but, as he was to show, he could do without it. He needed money, but he had done without it before and would do so again. He had been a seaman, he could always have worked his passage.

Why then did he not go? One good reason was that he was not an introspective man; he swung from contentment to misery and felt them both wholeheartedly. In his wretched periods he planned incessantly to get away from France; but except for the months before he left for Panama and Martinique he had always been overtaken, before he could go, by a period of praise, good companionship and a sale or two, which took away all wish to move. But the main reason was simply that he had a natural illusion of success always being just round the corner; and if that was where success really was, his place was in Paris or within reach of it. He was surrounded by admiring painters, and in the art world of Paris his work was talked about, written about, he was a figure—how much of one may be judged by Pissarro's bitter references to "the great Gauguin". Above all, Theo van Gogh believed in him. In his gallery Theo showed Gauguin pottery, sculpture in wood, paintings; he had no doubt about their importance; he had even sold some—the only man to do so. With Theo at his back, how could Gauguin fail to succeed?

Then, suddenly, Theo was no longer at his back. The heartbreaking circumstances of Vincent's suicide actually broke Theo's heart. Within three months of Vincent's funeral he was paralysed and insane; he was carried back to the Netherlands to die; in the gallery he was replaced by a man who looked coldly on Gauguin.

Gauguin received the news from Bernard in October with a despairing: "Van Gogh's attack of madness is a foul blow." Immediately all was black, and troubles that he had been carrying lightly began to weigh him down. He had no money and owed Mlle Henry three hundred francs. He felt desertion in the air: Sérusier, after too much talk about his "evolution", was in Pont-Aven preaching the Gauguin gospel but with a decided suspicion, Gauguin thought, of Sérusier in it. Laval had gone, Moret and Séguin were back in Pont-Aven. The previous winter showed every sign of repeating itself. He cried peevishly to Bernard: "I don't know who could have told you that I walk on the beach with my disciples. De Haan works outside, Filiger in the studio. I walk *en sauvage* with long hair and do nothing—don't even carry colours or a palette. All I've done is to make arrows and throw them in the sand like Buffalo Bill. *Voilà le soi-disant Jésus Christ!*"

He added a despairing, "When shall I be in the woods to live freely at last?" However, he was drawing close to the woods, there being no hope remaining to keep him away. The main question was, where it should be. For months he had favoured Madagascar. Then De Haan's relatives, making frantic efforts to disentangle him from Gauguin, persuaded him that Madagascar was unhealthy. De Haan withdrew.

Bernard was resisting Gauguin's honied descriptions, page after page of them, with alarming ease. He grew lukewarm about Madagascar. He complained that his work was being laughed at; no one would treat him seriously. This, the first murmur of what was to become a lifelong obsession, was stilled for a moment by Gauguin's "I cry to the rooftops, watch little Bernard—he's someone." But the drops were gathering into a stream. Bernard's latest work was received by Gauguin with a protesting "I see in this a great preoccupation with anatomy *à la* Michael Angelo which doesn't strike a chord in me. I don't exactly blame this scientific approach, you understand, but I much prefer the great love of Giotto." He had put his finger on the fact; Bernard, tiring of Synthetic-Symbolism, was flirting with a style of painting based on the Italian masters.

The hint of discord became more obvious when Bernard announced that he was trying to organise a Van Gogh exhibition. "What a blunder!" exclaimed Gauguin. "You know that I love Vincent's art, but it's quite out of place to recall his madness at the very moment when everyone knows that his brother has gone the same way. Plenty of people think our art is mad too, so all you'll do is to harm us and do no good to the Van Goghs." He gave a huge sigh: "All right, have it. *Mais, c'est IDIOT*."

Van Gogh as good as dead, De Haan doubtful, Bernard falling away, Schuff . . . "His letters tell me nothing, his banality is frightful." Schuff, in other words, was not committing himself. In November, Gauguin made up his mind, he would go even if he had to go alone, and he would go not to Madagascar but to Tahiti. He had been reading Loti, he had pored over a pamphlet on Tahiti picked up long since at the Exposition Universelle, he studied *Le Journal des Voyages*, a description of the free and easy life of Polynesia, he had perhaps recalled the legend that the Incas had sailed on rafts from Peru to the Marquesas and Tahiti—the islands were the nearest to Peru, the people even looked alike.

He explained himself to Redon, who had begged him not to leave Europe. "Madagascar is too close to the civilised world, so I'm going to Tahiti and shall die there. My art you love is only a seed, at Tahiti I hope to let it grow in primitive, savage soil. Let the others have the glory, I need peace. The Gauguin of France is dead, you will hear no more of him. I'm an egoist as you see. But I shall carry, in photos and drawings, a little world of comrades who will chat with me every day. In Europe death with its serpent's tail is probable, but in Tahiti I see it as the roots from which all the flowers will grow again."

This was rhetorical, but unlike other effusions this one was written by a man who intended to try out his theories on the spot. But money was essential. He came back to Paris before the end of the year and at once tried to arrange a grand sale of his pictures. He again went to the Schuffeneckers, but for a very short time and for the last time. Schuff made it clear that not one sou of his money was going out of France, but so innocuously that an open quarrel was impossible; the friendship was merely allowed to decline. Just before the new year Gauguin moved to the rue de la Grande-Chaumière, then took a room in a small hotel in the rue Delambre. He was uncomfortable, pinched for money and unable to paint.

He was rescued by De Monfreid, whose admiration had grown steadily. He suggested that Gauguin should share his studio in the rue du Chateau, off the Vaugirard. The sharing was merely a tactful device; Gauguin moved in with Juliette and De Monfreid paid the rent. He began by copying Manet's *Olympia*, which after a prolonged struggle had just been bought for the Luxembourg; but, unable to endure the stuffy surroundings, he finished it in the studio. He also made a study of Juliette for De Monfreid; she was the type he favoured—dark, strong, big, fierce. The two men had fallen into the habit of walking together during the previous winter and must have formed a striking couple, the dark, broad almost corpulent Gauguin and the tall, thin, gaunt-faced De Monfreid with hollow eyes, receding fair hair and long yellowish beard. De Monfreid knew his friend to be a difficult man, but had no doubt about his greatness; he was patient and he was rewarded—Gauguin liked his good talk and appreciated his kindness. He responded to the aristocrat in De Monfreid, and the gap left by the cautious Schuff was slowly and one must think more worthily filled.

There was another bond, or what would appear to be one, between them; De Monfreid was separated from his wife and hoping for a divorce. But the strength of this bond was limited. Gauguin was ready to sympathise with the trials of any husband, but he would listen coolly to stories of divorce; the mere thought of permanent separation from his own wife agitated him—it was the most sensitive point in the Gauguin that he kept hidden from all. All but Mette; to her he made no secret of his attachment, although it often took the form of reproach. The moment he reached Paris he gave her his news: he was invited to exhibit in Brussels, and he wanted to come on to Copenhagen for a month to see her and the children.

The usual squabble sprang up. Mette had complained of Schuff: Gauguin, he had told her (they wrote occasionally to each other), was a pirate, but above all the man who was making art incarnate. "Schuff always repeats what others say," replied Gauguin contemptuously. But what others said was a different matter. In his own way he struggled on, trying to bridge the gap: "It's probable that people find something in me that you don't, you Dane, you." And what was she using the word "affectionate" for?—the more gold, the more affection, that was about the size of it.

But his method of persuasion could not have been more unhappily chosen. Each was trying hard but hopelessly to alter the values of the other. Why talk of coming to Copenhagen, Mette asked; why didn't he drop his affectation of paternity? He became pathetic. "The affectation of paternity is forbidden, but not of maternity, which is never in doubt." He wanted to see his children, but of course he would never dare walk out with them, his clothes were much too old and tattered: "Scandal is forbidden in Denmark." As for Brussels, of course he couldn't go, he had not the fare. Probably he wouldn't come to Copenhagen either.

2

In February his letters became excited and triumphant. He had arranged a sale of his work at the Hotel Drouot, the popular art critic Octave Mirbeau was to introduce the sale with an article in the *Echo de Paris*, articles would follow in other papers, he would be released from poverty at last, go off to Tahiti and make a home for them all. "I'm playing a big game for the future." He might after all get to Brussels and on to Copenhagen. But "I can't have the family taxing me with '*a man who is not serious*'. I shall come incognito, stay at a hotel—don't worry."

For the Drouot sale and the Mirbeau article he had to thank his prestige with the Symbolists, and particularly his growing friendship with Morice. From the moment of returning to Paris he had made a point of dropping in to the Café Voltaire every Monday evening. There he found the bearded Verlaine "sickly, a scarf twisted round his neck, leaning on a thick stick" but with a look in his dark eyes, half glint, half twinkle that made one forget the limp and the sickliness. Denis had just illustrated a copy of his *Sagesse* and the poet was about to bring out *Extrêmes Onctions*—a title that, repeated in his sharp voice, made Gauguin chuckle. Verlaine had a look of Cézanne—the same short, round face, premature baldness, bold eyebrows and bushy fringe of hair—perhaps that was why Gauguin unbent before him. Morice was there, of course, elegant and vehement; he sat himself next to Gauguin whenever possible, as did Aurier "with the dark skin and long hair of an Italian Renaissance poet". Close by was Jean Moréas (of whom Gauguin made a drawing in charcoal and ink) rated by Mallarmé as, with Morice, the second of the three young men then writing great verse. Julien Leclercq, "looking, with his dark curly hair, like a Bellini portrait", was not the third, but he wrote on cheerfully, living from hand to mouth on the odd lyric and the more occasional loan. Gauguin took to him; he was a fellow spirit. Not so the reactionary Carrière, treated by Gauguin with uncharacteristic leniency. He admired Rodin, stared at the cartoonist Cazals, dressed in a frock-coat of the 1830s, and listened with eyes half shut to Maurice Barrès. He said little himself and took no part in the rather precious talk characteristic of this kind of group. One of his most refreshing traits, which lifted him head and shoulders above most of his contemporaries, was his dislike of cliques, labels and pretension. He hated cant. He had never taken kindly to the title of Synthetist, scribbling an ironical "Vive la Sintaize!" on one of his pots, and he liked Symbolist no better. He moved with the Symbolists for a time because he liked some of the members and because he was a businessman: but when Verlaine, being of his mind, commented one evening, "Hé! Zut! They bore me, these 'cymbalists'," Gauguin smiled sympathetically. His problems, as always, were practical ones—how to live and how to improve his work.

Records have been kept of his conversations—dicta rather—not at the Café Voltaire, where he was content to listen, but at a place more in keeping with his tastes and means, the Brasserie Gangloff in the rue de la Gaîté. This was a large hall with tables scattered round a central group of half a dozen billiard tables. A steam organ screamed airs from "Carmen" and "William Tell", waiters slid about bellowing orders, the hall was thick with steam, tobacco smoke, fumes of coffee, and rang with voices shouting over the music. In the midst of this bedlam Gauguin, a monument of tattered regality in beret, cloak and sabots, would prop himself, cigarette in mouth, against the bar or lean back in a chair, pour without appearing to notice it practically the whole of a *carafe* of brandy into his coffee, and read the papers. When roused by disagreements among the little group who followed him, he would unveil a keen eye and make great play with the decorated stick. It pointed at a billiard table: "A square centimetre of green in the middle is greener than a square centimetre by itself"—"Use your eyes"—"Line is colour"—"Ugliness can be beautiful, prettiness never"—aphorisms, practical every one, followed each other in the familiar emphatic drawl. He took a special pleasure in reversing shibboleths of the day. He demolished the "Paint stupidly what you see" with his "A painter may do anything he likes as long as it's not stupid." He contradicted the contemporary talk of "gaps" in nature: "All tones, even loud ones, join in an invariable harmony. The only gaps are those found in some paintings. The painter calls them 'values', but they destroy the harmony of the tones by introducing elements such as chiaroscuro, which are foreign to colour." The stick would veer round towards one of the oriental mats, shawls or jars that were beginning to appear in public places —"there's the proof".

Criticism of himself and his work, which followed the time-honoured formula of the frightened—he was either mad or making a fool of himself—he denied with a particularly grand sweep of the stick: "There's nothing ridiculous about me or my work. How can there be? I'm two things that can never be ridiculous—a child and a savage."

To Morice he explained, "The experience I won at Martinique was decisive. There and there only did I feel that I really was myself. That's why I want to go to Tahiti. I need money, about ten thousand francs. I think that a well-prepared sale of about thirty pictures from Martinique, Brittany and Arles could get them. But the preparation is ticklish." Morice, whose admiration for Gauguin had risen rapidly, took him to lunch with Mirbeau early in February and Gauguin explained why he was selling his pictures and what he planned to do in Tahiti. On the 16th Mirbeau's article appeared. It was reprinted as a preface to the catalogue of the sale and was quoted largely by *Le Figaro* and most of the leading papers.

"I have learned," wrote Mirbeau, "that M. Paul Gauguin is

leaving for Tahiti. He intends to live alone there for several years, to build his own hut, to try to understand many things that disturb him. The case of a man fleeing from civilisation, voluntarily seeking oblivion and silence in order to know himself better and be able to hear more clearly the inner voices which are drowned in the noise of our passions and disputes—this seems to me both strange and touching. Paul Gauguin is a most exceptional, most disconcerting artist who rarely shows himself to the world and of whom in consequence the public knows little. I have often wanted to talk about him but was afraid of the difficulty of the task and of speaking inadequately of a man whom I esteem so highly . . . never satisfied with what he has done, he is always looking forward and beyond, searching. He feels that he has not given all that is in him. In his soul there is confusion, he gropes vaguely but with power towards more abstract and mysterious ways and means of expression. His thoughts go back to the lands of light and mystery he has visited before; there, he believes, he can find new untouched elements in art conforming with his dreams. . . ."

His art Mirbeau described as "strangely cerebral and impassioned"—a remark of insight—"uneven but always poignant and impressive, the work of one who has known sorrow and the irony of sorrow which leads to the mystical. Sometimes indeed it rises to a mystical act of faith. At other times it grins in the darkness of doubt. . . . The splendour of barbarism, of the catholic liturgy, of Hindu dreams, Gothic imagery, symbolism subtle and obscure—all are here in this absolutely personal and altogether new art which Gauguin has created."

Gauguin hastened to send Mette a newspaper cutting, and promised more. "It's caused quite a stir in Paris and has even been mentioned in England." The effect was noticeable even before the sale: Gauguin was invited to show his pottery and sculpture in wood at the forthcoming exhibition of the Meissonier group. In his exultation, his imagination leaping ahead, he dropped all bickering: "I've loved you only and still love you even though my love isn't returned or is returned conditionally. The past exists, but it can be covered over with thoughts of the future."

As he wrote he was living with Juliette and she was with child by him. Many people, knowing this, have jumped to the conclusion that he was despicable in his dealings with Mette, that he lied and misled her. How, these people ask, can a man sleep with one woman and love another? The answer is that Gauguin could and did; this fact must be accepted if he is to be understood. The nature of his love for Mette was a blend of habit, conscience, love for the children, a wish for security, the knowledge that he was going far away and a something else that bound him to her, some attraction that a third eye cannot see. He deceived himself in thinking that they could live peacefully together again, but he deceived himself, not her. In the midst of anticipation, of talks, meetings, work, arrangements for the sale, two thoughts were constantly recurring: he must see the children as soon as possible and the family must follow him to Tahiti. After all, he was going alone; De Haan had been persuaded by his family to go back to the Netherlands; Bernard, forbidden by his father to leave France, had withdrawn with a noticeable lack of regrets. The accord of the Brittany years was waning. The elevation of Gauguin as the master Symbolist-painter while he, believing himself to be the real begetter of the Pont-Aven group, was treated as a clever child, one of Gauguin's pupils, understandably made Bernard bitter. He had not yet publicly complained that Gauguin had stolen his thunder, but the thought was in his mind.

3

The sale was held on February 23. Mirbeau's article had done its work. All thirty pictures were sold for a total of 9860 francs. Degas bought *La Belle Angèle* for four hundred and fifty francs and a Martinique landscape for two hundred and sixty. No picture sold for less than two hundred and forty. But the triumph of the day was the *Vision*, which fetched nine hundred francs—a bid that was applauded by the crowded gallery. Aurier, who was present, wrote an ecstatic appreciation of this picture in the new *Mercure de France*. Read carefully, this article, which proceeded to explain Gauguin's art, was far from being all that the painter would wish. Bernard, making a tentative beginning to his campaign, had urged Aurier to write the article on the grounds that Gauguin was a great artist. Who better fitted to help Aurier with the facts than Bernard himself, who had worked for so long with the master? Why bother Gauguin? Bernard supplied the facts and Aurier used them. The facts were cleverly selected, and the reader was given the impression almost without being aware of it that at the back of the master moved a young but brilliant controlling hand. That was all, but it was enough.

For the moment, however, Gauguin was too much occupied to do more than skim. His first thought was again Copenhagen. The total wasn't enormous, he told Mette on the day after the sale, enclosing another bundle of cuttings, "but the moral success is immense and I believe it will bear fruit very soon".

How great the success was can be seen in the attitude of those who disapproved. Pissarro could not contain himself when he read the Aurier article. "This man seems to think we are imbeciles! According to him drawing and painting can if necessary be dispensed with in a work of art—the only essential element is ideas, and they can be expressed by a few symbols . . . but 'the few symbols' have to be drawn after all."

Pissarro was one of the least envious of men; he did not grudge Gauguin the success, but he did disapprove of this kind of painting succeeding. Of the *Vision* he wrote, "I don't criticise Gauguin for having painted a rose background nor do I object to the two struggling figures and the Breton figures in the foreground, what I dislike is that he copied these elements from the Japanese, the Byzantine painters and others. I criticise him for not applying his synthesis to our modern philosophy which is absolutely social, anti-authoritarian and anti-mystical. That is why the problem becomes serious. This is a step backwards; Gauguin isn't a seer, he's a schemer who has sensed that the bourgeoisie are moving to the right, recoiling before the great idea of solidarity which is spreading among the people."

Here is Pissarro the ardent radical and the man with a long memory. He had never forgiven Gauguin for the boorishness at the Nouvelles-Athènes or the snub of his omission from the Volpini exhibition. He was not a profound man and he jumped to the conclusion that Gauguin, having used him and Cézanne to learn how to paint, had thrown him overboard. The ancient feeling against the "Sunday painter" revived: this was what came of encouraging a stockbroker to become a professional—he brought his beastly money-making schemes into art. The plans of Gauguin to conquer Rouen were never far from Pissarro's mind—businessman's trick; after that, he believed him to be capable of anything: Synthetism,

Symbolism, Cloisonnism were tricks to catch the public eye, every one of them.

Now he had to read of Gauguin, hear of nothing but Gauguin, at one of the most difficult moments in his harassed life. Soon after the Drouot sale Seurat died suddenly and, said Pissarro, "pointillisme is finished". He was right, but that was not the worst of it; he, who had sacrificed reputation, sales, everything, to join the Neo-Impressionists, who had been ridiculed, attacked, who was prepared to defend it with the last breath in his body—he no longer believed in it. He had, at his age, to develop a new style in which he could believe. At such a time to hear the praise of a "trickster" like Gauguin, who would sail in any colours that suited the mood of the moment—this was too much. "We are fighting against terribly ambitious 'men of genius' who are concerned only to crush whoever stands in their path. It's sickening. If you knew how shamelessly Gauguin behaved in order to get himself elected (that is the word) man of genius and how skilfully he went about it! We were left no choice except to smooth the way for him. Anyone else would have been ashamed!" Pissarro, who could never resist a tasty piece of gossip, then tells his son several dubious stories about Gauguin's "shameless" appeals for help, the most unlikely one being that Degas had bought his Gauguin canvases purely out of charity.

But Pissarro rushed on into his favourite topic of the moment. Why did everyone now think Gauguin a genius? "It's a sign of the times, my dear chap. The bourgeoisie, astonished by the immense clamour of the disinherited masses, by the insistent demands of the people, feels it's necessary to give the people back their superstitious beliefs. Hence the uprising of religious symbolists, religious socialists, idealist art, occultism, Buddhism, etc. Gauguin has sensed the tendency."

All this was as near nonsense as makes little difference. Personal antipathy, political fervour and his own difficult position account for it all. Rouen was far behind, forgotten by Gauguin. The various "isms" under cover of which Pissarro suspected that his old pupil had dishonestly leapt into favour were, practically, valueless. The public read, talked, laughed, but remained unmoved. The Gauguin pictures were bought only by dealers, fellow painters, rich collectors. In effect, he remained much where he was—financially a much poorer prospect than Pissarro, as time was to show. Had he wished to sell first and foremost he would have painted very different pictures. Pissarro was not just; Gauguin was as sincere an artist as he. But Gauguin had only himself to blame; he too was intolerant, his attempts to play the businessman, though absurd, were suspicious, and he appeared ungrateful. He acknowledged freely all his influences—Pissarro, Cézanne and Degas particularly—but he took his time.

At that moment, however, he did not worry about Pissarro or the murmurers, of whom there were plenty. He was satisfied that he must live and paint in the tropics. It was not the act of a showman or of an "escapist". Before the Drouot sale he had sold less than half a dozen pictures in the eight years since leaving Bertin. The Drouot sale was good only by comparison. It did not promise a livelihood—the price averaged just over three hundred francs against the three thousand for a Monet. How could he live in a place like Paris? The question was a double one—the prices and the atmosphere. He could not afford to live there, but did he even want to? Increasingly he felt that he did not; the commercialism of big cities disgusted him as sooner or later they disgust every genuine artist. Money was the be-all and end-all of everyone—shopkeeper, office worker, government official and, not least, art dealer—and the pride of all seemed to rest in the outwitting of all, their chief virtue a low cunning. Tahiti appeared paradisal by comparison.

Nor could he get comfort from his own people. In contempt and despair he saw discord everywhere. One might have thought that the artists, threatened by the exploiter on the one hand, the philistine on the other, would stand together. But not at all. Not only did they break into schools viciously attacking every other school, these schools split into cliques and factions which fought amongst themselves. He saw the older Impressionists exhibiting at the Salon, Cézanne agitating for a similar honour, the Neo-Impressionists breaking up; his own Pont-Aven school beginning to disintegrate; Pissarro neither one thing nor the other; Guillaumin, having won a hundred thousand francs in his lottery (at last!) retiring into the country to paint weak-kneed versions of an outmoded Impressionism; he would even, in a France riven by the Dreyfus affair, hear of his admired Degas publicly cutting Pissarro because he was a Jew.

But before going away he must see the children, meet Mette. He left for Copenhagen three days after the sale. All that is certainly known of his days there is that he was photographed between Aline and Emile. His appearance, as the photograph shows, was not likely to have ingratiated him with the Gad family; indeed, imagination reels at the thought of Gauguin in his Breton outfit walking with Mette and the children through the streets of Copenhagen. Yet his letter to Mette written on his return to Paris tells its own story—that Mette had been impressed by the result of the Drouot sale.For his letter (written nearly eighteen years after their marriage) begins "My adored Mette," and goes on, "I know how difficult life is for you at present, but *voilà* the assured future. I shall be happy, very happy if you wish to share it with me. In place of passion we can, white-haired, enter into a period of spiritual happiness surrounded by our children, flesh of our flesh." He ends "Love me well. When I return we shall get married again. It is therefore a fiancé's kiss which I send you today, a betrothal kiss." The only hint of discord was his mild "Perhaps you'll understand one day what kind of man you have given your children as father." He told her that he had been granted a "special mission" in Tahiti by the Ministry des Beaux Arts—a mission which consisted in a promise to buy a picture from him for three thousand francs when he returned, and which gave him a nebulous unofficial standing with the authorities as a man who would "accumulate documents to be used for painting in Paris".

He was in particularly good spirits when he wrote the letter. On the previous evening a farewell banquet had been given in his honour at the Café Voltaire. Thirty men and women were present —Symbolists, painters and one or two from the theatre. Neither Schuff, Bernard, Sérusier nor De Haan was there. Mallarmé, who was ill, could not take the chair, but sent a note ending, "I am, near or far, your friend"; verses by him—"delightfully obscure"—were read during the evening, Gauguin's health was drunk and his merits declaimed in a speech by the chairman. He replied shortly and with difficulty—too much smoking, explained one observer. Perhaps he was overcome by the tribute or, as is more likely, by the optimistic forecasts of all round him—a new art coming out of Tahiti, his pictures selling in France and, as a result, reunion with his family. No wonder that his heart was unusually light and that he wrote lovingly to Mette as a man at last delivered from the stigma of failure.

One final honour remained. A performance was to be given at the Théatre d'Art for the joint benefit of Gauguin and Verlaine. The foyer was to be hung with Gauguin's canvases, readings were to be given from Verlaine, Victor Hugo, Lamartine, Baudelaire and Mallarmé, and plays by Morice and Maeterlinck performed. It was hoped that three thousand francs would be raised, and Gauguin left on April 4 expecting his share to follow.

He was seen off by a group of friends at the Gare de Lyon and was followed by a gigantic sneer from Pissarro: "He will succeed. We who were so close to him know that he has great vitality, is used to the difficulties of life, and can take a new tack if need be."

Even more unpleasant was the letter sent by Mette to Schuff for him to forward: She could not remember the address: "I write to him so rarely and I think of him even more rarely." The letter was vitriolic. "My heart is filled with bitterness that Paul could be so criminally selfish. I've never seen or heard of anything like it."

Mette had just discovered that he had taken the proceeds of the Drouot sale, or what was left of them after he had paid his debts, to Tahiti.

Chapter Seventeen

TAHITI

1891-1893

I

He arrived at Papeete, the capital of Tahiti, on the eve of his forty-third birthday. At first everything exceeded expectations: "a voyage without trouble, in good health, to a marvellous country". His appearance, his letters of recommendation and the *Figaro* reprint of the Mirbeau article, which had reached Papeete ahead of him, caused something of a sensation in the small colonial town whose excitements depended on the rare arrival of a ship from France. Certainly such a figure as his had never before been seen in the streets of Papeete. He was besides a painter—an unknown species. He was received smoothly by the governor and was invited to appear at the royal palace. According to custom he was promptly given a name—Koki—by the people, and a girl—Titi—attached herself to him. He had money on him, he was expecting to receive fifteen hundred francs from the benefit performance, and regular sums to follow as his Tahiti pictures were sold. Even if the money were delayed, "I believe I'm going to earn money here which I had not counted on."

And the country! "The silence of the night in Tahiti is the strangest thing of all," he told Mette. "It only exists here, without even the cry of a bird to disturb one's repose. Here and there a big dry leaf falls but doesn't suggest the idea of sound—it is more like the slight touch of a spirit. The islanders often walk at night, but silently, with bare feet. Always this silence. I can understand why these people can sit for hours, for days without saying a word, looking sadly at the sky. I know that all this is going to take hold of me and I feel extraordinarily peaceful. Already it seems to me that the troubles of life in Europe don't exist any more and that each day will follow the other without change until the end."

Having written as much, it occurred to him that Mette might regard his present bliss equivocally; perhaps he had a premonition of the letter on its way to him, for he hastened to add: "Don't think from this that I'm selfish and am abandoning you. But give me time to live this way. Those who reproach me don't know all there is in an artist's nature. Why should they try to impose their duties on us? We don't impose ours on them."

But the beauty of the night was too much for caution. "What a glorious night it is! Thousands of people are doing just as I am. All of them give themselves up to living. . . . They go where they please, to no matter what village or by what road, they sleep in a house, they eat and they don't think of saying thank you for they know that one day they'll gladly do the same for others. And they are called savages! They sing, they don't steal, they don't murder, my door is never locked. Two words describe them: *Ia-ora-na*—Good-day, good-bye, thank you—and *O-na-tu*—What does it matter? I don't care. And they are called savages!"

But these feelings could not live long in Papeete. Tahiti, with other nearby islands of Polynesia, had been made a French colony ten years earlier, the King, though keeping his title and palace, had been deposed, and on closer view Papeete took on a disturbing likeness to St Pierre in Martinique.

Soon after Gauguin reached there the King died and even the pretence of Tahitian self-government was abandoned: "Tahiti is gradually becoming French and the old life will slowly disappear." He looked vainly in the capital for the Tahiti of Loti, of the highly coloured pamphlet of the Exposition Universelle, of Mme Redon's reminiscences; he saw instead "a European way of life aggravated by colonial snobbery and an imitation, grotesque to the point of caricature, of our customs, manners, vices and civilised absurdities" which had led to the island being ravaged by syphilis and consumption. To the indignant Gauguin the villains of the piece were first the missionaries, "they've already brought much Protestant hypocrisy with them and taken away much of the charm—not to mention smallpox, which has attacked the whole race", followed closely by the colonial authorities summed up for the moment in the person of the governor—a mulatto—whose smoothness proved to conceal suspicion of the "artistic mission" which, being unpaid, must, he assumed, be to spy on him.

No lucrative orders came Gauguin's way. When the next ship arrived with new passengers he was forgotten. Even Titi was a

Coll. Mme. Jeanne Schuffenecker *Photo: Vizzavona*

SOYEZ AMOUREUSES. 1889

Mme. Huc de Monfreid

EMILE, GAUGUIN AND ALINE. 1891

disappointment; he discovered her to be only half Tahitian—her father was English. She had the good looks of the island girls, the dark gleaming hair, golden-brown skin, regular features, proud carriage and expression, but she was already spoiled by a town life, ambitious and overdressed.

He decided to make a life for himself in the country. He hired a carriage and, with a proud and highly decorative Titi on the seat beside him, drove round the coast until he found a spot that suited him. After they had driven some twenty miles he saw at Mataiea a hut to let—the usual bourao wood hut of a Tahitian village with a roof of pandarus leaves, reed walls, cooking-stones on the ground before the door and a little eating-shed to one side. He arranged to rent it at once and drove back to Papeete to collect his belongings, but before he could get away he had a sudden return of the bronchitis that had attacked him after the privations in Paris years earlier. He was taken to hospital and coughed up a great deal of blood; the doctor shook his head over him, but his great strength pulled him through; in a few weeks he was in his hut at Mataiea, solitary (he had left Titi behind), weak, but contented.

Like all the coastal villages Mataiea faced a lagoon enclosed by a coral reef. From his hut Gauguin looked over blue water, broken by the arc of foam, to the high hills of the island of Moorea which, as the sun sank behind them each evening, stood up black and jagged. At his back the land rose steeply to mountains split by enormous rocky chasms. Between his hut and the hills the country was thick with cocoanut palms, breadfruit trees, the bourao, iron-wood and vast ferns that came up to his shoulders. "In the evening I go down to the sand by the edge of the sea to smoke a cigarette. The sun sets quickly on the horizon, half hidden already by the island of Moorea to my right. The contrasts of light are accentuated clearly and strongly, black on a fiery sky, the peaks of the mountains appearing like the crenellations of old castles. The silence—I am learning to understand the silence of a Tahitian night . . . Between me and the sky nothing but the great roof, light and lofty, of pandarus leaves where the lizards live. In my dreams I can imagine the free space above my head, the celestial way, the stars. I am very far from those prisons, the European houses. . . ."

He watched the men fishing naked in the lagoon, the women, stripped to the waist, arranging the nets. Down the path from the mountains, outlined against the mango trees growing on the face of the chasm, men and women walked, upright, elegant, carrying baskets of breadfruit on their heads. A small girl was sent to greet him, silently laying before the hut freshly cooked fish and breadfruit wrapped between giant banana leaves. At night the villagers serenaded him, sitting in front of their huts playing soft melodies on their flute, the *vivo*.

Was not this the life he had dreamed of? Tahiti was another Martinique but a healthier one, without the swarms of mosquitoes, with food that was good to eat and easy to gather. It was another Martinique but with a beautiful people, a brotherly people, dignified and gentle. What work he could do here, with such models, such colours! "The landscape with its pure and ardent colours dazzled and blinded me. Once I had always been uncertain and groping. . . . It was so simple after all to paint as I saw, to put a red, a blue on my canvas without so many calculations. Golden forms in brooks enchanted me. Why should I hesitate to make all this gold and all this joy of the sun flow on to my canvas?"

But at first it was not so simple as he imagined. He was truly dazzled; the brilliance of colouring that was to make his Tahitian landscapes notorious then famous—the purple earth, orange flowers, scarlet leaves, the glare of green—was, after France, after the cold rocky Pouldu, too great a change. He could not acclimatise himself. "Sometimes I find it good, at other times I find that it looks horrible," he told De Monfreid, who had asked how his work was getting on. "So far I've done nothing up to much."

He lived the village life, fishing, swimming, wood-chopping and breadfruit-gathering with the villagers. At night, more often than not, one of the village girls would come to his hut and sleep with him—it was the custom, and in this case it was considered an honour to sleep with the white man. The custom flattered and pleased him; he was entirely sympathetic towards the Tahitians who in spite of the missionaries remained proud of their bodies and very ready to enjoy them. They were oblivious of sin and no explanation could make them understand it; was it a sin to eat, to walk, talk, laugh or sing? Well, then.

This was Gauguin's attitude precisely—the attitude that distinguished his nudes from others. He began to write down his impressions in a rough notebook that he called *Cahier Pour Aline*, hoping that one day this favourite child might benefit from them. In this book he dealt, amidst a medley of subjects—art, politics, literature, metaphysics—with sex, illustrating his theories with his observations of the islanders. "In Europe intercourse between men and women is a result of love. In Oceania love is a result of intercourse. Which is right? The man or woman who gives their body is said to commit a small sin. That is debatable, and in any case sin is wholly redeemed by creation, the most beautiful act in the world, a divine act in the sense that it continues the work of the Creator. The real sin is committed by the man or woman who sells their body." He narrowed the question down in another remark about women. "Their nature is to love, but love of a special kind, one that conceives and in conception gives itself completely. Woman only fulfils herself when she gives herself. She will be free —and healthier—on the day when her honour is no longer placed below her navel."

2

Months passed. He had been accepted by the village; his eye had settled to the blaze of colour everywhere; his physical needs were satisfied; yet he remained somehow empty—he could not work. The people were kind, obliging, but they did not belong to him. The girls who came to his hut at night left it—and him—in the morning. And he, praising promiscuity, found himself at a loss when he practised it; neither this nor the free and easy life in the sun he had dreamed of could compensate for his creative sterility. A savage he might be, but he was a European too; above all he was a painter. He needed at least the illusion of permanence and stability; he wanted the encouragement of love and a home. Mette was too far away; a substitute must be found—the kind of substitute he envisaged when he had first written to her about Tahiti. Without the illusion and the substitute his venture would fail, Tahiti for all its charms would not bring from him a single worthwhile painting, he would have crossed half the world for nothing. In despair he summoned Titi, but sent her back to Papeete after a week or two—she was hopelessly out of place. At last he went off on a tour of the island—perhaps he would find his "vahine" that way.

He walked, then rode a borrowed horse for some miles until, at

Faone, he was invited to share the villagers' meal. Even so far away he was known, the painter "who made men". He went into a hut and joined the group of men, women and children sitting on the ground talking and smoking. A good-looking woman in early middle age asked him where he was going.

"To Itia."

"Why?"

"To find a vahine."

"If you want one there are several here, good-looking too. Do you?"

"Yes."

"I'll give you one if you like. She's my daughter."

"Is she young?"

"Yes."

"Is she healthy?"

"Yes."

"Good. Fetch her."

The woman went away. She came back a few minutes later with a girl of thirteen or fourteen. Her name was Tehura and she was from the island of Tonga. Gauguin watched her as she put food before him on a banana leaf—fish, shrimps and bananas. She was tall and strong, with big firm breasts. Her golden-brown skin shone through a thin pink dress. She moved gracefully and with composure. Her dark hair, parted in the centre, fell over one shoulder; it was slightly frizzy and deep yellow glints struck out of it when the sun caught it. Her forehead rose, broad and high, from black level brows, her eyes, dark, enigmatical, met his calmly. She was not beautiful, but she was impressive, even formidable. A child? How could one believe it? Her face was serene, like his paintings, proud, independent. Her mouth, sensual, tender and mocking by turns, perplexed him. For the first time in his life he felt at a loss with a woman. How to know what was going on behind those eyes? At first he was afraid that she was being forced to go with him, to give the family the honour of being connected with a European. Another look at her face reassured him—no one could make that girl act against her will—but he questioned her nevertheless.

"Are you frightened of me?"

"No."

"Do you want to live with me in my hut for ever?"

"Yes."

"Have you been ill?"

"No."

After the meal was done, he began to ride back slowly, followed by Tehura, carrying a small bundle, and members of her family. Soon they came to another hut, a large one with hay spread on the floor and mats placed on top of the hay. All sat down beside a youngish woman—Tehura's foster-mother, she explained. After a glass of water had been passed round, this woman, who seemed anxious, said to Gauguin, "Are you a good man?"

He hesitated then, judging himself by his intentions, answered "Yes."

"Will you make my daughter happy?"

"Yes."

"She must come home in a week. If she isn't happy with you she won't go back."

At the end of the week Tehura went home, and so little did Gauguin understand her that he was astonished when she came back—astonished and absurdly elated. He told her that he loved her; she merely smiled. Child though she was, she could not have bound him more closely to her; the European gambits of love were nothing to her, she made them appear shoddy. He no doubt read into her looks and smiles and silences a profundity that was not there—all his reverence for primitive peoples inclined him to do so—but some innate wisdom she must have had to satisfy him. There she was, in his hut—his woman, never leaving him, giving him company, youth and gaiety, for she had moments when she behaved like her age. She slept with him, cooked for him, bathed with him, walked with him and showed by European standards an extraordinary tact for one so young, talking to him when he was in the mood, watching grave and impassive beside him for hour after hour when he painted.

For he had at last begun to work; she had done that for him. He made study after study of her—the *Tahitienne*, the *Rêverie*, above all the *Vahine No Te Tiare*. He felt that he had never painted better. He felt that through Tehura he was beginning to bridge the gap—the gap that had kept him from work of any moment—between European and islander. The artist is not always the best judge of the workings of his mind; Gauguin persistently overrated the effect and the extent of his affinity with "savages"; in so far as the gap could be bridged it was due as much to intelligence as to the savage in him. At times, when he described how he painted a picture, he admitted as much. He could not, in fact, "go native", and he never seriously tried to do so—his intention was to return to France if he could not persuade Mette to join him. However, he did live (with certain important exceptions) as the islanders lived; and by taking Tehura into his hut he made it into a Tahitian home and drew as close to the people as a foreigner could hope to do. "Bit by bit civilisation is leaving me. I'm beginning to think simply and to lose hatred for my neighbour—or even better, to love him—I live a free life, enjoying animal and human pleasures. I escape from the factitious, I identify myself with nature, knowing that the next day will be like the present one, just as free, just as beautiful. Peace is taking possession of me."

3

He worked hard. One year after Tehura joined him—before the end of 1892—he sent eight canvases to Mette with "In the eleven months since I've really got down to work I've made 44 important canvases which ought to bring in a yearly income of 15,000 francs." He was, he said, "well satisfied with my recent work. I have the feeling that I've begun to grasp the Oceanian character. I assure you that what I am doing here has never been done by anyone and is unknown in France." A month later, "I'm in the thick of my work now I've got to know the very smell of the earth. The Tahitians of my canvases, though enigmatic, are really Maoris and not orientals from Batignolles."

By the end of the year he was writing triumphantly to De Monfreid of three more canvases: "I think they're the best I've done, and as it is only a few days to January 1st I've dated one, the best, 1893. For a change I've given this one a French title, *Pastorales Tahitienne*, because I can't find an equivalent in Kanaka. I don't know why—I've used pure veronese green and vermilion—but this one looks to me like an old Dutch painting or an old tapestry." This was the canvas that was to cause such a sensation in Paris. Something of this he surmised—"these canvases are advanced, that's to say even more difficult to sell than my earlier ones"—and he sighed for Theo van Gogh, lying beside his brother in the churchyard at Auvers: "If Van Gogh of Goupil's weren't dead. . . !"

How much he really believed that his Tahitian canvases would not sell it is difficult to say. He contradicted himself, telling Mette, "I hope that this novelty will count in my favour." It was not in his nature to think that his work could be ignored. He was more satisfied with it than ever before; so much so that when, a few months earlier, Mette's bitter letter at last reached him—the first time he had heard from anyone except De Monfreid—he felt so justified in the step he had taken that he ignored her complaints and replied with a burst of proud optimism, or defiance one might call it, to the only remark that could be taken favourably.

For there were signs of a change in Mette, not towards him (though perhaps he chose to take it so) but towards his potentialities. His disappearance with the proceeds of the sale was a scandal, of that she had no doubt. But what of the fact that there were proceeds to be taken away? The more she considered the matter, the more astonished Mette became—astonished and impressed. This ne'er-do-well husband of hers had put thirty of his absurd pictures into a sale and had sold every one of them, had made nearly ten thousand francs from them. He could send her as many press cuttings as he chose—didn't she know the backscratching among those artists?—he could promise and predict good times to come—words, all of it. But this sale was different, this was business, hard cash. Was he, after all, an artist—or, if one put it another way, had he at last managed to impose his work on the public? It came to the same thing—he was suddenly, unexpectedly an asset. She had at Copenhagen many of his early works, including *Etude de Nu*, as well as the bulk of his collection of other painters. So with her reproaches was mingled an acknowledgment that perhaps after all he had chosen a career not utterly worthless, together with a suggestion that he send her some Tahiti canvases; she would then try to arrange an exhibition in Copenhagen of his early and late work.

He sent the canvases with an injunction (he had never shown greater optimism), heavily underlined, "It is ESSENTIAL that the money from any sale be put to one side until I come back to France." But he was chiefly concerned to widen the first sign of a gap in Mette's disregard of his art. With an eagerness that is a curious mixture of pathos and pride he insisted, "You're right, you aren't foolish, I am an artist, I am a great artist and I know it. It's because I am that I've endured so much suffering in order to follow my calling, otherwise I should feel like a brigand, which, for that matter, I am to many people. But why worry? What most annoys me is not so much the misery as the perpetual hindrances to my art."

Mette, with this new view of him before her, had criticised his move to Tahiti not only as a fresh desertion of her but as unbusiness-like just when he was becoming known. The reproach stirred him. "You say that I am at fault in living far from the centre of the world of art. No. I'm right. For a long time now I've known what I should do and why I should do it. My artistic centre is in my own brain and nowhere else. I'm strong because I'm never led astray by others and because I know myself. Beethoven was deaf and blind, he was cut off from everybody, that's why his work shows an artist living in a world of his own. Look at the stuff Pissarro puts out now as a result of always wanting to be ahead of everyone, to be perpetually up to date; he has lost all personality of his own and his work is absolutely without unity. He follows every movement from Courbet and Millet right up to the young chemists who pile up the dots. No, I have an aim and I'm always after it, accumulating evidence. There are changes in my work each year, it's true, but it always follows the same road. I'm the only logical one. That's why I find very few who will follow me for long."

Schuff had enclosed Mette's letter with a mild complaint of his own. Gauguin ignored it, but commented to Mette, "Poor Schuff reproaches me for being self-willed. But if I didn't behave as I do, how could I stand even a single year of this struggle to the death that I've taken on? My acts and my paintings contradict each other at first, but in the end people see that I'm right. I'm always beginning again. I believe I'm doing my duty and, strong in that belief, I refuse to accept advice or reproach."

This letter, like all those to Mette from this first stay in Tahiti, was affectionate: he signed himself "Your faithful lover and husband", wrote "I think tenderly of you all and embrace you", and spoke often of a future in which "when we are old we shall talk with one another and shan't fear to have more children". All was to be well when his paintings brought in a regular income and a joint home could be set up. Mette gave him no encouragement in her occasional letters, but he persevered. He found the weaving of such plans essential to his peace of mind. He had filled a shelf on the wall of his hut with photographs of Mette and the children, two of them quite grown up. He did not tell Mette about Tehura. He had warned her that he would make a home across the sea. Tehura was necessary to him as model, companion and link with Tahiti. In any case he thought nothing of it; it was the custom; the Tahitians were offended if a man would not sleep with their women; and if Mette didn't remember that he could not do without a woman, who did?

4

Tehura was not an easy vahine; after six months, after twelve, he could fathom her moods little better than during their first trial week together. She was not only of another race, she was youthful for a people who matured early. She passed with bewildering rapidity from one mood to another, from pensiveness to frivolity, from submission to defiance, without any obvious cause. The thought of the experienced Gauguin baffled by this inexperienced child is not without its amusement. The consciousness of his age which her youth and liveliness brought out reads with some pathos in his remarks to De Monfreid: "I have grown older with astonishing speed."

But on the whole the ménage was successful, remarkably so. Except for one falling away, Tehura remained faithful, attentive, even devoted in an impenetrable manner; she made a superb model, and by her chatter when Gauguin was resting she gave him an insight into the mind of the islanders. Like most of the coastal dwellers she was nominally converted, and after a ritual of hair-washing and scented oil went off every Sunday morning to the Protestant chapel in her frock, repeating the psalm for the day, wearing a flower behind her ear and carrying one of Gauguin's handkerchiefs in one hand—the ultimate sign of respectability. But her conversation remained obstinately fixed on the island deities, Hina, goddess of the moon, and Tefaton, god of the earth, whose statues were still preserved all over the island, and on the evil spirits which she believed lay in wait for all after nightfall. She was particularly terrified by the *tupapaus*, the spirits of the dead; she begged Gauguin not to go into the interior; anyone caught there by night, she assured him, would be tormented, for it was then that the spirits became visible in the form of a strange phosphorescence hovering between earth and sky. He took no notice—he was given to walks after dark, enchanted by the silence and the scents of night. He had seen the phosphorescence; it was thrown off, he believed, by a fungus growing on dead trees in the forest; but he could not reassure her. She dreaded darkness even in the hut and tended the solitary oil lamp with desperate care. Gauguin suspected that she still secretly prayed at the shrine of Hina.

Idols began once more to appear in his pictures. In his hut prints of Manet, Degas, Ingres, Rembrandt and his other mentors were flanked by wooden images—for he turned easily from brush to mallet. One may deplore these idols and the whole supernatural atmosphere with which Gauguin invested some of his Tahiti work, but at least his material was obtained at first hand, not borrowed from Bernard. Occasionally, as in his *Manao Tupapau*, he turned some of this material to original use. He visited Papeete, had unexpectedly to walk part of the way home, and did not reach Mataiea until after midnight. No light shone from the window of the hut. He remembered that he had forgotten to get in a fresh stock of oil for the lamp. He walked quickly to the door, fearful that Tehura had run away, pushed it open and struck a match. She lay on the bed naked, face downward, not moving. When she lifted her head her eyes, large and terrified, seemed to throw off the phosphorescence she had described so often and the hut appeared to be filled with her fear.

When he managed to calm her she explained that, unnerved by hours of darkness, she had taken him to be a *tupapau* come to torment her—his face at the door, heavily shadowed and unsubstantial in the flickering matchlight, appeared ghostly, obscurely threatening. She had never seemed so lovely and so desirable. He promised never again to leave her without light; he vowed to cherish her; he felt that he loved her truly, not exactly as wife or daughter but something of each. He meant what he said and he felt sincerely. But he was an artist, and the artist is a dedicated and a damned man. His art respects nothing, least of all his private life. Even while he first looked at Tehura prostrate with dread, Gauguin's compassion had been challenged by the implacable eye. What a picture she would make lying there! On that one canvas, could he but achieve it, would be found the quintessence of Tahitian life, the mystery, the beauty, the terror of it. He was thinking, while he comforted her with tender embraces, that technically, to say no more, such a study would test him as never before; the dark hut, the dusky figure on the bed were subjects as far removed from bright light and blazing colours as one could imagine.

Manao Tupapau (*L'esprit des morts veille*) was one of his triumphs. But he did more than paint it, he explained at length to Mette (to whom he sent it for exhibition) how he did so. "I made a nude of a young girl. In such a position the slightest thing could make it indecent. However, I wanted her that way, the lines and the movement interested me. So I gave her face a frightened expression. This terror serves as a pretext for the position even if it doesn't explain it, and it is in the character of the model, a Maori. By tradition these people have a very great fear of the spirit of the dead. A young girl at home would be afraid to be surprised in such a position (women here not at all). I wanted to explain this terror with as little as possible of the old-fashioned literary means. So I did this: general harmony sombre, sad, fearful, sounding to the eye like a funeral knell, violet, dark blue, orange yellow. I make the bed linen greenish yellow: (1) because the linen of these people differs from ours (made from the bark of a tree); (2) because it creates and suggests artificial light (the Kanakan woman never lies down in the darkness) yet I don't want the effect of a lamp (that's common); (3) this yellow, connecting the orange yellow and the blue, completes the musical accord. There are some flowers in the background, but being imaginary they must not seem real, so I make them look like sparks. To the Kanakas the phosphorescences of the night are the spirits of the dead—they really believe this and are afraid. Finally I make the ghost simply a small ordinary woman because the girl, not knowing the playhouses of the French spiritualists, can only imagine the dead as people like herself bound to their own spirit."

To De Monfreid, who was to send the canvas on to Mette, he added a few details: chrome 1 was used for the orange-yellow background, chrome 2 for the bed linen "because this colour *suggests* night without explaining it"—an interesting point, showing that he made the colour serve two purposes, the suggestion of darkness and the suggestion of artificial light. He also explained to De Monfreid how he intended the imaginary flowers in the background to appear "at the same time (in the mind) like night phosphorescences"—so creating atmosphere without straining after effect. He thought the study "excellent" and talked hopefully of it fetching as much as two thousand francs. He wrote another detailed explanation into the *Cahier Pour Aline*. Never before and only once in the future did he write at such length about a canvas. Understandably; for this picture more than most summarises what Tahiti had done for him as a painter.

The purpose of the long note to Mette, for which he apologised, was "to give you something to say about the picture when the critics bombard you with their malicious questions". For the present-day reader it has another function; it reveals how Gauguin composed his pictures, shows what a "cerebral" painter he was and makes nonsense of the argument, sometimes heard, that he was a painter *malgré lui*, that some subconscious force arising out of this brute of a man "miraculously" painted pictures. In truth, the subconscious had little or nothing to do with his work; before he began to paint he knew what he wanted to do and how to do it. To some this businesslike approach will seem disappointing, to others refreshing, but it is the man, and the man is his work. When Gauguin fails he does so not because "inspiration" is suddenly withdrawn but simply because certain weaknesses in him—his tendency to decorate for decoration's sake, his love of dabbling with mysticism, his occasional lapses into sentimental symbolism, for example—get between him and his original conception.

During this first visit to Tahiti, however, he rarely failed badly once he had settled down with Tehura. By the beginning of 1893 he had painted more than fifty pictures, he had made innumerable drawings, he had done much sculpture in wood. Much of this work was as good as anything he had ever done—particularly his landscapes, his *Arearea*, *La Siesta*, two beach studies *Tahitiennes Nues sur la Plage* and *Nafea Fo I Poipo*, and the crouching figure *Otahi*—and was certainly more original. Regarding it, he felt enormously satisfied; he had demonstrated that a return to the simple life combined with tropical light and colours could produce a new style of painting freed from artificial restrictions. In his life with Tehura and his neighbours he felt that the "savage" in him, so long repressed, was being fulfilled. "The real self", he said in the notes he began to keep about his experiences in Tahiti "is developing normally in me. I no longer have petty, useless troubles." He was learning wisdom from the "savages". "I'll tell you a bit of my secret," he writes to De Monfreid. "It consists of a great logic and I'm behaving very methodically. I knew from the start that I should have to live from day to day, so logically I've adjusted my temperament to such a life. Instead of wasting my strength in work and worry for the future I put all my energy into the day itself like the wrestler who moves his body only when he's ready for the struggle. When I lie down at night I say to myself 'that's another day won, tomorrow I may be dead'."

5

In some respects his life lived up to the idyll he had dreamed of. But it was not always so. There are two men in most of us and there were two in Gauguin. He lived parallel lives in Tahiti. There was the life of sensuous pleasures he was to describe in his *Noa-Noa* —the ear, eye, nose all enchanted, body satisfied to the point of excess, the artist enraptured, the breaker of new ground triumphant, the savage reunited at last with his own. This was the Gauguin who sat and stood for hours in the sun, beret on head, cigarette in mouth, bare-chested, bare-footed, coarse-trousered, sketching, painting with the silent Tehura squatting beside him; the man who swam half a mile up a cavernous creek because Tehura suggested that he would be afraid; who fished and cut wood with the villagers, and attended the village feasts in solemn state; who sat on the sand strumming his guitar and singing Parisian ditties and Breton folk songs or trying his hand at a Tahitian melody; the man who would stare motionless, absorbed, at the colour, the luxuriance of growth everywhere about him; who would stand at the door of the hut listening to the small noises of the night which emphasised the silence; who, lying on the bed inside the hut, would listen to the stories of Tehura until, having frightened herself by her imagination, she gave herself up to forgetfulness in his arms.

But there was also the life of his letters after the first few months, the life of the frustrated European who found himself stranded far from his true centre, neglected, even betrayed. In these moments—and they increased rapidly from the end of his first year—Tahiti, Tehura could do nothing for him. What use was exotic beauty, colour, freedom, to a man who rarely heard a word about his work and never received a penny for it? He was there to paint, but why paint if his paintings were ignored? Mentally he was back again in the Paris of those awful early winters, stranded in Martinique, in Pont-Aven and Pouldu at their barest and bleakest, lonely, hungry, disillusioned, but this time worse than ever as the difficulty of a return was greater. Nor was that all; the bitterest pangs came from another kind of suffering: "I left Paris after a victory, a small one, but a victory nevertheless. In the last eighteen months I haven't had a penny from my painting, which means that I've sold even less than before. It's easy to draw the conclusion." So he told De Monfreid, the one man who tried to keep him in touch with his world, the one man who showed any practical appreciation of his effort to widen the scope of painting.

What had happened to the men who had toasted him at the Café Voltaire? No one wrote to him, he heard nothing from the dealers who had taken his pictures with confident words after the Drouot sale. Morice, who had promised to send on the proceeds of further sales, did nothing of the kind; in two years Gauguin received one short note from him. None of the others troubled their heads about him; it was out of sight out of mind; he had made something of a sensation with his Breton clothes and weighty words and curious canvases and plans to go to the tropics, but there was always another and better sensation round the corner.

To a vain man—and Gauguin's vanity was strong—this wordless abandonment was hard to bear. To a man with a mission, believing in the mission and in his ability to carry it out, the neglect was criminal. His letters blazed with accusations, recriminations. His optimism and trustfulness, as unquenchable as his vanity, had led him astray. Once more the pattern repeated itself. He had gone to Tahiti with a reputation, his pictures were the talk of Paris, he had sold every one put up for auction. Learning no lesson from the past he believed that he would sell more—that money would flow out to him, enabling him to paint in this new-old world with a mind free from distraction.

The first sign that all was not well came with the news from De

Monfreid that the theatrical benefit had been a financial fiasco—there was for him what the other beneficiary, Verlaine, described as "the magnificent sum of 100 francs". Then, in place of money from Morice, from dealers, from friends to whom he had made loans after the sale, came—silence. The mail boat called in every month, but time after time there was nothing for him, not only no money, not even a word. De Monfreid wrote when he was not on his yacht, Mette wrote three times coldly, reproachfully, the businesswoman, there was the note from Morice at last and one from Sérusier. As for Schuff: "He complains to my wife of my character. God knows if I have a bad character—you can judge for yourself." And that was all. In two years that was all.

All who have waited in vain for vital letters will understand something of his feelings if they can imagine themselves stranded thousands of miles from home. Standing there by the mail boat, his hands empty, he felt himself to be the forgotten man. Why was he there was it for himself alone? No, he told himself; he was there to lead the way; others would follow, not in the body perhaps but in their art; a new painting, free, calm, bold would spread over the world, it would begin in France and spread outward until all men knew it and were the better for it. That was why he was there. Silence can be a positive evil; silence week after week, month after month became the malicious voice of disapproval, disregard, contempt. But "I no longer have vain troubles," he had written, "I train myself to follow these people and not worry about tomorrow." But alas, he was a European too, the troubles thickened, the shadow of tomorrow could not be avoided. He was not commonly given to heroics and his banal words covered much suffering: "It's extraordinary the way I get stuck every time I leave Paris."

6

This was in May 1892, almost at the end of his first year in Tahiti. He was then down to his last forty-five francs. When the year was completed, a week or two later, he was free to apply for repatriation, and as no money and no messages had arrived he went in to Papeete to see the governor. He went reluctantly and in a very bad temper; Tehura had enlivened him, he loved the island and its people, he was working well and getting something of the

spirit of the place into his pictures. All this, and
the mulatto for a free passage, he had to craw
a pauper because his so-called friends and
bothered to bestir themselves on his account.

His bad temper vanished when, before
governor's office, he ran into a man he h
skipper of a schooner that traded, illegally
the islands. He was a man after Gauguin's hear
a rascal, foul-mouthed, fearless, contemptuous of the local gov
ment and with an ever-open pocket for the right peop
wasn't broke himself.

Why on earth was Gauguin going into that sink of
he wanted to know, indicating the governor's off
explained. The man put his hand in his jacket,
hundred francs; he would take a painting for it s
Gauguin was hard up, perhaps the wife could be pers
for a portrait; if so, it would be worth thirteen hund

Gauguin went home after celebrating his luck
he arrived back late to find Tehura in dark
money, worried no more. But money never stay
few weeks later, in July, he was down to fifty fra
end of my tether," he told Mette; and as there had
"thanks to Morice who talks of his affection but
prove it". There was a reason for the admission
Mette had visited Paris to collect his canvases, had
was charmed. Gauguin could tell, he growled,
you're infatuated". He found her letter "much
than usual as though you felt the need to beg forgiver
thing. I hope you've only sinned mentally." He
jealous, he reminded her. She might think that he h
right to be jealous; no matter, he was jealous and
if given cause.

This admission gave Mette nothing but annoya
away husband, to talk of jealousy! It never once
that he might, given so little encouragement, have
of her long ago as so many other men would have
occurred to her that he could have quoted Matthe
Luke 18.29 at her and disappeared with a clear c
thoughts were predominantly of legal rights; th

Coll. Mme. Huc de Monfreid *Photo: Vizzavona*

SELF-PORTRAIT. 1896

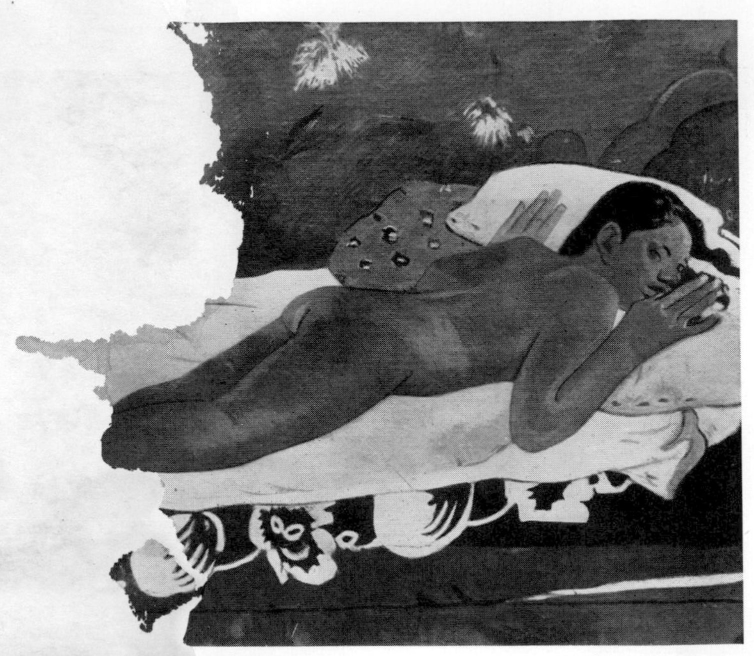

ear Photo: Vizzavona

MANAO TUPAPAU. 1892

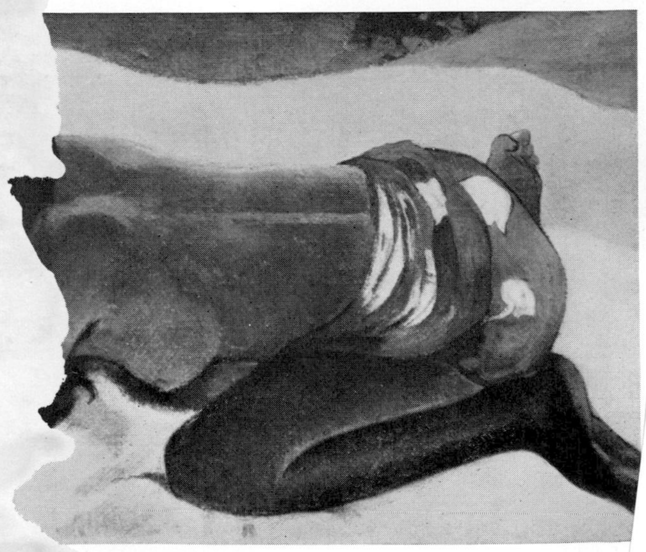

Photo: Vizzavoı

ƞTAHI (SEULE). 1893

interested her less. He too misinterpreted her, though more charitably; when she spoke of Morice as charming, his mind could imagine only sexual attraction—business never entered his head. Yet what charmed Mette in Morice was not his manner or appearance but his faith in her husband's work. His pictures would be famous, he was a genius, she was assured. She began to think that he must be. Helped by a Schuff deep in domestic discord, who ranged himself by her side as an injured party, she took back every canvas she could lay hands on and left for Copenhagen comparatively lighthearted; at last it seemed that there was a chance of making her husband contribute substantially to the family expenses. True, she was disposing steadily of his collection—he reckoned later that she must have obtained thirty thousand francs from it in all—but she preferred to think of that as a reserve against her old age.

Without money or letters (De Monfreid was on his yacht most of the summer) Gauguin was forced to go into Papeete again. The skipper's wife, after one horrified glance at the Tehura portraits, had resolutely refused to sit for her own. Nothing was left but an appeal for repatriation. At the end of November he was told that he could be repatriated when he wished. He did not wish it—Tehura, now with child, was more amenable though no less charming, he was fascinated still by the country and the life, he was full of projects for new pictures—but he had given up hope of attention from France and believed that if his Tahitian canvases were to be sold he must return and do the job himself. And sold they must be; to keep him alive, to spread the news of his discoveries, and above all to bring nearer the time when he could settle down. Undeterred by coldness, he continued to write to Mette of an old age spent peacefully together, himself an established painter with a regular income. Tehura was a will o' the wisp for all her charms, she embodied Tahiti and was as elusive. One moment one had her, the next moment she was away, uncapturable the essence of impermanence.

He decided to leave in January 1893, which would give him time to finish four canvases—the best, he believed, that he had yet painted. A few days after he had made his decision he received three hundred francs from De Monfreid, just back from the sea. He decided nevertheless to go ahead with his plans; the silence from dealers and friends was unnerving him; he must see for himself since no one would see to it for him—De Monfreid, though kind and generous, was not a man of authority, he wasn't in with the crowd, he was no Gauguin. The one note from Morice said only that he'd never heard a word, that he had sent money. Was he a liar and a thief? Gauguin would see.

But he had De Monfreid's money to play with and he lashed out as people will after they have had to go short; in a month half of it had gone. Then he heard that he could not be repatriated in January—the colonial office in Paris must send the fare; April was the earliest he could leave. At once he was struggling again with poverty; by February he was penniless.

He read Mette's next letter with mixed feelings; she had sold some of his pictures for eight hundred and fifty francs; she enclosed nothing because (and her pleasure in this tardy stroke of justice glowed coldly in every word) she needed all and more to support the children. "What can I say?" Gauguin asked De Monfreid. He concentrated on his sufferings—like many men he appeared at his worst with his wife. His eyes were troubling him. The explanation was simple—too much tobacco, too much sex—but he did not see it like that. He had become a chain smoker, but he claimed that he was also undereating and he assumed, without much foundation, that in France both states would be remedied: "Because I deprive myself of food my stomach is sinking in atrociously and I'm getting thinner every day. But I must keep up the struggle always, always. And the blame rests on society. You have no confidence in the future but I have *because I wish to have it*. Without it I should have blown my brains out a long time ago. To have hope is to have life. I must live to do my duty to the end, but I only manage it by straining my illusions and by imagining hopes in my dreams. When I eat *my slice of bread* here every day with a glass of water, I force myself to believe that it's a beefsteak."

7

Another three hundred francs from De Monfreid again rescued him from bread and water. But the question is inescapable—if his picture to Mette is not excessively overdrawn, where did his money go? When he had set off more than a year earlier to search for a "vahine", his landlord and wife, thinking that he was going for good, wailed in dismay—not for the loss of the pittance of rent but because they liked this white neighbour and were proud of him. In tears, both of them, they begged him to stay; if he was without money, what of it? They would feed him—to live in Mataiea cost next to nothing. This was a fact; Gauguin's enthusiastic boast before leaving France that one could live for nothing in the tropics was no more than the truth; at Mataiea were fish, bananas, breadfruit—to name but three—for the asking. None of the villagers spent money on their food—most of them had nothing to spend. But Gauguin had spent several thousands of francs since landing at Papeete less than two years earlier.

When actually faced with life on the fruits of the earth, he found it unexciting and indeed almost unendurable. He had developed a taste for wine, for spirits, for sophisticated food. All this, in Tahiti, cost money, a great deal of money, but he did not stint himself. His smoking cost him dearly. He liked to buy trinkets for Tehura. To explain this is not to criticise unless it be his absurd optimism; no one but a fool or a Gauguin would imagine that a Frenchman of more than forty would willingly sit down day after day to fish, breadfruit, banana if tastier foods were to be bought.

When he lived on bread and water, then, it was because he was too busy painting to go out and gather food or because he preferred like Vincent to spend what he had on paints and canvases. Often enough, however, the bread and water was embroidery for Mette's benefit, but always useless. In March she told him that she had sold four more Brittany pictures for fifteen hundred francs and the *Etude de Nu* for nine hundred. "Some money at last, you'll be thinking," wrote Gauguin to De Monfreid, "but my poor wife needed it." She did, in fact, talk of sending him about six hundred of the three thousand odd she had received in the last few weeks, but they never arrived.

On the whole Gauguin took it very well; he was neither a mean man nor unjust—he tended to chuckle at the thought of Mette getting her own back, and he still hoped that he could draw on her when he returned. In any case, he was not long without funds; De Monfreid, moved by his tales of woe as Mette was not, sent him a third and larger sum—seven hundred francs—in April. So Gauguin, replying to Mette, concentrated on the children. Mette was never backward with photographs of the children—it was the one request of his that she granted freely, doubtless with the faint hope of stirring his conscience. They never failed to produce cries of delight: "How the children alter almost every day! Clovis now looks just as I did at his age"; and of Emile: "1 metre 96 at 18½ years old—that's promising—one will soon be able to say 'the Great Gauguin'." He added a few comments on himself: "You're right enough to think that I shall have grey hair when I come back. In revenge I've given up cutting it as I used to, and I've lost that tendency of mine to stoop—the custom of walking naked or nearly so and the physical exercise have given me back my youthful step."

The incongruity of this picture with the bread and water did not strike him; he had not his letters before him, and wouldn't have cared if he had. One day he felt young, another old; he wrote as he felt, and that was all. And what he most felt, after he had dealt with the children and himself, was amazement that in Denmark of all places his work was being accepted: "Yes, in Denmark there are a bunch of imbeciles who believe what the papers say now that they find I have talent."

Before he could leave for France he had news of friends there—bad news all of it. The worst was the premature death of Aurier at twenty-seven, the only man who had praised him steadily and who in his last article had used one of the Pont-Aven pictures to illustrate the essence of symbolism. "We certainly have the vilest luck," Gauguin told De Monfreid. "First Van Gogh, then Aurier, the only critic who understood us well and who would have been very useful to us one day."

Joyant, the man who had succeeded Theo van Gogh, wrote at long last; he had sold some pictures nearly two years earlier and had handed the money to Morice. This aroused Gauguin's wrath. Nearly two years—and he penniless for months! He hastened to disillusion Mette about her "charming" companion in Paris—evidently he had been brooding about her supposed infidelity: "Morice has stolen 1350 francs from me!" he shouted; and had the audacity to claim that he had sent it—"A lie!"

The once faithful Schuff seemed little less traitorous: "You tell me that Schuff has written to my wife," he wrote disgustedly to De Monfreid. "What for? He'd have done better, knowing the fix I'm in, to have sent me my fare. I would willingly have paid it back plus 25 per cent. and I'd still have been the gainer. But no, there are some people who never know how to be useful at the right time and don't know a good bit of business when they see one. They prefer to invest in Panama loans. . . ."

Schuff perhaps had doubts of the repayment, let alone the 25 per cent. interest. Whatever the reason, he made no offer of help, and Gauguin, who was running rapidly through his seven hundred francs, was obliged to wait for the official repatriation in April.

Tehura saw him off. She sat on the wall of the quay swinging her legs. Her feet just touched the water. She had wept often since he had broken the news, but she was now quiet. She looked unhappy, but Gauguin did not worry overmuch; she would find compensation—they all did. As for the child, Emile, she carried, children were practically public property since so few Tahitian mothers could be sure who the father was. His would be well cared for. For the rest, Tehura was Tahiti, not France, and at the moment he needed France.

He arrived at Marseilles in the first days of August. He had left Papeete with a fair stock of money, but it dribbled away—on the shipment of his canvases and sculptures, on an hotel room during a change of ships at Nounes, on a second-class supplement on the crowded troopship that took him to Marseilles. When the ship docked he had four francs left.

Chapter Eighteen

LAST FLING

1893-1895

I

BEFORE he left the ship he sent wires to De Monfreid and Joyant asking for money to pay his hotel bill and fare to Paris. He also wrote to Mette begging for a letter: "I've been five months without news of you," asking, "what is the state of our finances?" and assuring her that, "you will have a husband to embrace who is not too much like a skinned rabbit and not too exhausted."

Mette did not reply; she did not care for the "our finances" or the embraces. She was, if possible, more than ever disgusted with her impossible husband; how like him, to bounce off to Tahiti full of grandiose promises and with every penny he could get hold of, and to come back, a burst bubble, with four francs in his pocket!

De Monfreid as usual was kinder hearted. He had gone off in his yacht to Algiers, but before leaving, anticipating the inevitable, he had appealed to Sérusier for a loan. Sérusier, who now spent much of his time in Brittany, sent two hundred and fifty francs and the address of a friend in Paris from whom Gauguin could borrow a little more. The two hundred and fifty francs Gauguin found with a covering letter in the Poste Restante at Marseilles when, having had no reply to his telegrams, he thought of asking there.

Within a couple of days he was in Paris, but it was August and Paris was dead; not a soul there; even Schuff's house was shut up. And no letter from Mette. He spent a night or two in De Monfreid's studio, then, his money exhausted, he went to the only place he could think of where he could get a square meal and board on credit. A certain Madame Caron kept a small restaurant next door to the Académie Collarossi in the rue de la Grande Chaumière. He knew her well; it was at her café that the students used to meet when he was attending classes. She was a shrewd woman who would on occasion let a room with board to promising painters.

They paid her in canvases. To her growing collection (on which she was soon to retire) she now added some Gauguins.

He sent a telegram to Mette giving his new address. No reply. He wrote again: why did she not write? But for Sérusier's friend from whom he had borrowed an extra hundred francs he would be penniless. Her silence was heartless: "Why can't you or Emile come down to Paris to say a word of greeting? It wouldn't kill you." When he met someone he knew and they asked after her, must he tell them that she had not even troubled to write to him?

These protestations as usual covered both falsity and truth. The enquiries of his friends—the few who were about—could scarcely embarrass him after years of separation. On the other hand he felt himself to be a man returned as it were from the grave, a man who had dared greatly and who deserved at least a welcome from wife and children. Besides, Mette had made money from his Breton canvases and she either possessed or had sold some of the work he had sent from Tahiti. He didn't know which. He should be told—the work was his, when all was said and done—and, if she had sold more canvases, be given a share. Finally, he had determined to hold an exhibition of his Tahiti work as soon as possible; it would, he believed, re-establish him at once as one of the foremost painters of the day—certainly as the most progressive. At worst it should give him something to live on until he could take his bearings. He called at Goupils, found that Joyant had been replaced by a man who looked indifferently at his new work. He went on to Durand-Ruel, who had made money out of Monet and Degas and was beginning to sell Pissarro and Guillaumin. He had never shown much interest in Gauguin and seemed scarcely the man for the Tahiti canvases, but did not reject out of hand the idea of an exhibition. But Mette had in Copenhagen some of the best Tahiti work; an exhibition without it would be incomplete.

His anxiety was understandable and his annoyance when day after day passed without a word. Where the next franc was to come from he had no idea; Sérusier had been tapped; De Monfreid, Schuff, and all other possible lenders remained obstinately out of town. What kind of welcome was this for the man from Tahiti? He was back again in the dark days, scratching after a meal, dunning the dealers.

Before the month was out he was rescued from despair. From

Orléans came a message; his Uncle Zizi was seriously ill, He hurried down; Uncle Zizi "had the wit to die"; his estate was to be shared between his niece and nephew.

On his return to Paris Gauguin found a letter from Mette, cool and businesslike; was he insane to think she could afford the journey to Paris just to greet him? Where was the money to come from? Not from his Tahiti pictures; they had been "a moral success with some artists in comparison with the attitude of the general public, but the result in cash was—not one centime".

Nothing was to be looked for from Denmark, that was certain; all the more reason to press on with the Paris exhibition. Degas proved his good angel once more; he looked at the Tahiti work, liked it, and put in a word with Durand-Ruel. He was too good a source of income to be denied; Durand-Ruel agreed to exhibit Gauguin for a month from November 4.

Gauguin had not yet got his hands on his inheritance—it would come, he hastened to tell Mette, to less than ten thousand francs after he had paid a legacy to his uncle's housekeeper—but he lost no time in anticipating it. Five hundred pounds, which was about what it amounted to, was not a fortune even in those days, but it seemed so to him and he began to strike out like a millionaire. He rented and completely redecorated an apartment, he had all his canvases well framed (Mette after a prolonged wrangle had released some), he looked up Juliette and her daughter to whom he had sent a few francs from Tahiti and whom he now treated lavishly, he sprinkled large loans among all his needy friends.

But his first thought was for his family; he pressed Mette to let Emile finish his education in France, and he invited her to bring the young Paul to Paris: "that would rest you for a bit and I should be happy to embrace you. Besides we should be able to talk things over and we need a chat, one can never get anywhere by correspondence. I have a studio almost ready for me to move into in which there will be neither trouble nor expense for you. From every point of view a meeting would be very useful." Unhappily he added, "If you can find the fare I will pay you back in a couple of months or so."

This suggestion sent Mette into a paroxysm of rage. Perhaps she was insulted by the casual call to Paris. Possibly she thought that she was being treated like a prostitute. The mention of a new studio, with its implications of large sums of money slipping away, may have been more than she could bear. Her view as expressed later seemed to be simply, "give me half your share and spare me this ridiculous pretence of affection". Encouraged as always by her family, she refused to go to Paris. She did not even reply to the invitation for many weeks. As far as one can judge she never seriously considered it.

She chose instead to fasten on to the suggestion that she should pay her own fare—the offer to pay it back she ignored. She worked off her rage, not on Gauguin (which is an interesting sidelight on her character), but on the unlucky Schuff, who, having come once more under Gauguin's charm, was still trying to keep a foot on his side of the wall. "So he has come back!" she wrote "and, to judge by his letters, just as he went, steeped in the most monstrously brutal selfishness, to me phenomenal, incomprehensible! No, Schuff, with him one can hope *nothing!* He will never think beyond himself and his wellbeing, he remains lost in admiration of his own greatness! That his children have to get their bread from his wife's friends, this is all the same to him, he doesn't want to know it! Well, he doesn't know it! Yes, this time I'm indignant."

The "this time" was superfluous; she had been indignant for years; but she did not spare Schuff. She reminded him of Gauguin's departure for Tahiti with the proceeds of his sale, of his request when he got back for a share of the money from the pictures she had sold, of the way she had spent this money on the children, of the legacy: "he doesn't even say anything about giving me a part of this 15,000 francs" (for so she persisted in believing it to be). "And now he asks me to find the money for a little trip to Paris!!! I am more than ever determined to stay here, I can't leave five big children for whom I am *entirely* responsible! If he wants to see us he knows where to find us! As for me, I'm not chasing all over the world like a fool!"

Mette felt that this outburst called for further explanation. "Perhaps, dear friend, you will think me cold, severe, *venal* as Paul used to say, but frankly there is every reason for feeling tired of the whole thing. I have been preoccupied by Emile's future, I have spoken of it to Paul, who tells me that we are worrying our heads over nothing, that the boy is big enough to shift for himself!! Yes, he is a big boy, but not big enough to look after himself if one wants to see him take his proper place in society. . . ."

She explained what she considered a "proper place" to be; a friend, a countess, was using her influence to get Emile a job as civil engineer. "When I see the goodness of others compared with the selfishness of Paul I don't know whether to laugh or cry but I don't do either, I am too busy trying to make sure that the children grow up into useful citizens".

She spoke of the children "beautiful, healthy, intelligent", and the mere mention of them aroused all her bitterness again; "Perhaps, Schuff, the worst is over and one day I shall be repaid for my work in some other way than the mere satisfaction of doing it which, between you and me, isn't very obvious! But can you understand a father who feels nothing, nothing, nothing! I believe that he would see us all dead without turning a hair!"

This is not only the letter of an indignant and embittered woman, it is the letter of a foolish one. The bitterness is understandable; it is not pleasant to be left to one's own devices, saddled with five children and no certain income after ten years of prosperous married life; it is humiliating to be forced to rely on the charity of relatives who lose no opportunity of decrying the missing breadwinner and treating the wife as an unwelcome dependant. In her sufferings and her struggles Mette has the sympathy of every fair-minded onlooker. But it is less easy to sympathise with her constant self-pity, her self-righteousness, her implacable cold resentment. She declared repeatedly that she lived for her children, she was for ever talking of their welfare. Yet she allowed bitterness and pride to come before it. Something would have been gained from the journey; to put it on the lowest plane, with Gauguin in his present expansive mood, she would have got money for the children. And she would have given one child at least enormous pleasure in meeting the father whom they all, in spite of everything Mette and the Gads could say, continued to love and admire.

But she did not go; and one has the strong feeling that she had done with Gauguin except as provider of money and outlet for her spleen, and that she would have been secretly dismayed had he lived up to his words about reuniting the family. She was anxious that her children should be respectable; that is, as unlike their father as possible; and the thought of his influence on them if they lived together again, or even stayed in Paris, was obviously unwelcome. When at last she replied to his letter, she asked simply for her share of the legacy; six thousand francs, she reckoned.

Exactly what had she received from canvases she had sold from his collection? he wanted to know. He had no idea what she had sold, what canvases she still possessed. Some of them, a Cézanne in particular, he was anxious to keep. Before there was any question of sharing the legacy he must have the facts. She refused to give them. He drew his own conclusions. No money went up to Copenhagen.

Two months later she asked him why he did not come to Copenhagen. By then the chance had passed; he was in his new apartment and not alone—he had, inevitably, consoled himself elsewhere, and disastrously. So disastrously, so madly had he consoled himself that only the severity of Mette's rebuff can explain it. For the first time since he had left Bertin ten years earlier he was in a position to keep Mette and his children in France. Her refusal even to meet to discuss a rapprochement was a damaging blow to his pride and his affection. She didn't want him, she only wanted his money—that was now inescapable. He reacted from the hurt by the most foolish act of his life—an act that he conveyed by a curt, "Thanks, but I'm tied here all the winter by a great deal of work. Many receptions. People who come to see my pictures—buyers, I hope. And a book on my travels is giving me a lot to do."

2

He was undoubtedly tied to the rue Vercingetorix, but not by hard work. Not for years had he worked so little. He had money and was determined to spend it, he had fame and was determined to enjoy it.

Fame was perhaps too favourable a description; notoriety would be nearer the mark, but he didn't object to that either; the one thing that he could not abide after the solitary years was neglect. Of that there was no fear: he had money, and a monied man doesn't lack company; and his exhibition had just run its course at the Durand-Ruel gallery.

A stormy course. Before it opened, Morice wrote to beg for an interview; he could not bear the misunderstanding. Somehow he and Gauguin patched up the friendship. Perhaps he managed to convince Gauguin that he had sent the money to Tahiti and that it had been lost. Perhaps—and this is more than likely—Gauguin was in the mood to overlook even this lapse: one can hear the expletive that put a stop to Morice's explanations, see the large buffet on the shoulder and the two glasses drained. Whatever the means, Morice came back into Gauguin's good graces with a vengeance; he arranged to preface with appropriate poems the stories of the years in Tahiti that Gauguin was thinking of finishing—the whole to be published under the title of *Noa-Noa*—and to write the preface to the exhibition catalogue.

Gauguin, wrote Morice, "is angered by our habits, our prejudices, our conventions about art and everything else, and by the tradition of imitation which in particular bears heavily on the painter. He intends to find his own poem and his own way of expressing it. He wants to be—in the words of a saying I used to be fond of—'the digger and the smith of his gold'. That is what he went to look for so far away." His work, Morice claimed—there were thirty-eight canvases from Tahiti, six from Brittany and two sculptures—"reminds me of the ritual of a religion of joy; to see it is to be given an opportunity of happiness".

This was true enough; they were happy paintings, with the serenity which is the hallmark of Gauguin's work. They were also original—too original for that generation. But Morice went on to present Gauguin's work as a reaction to Impressionism. This was not true, as the early Tahitian canvases showed clearly; Gauguin was trying to follow his own star but he never denied the constellation from which it sprang. All Morice did by his anxiety to set Gauguin apart was further to antagonise the Impressionists—Monet, Renoir, Guillaumin, all detested the Tahiti work—and to increase the bewilderment of the educated public. To them this was the Volpini show all over again. There, having become accustomed to the Impressionists, they were faced with something that looked like the meanderings of a peculiar child. Since Volpini, four years earlier, they had with a struggle begun to accustom themselves to the Brittany paintings; by the time of the Durand-Ruel exhibition there was a certain demand for them among the collectors. Now they were asked to throw off the knowledge so hardly won and accept these bizarre canvases as the true direction that the painting of the future must take.

Gauguin's Tahiti pictures differed from those of Brittany mainly in colour and subject. The difference was considerable; one must imagine the feelings of the people who crowded into the gallery in the rue Laffitte as they stared at brilliant colours never before seen in juxtaposition—yellows, blues, reds, greens; a country and a people absolutely foreign to them; and titles that no one could understand. There was another peculiarity—a hint of it—to be seen; the extreme simplification of design, the flatness of treatment, rather as though the artist were painting murals or fashioning bas-reliefs. This was not new in Gauguin, but became more obvious in the new canvases. But the subjects, the colours—these gave the offence, the colours particularly. "A red dog!" shrieked an English visitor, pointing to *Pastorales Tahitiennes*: and the sensation this caused was typical of the exhibition; Gauguin and his Tahiti pictures became a cross between the latest Paris joke and the latest scandal.

There was of course a more intelligent opposition. Pissarro voiced it. He had not changed his views about Gauguin—Tahiti was a "stunt" to capture a new market—and the fact that he had been accused of much the same thing when he followed Seurat did not help him to charity. But he was now, painting after his own fashion, becoming accepted; that mellowed one. In any case he could not keep away, ran into Gauguin in the gallery (they had not spoken for years) and remonstrated with him; to remain silent in the face of what he saw was impossible—dignity, resolutions all collapsed. The words rushed out: why, why, why?

Degas, indeed, had explained Gauguin's painting in his fashion; his reply to a bewildered enquirer was the talk of the cafés. "You know La Fontaine's fable of the wolf and the dog? Well, Gauguin is the wild wolf in the wood." But that did not satisfy Pissarro. Nor did Gauguin's own explanation. The artists of the future, he said, must be saved from cramping tradition, academic and otherwise. They must be free to develop their "sensation"; the freedom and the strength to pursue it they would find in the tropics—"those far away and savage sources", as Pissarro put it. No, replied Pissarro, "that kind of art doesn't belong to you; you're a civilised man and must show us harmonious things."

Gauguin's contemptuous silence did not hide his thoughts: mixing the civilisations as usual! unable to imagine the Tahitians living a civilised life that the Parisian—even the Parisian with a palette in his hand—hadn't the faintest conception of. "Doddering old imbecile" (Pissarro was only sixty-three, but his beard was quite white). "We left each other unconvinced," Pissarro told his son. He understated for once.

Accusations of theft flew about freely. Bernard, looking longingly towards Egypt, remained outwardly the admirer, but the effect of his whispering campaign was becoming obvious. Another man, who saw what neither Pissarro nor Bernard could see, was to attack Gauguin even more fiercely. "Trailing my *petite sensation* through the Pacific," snarled Cézanne. But Cézanne was mistaken; it was no longer his "sensation"; it was Gauguin's.

The exhibition was a financial failure. Only eleven pictures were sold, including all six Brittany studies. The receipts barely paid the expenses. But Gauguin had put himself in the public eye once more; his work was discussed, abused, dissected—discussed above all. Degas admired. Mallarmé exclaimed, "It is extraordinary that anyone can put so much mystery into so much brightness." Manzi, the dealer, spoke enthusiastically of the possibilities of such paintings. The advanced critics praised him. The painters of the future swarmed before the canvases; the Nabis—Bonnard, Vuillard, K.-X. Roussel in the lead—and with them a crowd of disciples of these disciples.

"The most important thing," Gauguin told Mette, "is that my show has been a very great artistic success as well as rousing jealousy and anger. The press has treated me as it has never yet treated anyone, that's to say reasonably and with panegyrics. For the moment I pass with many people for the greatest modern painter."

He did not exaggerate unduly, nor did he try to hide the general impression of his work. "These people understand nothing! Is it too simple for these Parisians, too spiritual, too refined?"

He tried to enlighten the scoffers. "Wishing to suggest a wild luxuriant nature and a tropical sun which sets everything ablaze, I had to present my figures against such a background. It is a truly open-air life, however intimate in the thickets and by shady brooks where women whisper; it is like an immense palace decorated by

Nature herself with all the riches of Tahiti. Hence these fabulous colours on my canvases, this fiery light purified and silent."

He put an argument into the mouths of his opponents—"But all this doesn't exist!"—so that he could demolish it with a "Yes, it exists. It is the equivalent of the grandeur, profundity and mystery of Tahiti when one has to express it on a canvas one metre square."

His Tahitian women offended in the opposite direction. Hard things were said about these robust creatures. To a public brought up on advertising brochures and the novels of Loti, this realistic version of a sylph lying voluptuously on the golden sand with a coral necklace round her slender throat was more than a little distasteful. They would not believe it. Gauguin was merely indulging his love of large women, his passion for sculpture, they said. This contained a sufficient pinch of fact to infuriate him. "She is very subtle, very wise in spite of her naïvety, the Tahitian Eve. The enigma hidden at the bottom of the childish eyes remains incommunicable. There's no more of the pretty little Ravalon listening to a pretty ballad by Pierre Loti playing his guitar, Pierre Loti who is also pretty. This is Eve after the Fall but still able to walk naked without shame and retaining all the animal beauty she enjoyed on the first day. Motherhood doesn't deform her, so firm does her womb remain. She has the feet of a four-handed mammal. Like Eve her body remains animal but her head has progressed with evolution, her mind has developed a subtlety, love has imprinted an ironical smile on her lips, she seeks naïvely in her memory the *pourquoi* of the present day and she looks at you enigmatically."

"All this is intangible, you say? So be it, I accept it."

But to accept criticism was beyond him. Imbeciles! However, he had a useful, if rather broad, sense of humour. How should the greatest modern painter conduct himself? How should a mad painter of bizarre pictures, a charlatan, conduct himself? He would live up to both reputations. Nothing would please him better; he could indulge his passion for dressing up, his taste for the flamboyant, his love of shocking the philistines. He began to walk the streets of Paris in a blue Russian shirt embroidered in yellow and green, a blue frock-coat with mother of pearl buttons, beige trousers and a large grey felt hat with a band of sky-blue ribbon. On his feet were the brightly ornamented Breton sabots. Between his hands, enclosed in white gloves, he twirled a large stick, the knob of which (a blister pearl) he had carved into nude male and female figures in the act of copulation. On fine days there walked by his side a tiny brown-faced woman dressed in gorgeous silks. A parakeet, brilliantly coloured, balanced itself on one of her arms, a monkey trailed behind on a decorative chain or leaped on to Gauguin's broad shoulders chattering and scratching.

The guests who began to crowd into his apartment just across the street from his favourite rue de la Gaîté were greeted by a large sign *Te Fararu*, which he was eager to translate—"Ici l'on aime". The studio walls had been painted in his beloved Chrome No. 1—a bright orange-yellow. Against this vivid background were hung his unsold Tahiti paintings, the one or two Cézannes, Pissarros and Van Goghs he had been able to keep from Mette, and an array of weapons brought back from Oceania—tomahawks, boomerangs, spears, axes.

When one had recovered from the shock of the Chrome No. 1, the blazing canvases, the weapons, the squawking of the parakeet, the silent bounds of the monkey, the woman would strike the eye. She would be lying, most probably, on the sofa and she might or might not be clothed. This was Anna, a half-caste Javanese whom Gauguin had in an unlucky moment picked up round Montparnasse and brought home as a model. He made a study of her in the nude with the monkey in its usual place at her feet—not one of his best works. She stayed on, and not even the infuriated Juliette, whose interests were not confined to Gauguin's money, could get her out. He would listen to no one. The exotic touch provided by Anna, he explained, was exactly what he needed to complete the tone of his studio and to titivate his guests.

For the studio was filled with people. He instituted a Wednesday evening soirée which became very much the thing in certain circles. If a man is to be judged by his friends, Gauguin's reputation will not suffer from the Wednesday visitors. There were the sculptors Rodin, Aristide Maillol, Francisco Durrio and Gauguin's neighbour the cigar-smoking Ida Erikson. There were the poets and playwrights Mallarmé, Strindberg, Verlaine, Morice and Leclercq. There were the Symbolist friends of Morice. There were the painters, mainly his old disciples from Pont-Aven together with De Monfreid and the Nabis, but including often enough the lively Bernard who, like Schuff, found positive disapproval difficult, perhaps dangerous, when Gauguin was at hand. There were the people from next door, the composer William Molard, his wife and step-daughter Judith, a thirteen-year-old girl so much devoted to Gauguin that she practically lived in the studio and fetched and carried for him at the soirées. Some of his guests were chronically hard up; he lent them money, put them up in his apartment, paid the fares of those from Brittany, fed them; he remembered his own years of semi-starvation, he was absurdly generous.

The gatherings in the studio were not confined to Wednesday evening, and Paris was soon whispering of orgies in the rue Vercingetorix. Gauguin, one may be sure, encouraged these horrific rumours with amusement; he was also the businessman—let them talk! When the rumours are examined they become disappointingly vague. Gauguin drank too much, smoked too much, but that was no novelty. He, the Molards, Leclercq and De Chamaillard made music together. Charades were played extravagantly but, as far as Gauguin was concerned, "with a divine clumsiness". And it seems that on one evening at least, stretched along the couch elevated on the painting platform at one end of the studio, he listened, puffing his pipe approvingly, to tributes from an adoring group below—Leclercq reciting, between profound obeisances and to the accompaniment of a mandoline, verses acclaiming the host as the Demi-God, the great Master of painting, supreme among men.

It is difficult to take this seriously or to imagine that Gauguin did. Yet this is all that can reasonably be recovered from the Parisian gossip. The proceedings scarcely live up to the *Te Fararu* over the door. Gauguin, it may safely be conceded, played the fool. But fundamentally he was a serious man. A few months of fooling were enough. By the early spring of the next year, 1894, he had sickened of the adulation, the waste of money, the idleness. He had finished *Noa-Noa* (a very short book), a portrait of Molard, one or two self-portraits, and that was all.

He left Paris to attend a dinner of the Vingtistes in Brussels given in his honour. At Bruges he discovered Memling; and if he had any further hankerings after the life of the rue Vercingetorix they left him then. "What marvels, my dear chap!" he told De Monfreid, "and specially when one looks at Rubens afterwards (the beginning of naturalism). What a falling away!"

He came back and unceremoniously swept Anna and her retinue off to Brittany. He tried Pouldu first, but Mlle Henry had given up her inn. He stayed for a few days with a Polish painter, giving him the *Bonjour Monsieur Gauguin* for his keep, but soon moved—the solitary sea-coast being no place for Anna—to Pont-Aven. There too he found unwelcome changes; the Pension Gloanec had been sold and Marie-Jeanne Gloanec had moved to the smaller *Ajoncs d'Or*. She welcomed him rapturously in her stiff way and proved her devotion by accepting Anna, the monkey and the parakeet without a word. She took them all in; gave them the best of everything. The remnants of the old group—Séguin, De Chamaillard, Maufra, O'Conor—gathered round Gauguin. Morice followed him to Pont-Aven. There was for a moment an illusion of time leaning back.

The one cloud in the sky was Sérusier, who had formed a school of his own in Pont-Aven. He felt that, Gauguin having gone off to Tahiti, someone must carry the flag, and he believed that he was Gauguin's natural successor. Then Gauguin inopportunely returned; Sérusier was generous with money, but not with his school. It was now his school, he decided, in which he taught the Sérusier technique—the true forward movement of the future. Gauguin discovered with pardonable irritation that this technique was no other than an inferior version of his own manner. He examined Sérusier's work with disdain. It was a travesty of the truth. He heard of the sketch Sérusier had made of him, knapsack on back, staff in hand, setting out on his travels while his disciples sat on the banks of the road saying, "As for me, I stay where I am." This was too close to the bone; he ostentatiously avoided Sérusier, the loans of the previous year forgotten, and commented mordantly on the tricks of his pupils. "They're young, they're cunning, they have all the trumps in their hand. Soon they'll be walking over me, grinding me into the dust." A pathetic picture, but fortunately not an accurate one. To set against it were the faithful followers, the joy of feeling a brush between his fingers and of having the familiar scenes before him once more.

For a few weeks it seemed that Brittany might repeat its effect on him. He worked hard; the violence of the change from Tahiti stimulated him. For Mère Gloanec, who heard his tales of Tahiti with astonishment and perhaps with some incredulity, he painted

Arearea No Varua Ino, a study of two Tahitian girls resting in the hot sunshine. It was a strange picture to hang in the cold stone house of a people who scarcely knew what it was to rest. It was far from being one of his best works—showing the limitations of painting by memory—but his Brittany pictures were very different. He painted three of them—*Paysage de Bretagne*, with its strong composition and glowing colours, and two studies, *Les Blanchisseuses* and *Deux Bretonnes sur la Route*, in which his tendency to "sculpt" his figures is used with a conviction (because of the natural rigidity of the Breton clothes and attitudes) rarely found in the tropical canvases. There is, in fact, a verisimilitude in this last Pont-Aven work that places it above most of his paintings; regarding it, one wonders whether he was about to enter a period in which the restraint of the Breton scene and character would govern his weakness for the exotic and the purely decorative and turn it to great use. He was, after all, not quite forty-six, virile, ambitious, confident. A wonderful future could be seen opening before him.

3

It was not to be. Anna not only prevented him from concentrating on his work, she was a troublemaker, a disaster. She brought out all the "spiv" in him, the annoying little boy. He adopted—perhaps in an attempt to live up to her, perhaps as a protest against the bleakness of Brittany after Tahiti—an excessively wintry outfit consisting of an astrakan hat and waistcoat in addition to the gaudy finery of Paris. Clad in this conglomeration he walked magisterially and incongruously over the Pont-Aven cobbles accompanied by Anna, the monkey and parakeet.

The amused curiosity of Paris was not repeated; the villagers resented the fantastic clothes, the arrogant air, they resented particularly the presence of Anna, perky, primping and treating them like dirt. Gauguin's action in setting up house with Anna in Paris, though foolish, was excusable; but there was nothing to be said for his taking her to Brittany. He had been well treated in Pont-Aven; Marie-Jeanne Gloanec had mothered him, the villagers had provided him with free models and more—for their country and their way of life had first released the great painter in him and had inspired some of his finest works. He now gratuitously insulted them by bringing into their midst a woman whose way of life was an offence and whose attitude was a disgrace—for Anna was out only for what she could get; her one discernible merit, her charm, was not wasted on the people of Pont-Aven; she flaunted past them disdainfully in the manner of a great lady.

This was the most discreditable episode in Gauguin's life, the only one for which no excuse can be found. But like all transgressors he paid, and paid heavily. Sooner or later there was bound to be trouble. It came in May when he, Anna and De Chamaillard walked to Concarneau to see Séguin. Some children jeered at Anna. Séguin slapped one on the face. The child ran off to his father, a fisherman, while the others began pelting the party with stones. The man came up from his boat, cursing and threatening. Gauguin knocked him down.

At once the place was in an uproar. The man called for help. Seamen climbed from their boats and set on Gauguin—fifteen of them. The nervous Séguin jumped into the harbour and waded off to safety. De Chamaillard tried to protect Anna. Gauguin was an excellent boxer and more than held his own until, driving the ring of men back towards the harbour, he caught a foot in a hole in the granite, tripped, fell and broke his leg close to the ankle. The men closed round him, kicking savagely with their heavy sabots. They did not leave him until he was unconscious.

He soon came to and was carried back to Pont-Aven smoking his pipe, but he was badly bruised and the bone of his broken leg had been shattered by the blows from the sabots and driven through the skin.

This was the virtual end of France for him. The local doctor was a bungler, he failed to set the broken bone correctly and the wound would not heal. For week after week Gauguin lay in bed; he could not sleep, work or read for the pain; he lived on drugs. He could not move, his pictures did not sell, Anna sulked. He was no longer fun, she disliked illness, she would do nothing for him. He begged the Molards to spare the young Judith to look after him, but the plan fell through; he remained for all practical purposes alone. "I'm looking after myself," he told Molard.

Everything looked black, hopeless. The news outside his bedroom matched the pain inside it. Laval, painting like a ghost of Gauguin to the end, had died of consumption; Madeleine Bernard, defiantly engaging herself to him too late, was dying of the same disease. De Haan was dying in the Netherlands; Taoa the monkey died: "a great pity . . . she used to follow me like a dog even into the sea". The action for assault that he brought against the Concarneau seamen was delayed for months. At last he was awarded six hundred francs, but by that time had spent nearly five hundred on the doctor and a hundred on the advocate. When he tried to collect the money the men had nothing; he never got a sou.

Towards the end of September he managed to hobble outside the village to second Morice in a duel, but his ankle was still so painful that he could not work. His money was running low and he longed to get back to Paris. He was sick of Pont-Aven, of his bedroom, of himself: "I've lost all courage to bear up against the suffering and specially at night when I get no sleep. Naturally I've done nothing—four months wasted with plenty of expenses to pay."

He sent the sullen Anna ahead to open up the apartment. His trustfulness had no end, it seemed; he gave her the keys and wrote almost cheerfully to the Molards that "the good little woman" would soon be settling down again. He had visions of a warm and comfortable studio waiting for him as soon as he was well enough to travel. Anna left with the parakeet and was never seen again. She called in at the rue Vercingetorix, ransacked the studio, took all the money and valuables she could lay her hands on, then disappeared.

At a blow Gauguin found himself struggling once more and, what hurt him much more, deserted by a woman. That settled it. "I've made up my mind," he told De Monfreid, "to go back to Oceania and live there for good." He would sell every picture he possessed—everything—no matter what the price, "then I will end my days free and peaceful without for ever having to worry about the next day and without this eternal struggle against the Imbeciles". He would not go alone this time; Séguin and O'Conor would go with him for a year or two—that is, if he could find the money, for they had nothing. But he: "I shall stay there for good."

Beyond the window of the comfortless bedroom of the Breton pension, his prison all the summer and autumn, the skies were often gloomy, the winds strong and cold, the voices bleak and impersonal, the bodies hidden in ugliness. He looked back longingly to the sun, the colour and the friendliness of Tahiti. He even managed, such wonders can the imagination perform, to think once again of Tahiti as a place where he could live and work for next to nothing.

But what most attracted him was a return to love; love in the larger sense of a people to whom competition and all its meannesses meant nothing. Marie-Jeanne Gloanec was kind and motherly in her brisk way; she had to present him with bills because she had to live; she knew nothing of a life without the fight to keep body and soul together, where respectability had no equivalent word in the language.

And beyond Pont-Aven, in Paris, what a scene was there! So-called friends cutting each other's throats to earn a living and make a name. Every imaginable dirty trick played to come out on top of the never-ending war in the heart of "civilisation". He, Gauguin, acknowledged great, unable even now to live on his work; the young men who should have been humbly at his feet, trying to outsmart him—daylight robbery, and no one cared: "No point in my saying more. Nothing will stop me from going, and for good. What a vile existence this European life is!"

From his wife and children, who might at least remember him—silence: "I begin to wonder if I exist for my family when I see my birthday pass, then Christmas, and still not a word." When he did get a word, what a word it was—pay up, pay up! "Oh, the devil!" he snapped at Mette. "Can't you find anything else in life to write about except money?"

By and large his attitude was precisely that of four years earlier. The only difference was that he knew himself to be a greater artist now than then and—he had been to his paradise. He had been and he had come back. If he asked himself why he had come back he said nothing, choosing the lesser evil.

4

At the end of the year he was well enough—though lame and in pain—to go back to Paris. He at once began to organise another sale of his work.

There is a tradition—it is no more—that he paid a final visit to Mette and the children at Copenhagen, that he tried to persuade her to come to Tahiti with him and that she refused. It is not impossible—he had never before left France without seeing her—and if he did see her his request and her refusal were both to be expected. All that is certainly known is that he gave or sent to Mette fifteen hundred francs and refused to give her any more—indeed, by that time he had little more to give. He had discovered that Brandes, his brother-in-law, had paid her ten thousand francs for some pictures from his collection, but what pictures and how many Brandes refused to say. She had still some pictures, pottery, sculpture; she would not let him see them.

His sale was to be held at the Hotel Drouot on February 18, 1895. This time, having had small satisfaction from Morice's preface, he asked Strindberg to write one. Strindberg was then something of a hero to the men of the Latin Quarter; a few months earlier he had been tried in Stockholm for blasphemy (he had written in one of his stories of "the popular agitator Jesus of Nazareth"), had defended himself and was acquitted. He came along to the rue Vercingetorix one evening and Gauguin, struck afresh by his appearance and his astonished stare at the Tahiti canvases, and remembering that his was now a name to be reckoned with, jumped at the chance of associating him with the sale.

The next day Strindberg sent him a long letter of refusal: "I reply at once to your request with an 'I cannot' or, more brutally, with an 'I don't want to'. At the same time I owe you an explanation. . . . Here it is: I can't understand your art and I can't like it (I can't get a grip on your art, this time exclusively Tahitian). But I know that this avowal will neither astonish nor wound you because you seem to me to be strengthened rather than otherwise by the hatred of others; your personality, anxious to remain whole, delights in the antipathy it rouses. And perhaps you're right; for the moment you, admired and approved, won a band of followers your art would be classified, tidied up and given a name that after five years or so the young would use as a nickname for an out-of-date art which they would do their best to make even more old-fashioned. I have myself tried very hard but in vain to classify you, to insert you as a link in the chain, to understand the history of your development. . . . I thought of Puvis de Chavannes last night when, surrounded by the southern strains of the mandoline and guitar, I saw on the walls of your studio the hubbub of sunny pictures which pursued me in my dreams. I saw trees which no botanist would ever find, animals which Cuvier has never even suspected, men whom you alone have been able to create, a sea which must have flowed from a volcano, a sky in which no God could live. Sir, I said in my dream, you have made a new heaven and a new earth, but I don't feel at ease in the sphere of your creation; it is too sunny for me who like light and shade. And in your paradise lives an Eve who isn't my ideal, because I too have an ideal or two of women!"

That morning, Strindberg wrote, he had gone off to the Luxembourg to look again at the Puvis de Chavannes, but he could see no trace of Gauguin in them nor in the Manets. Who then, he asked himself, is this man? And answered: "He is Gauguin, the savage who detests a troublesome civilisation, something of a Titan who, jealous of the Creator, makes his own little world in his spare time, the child who takes his playthings to pieces so as to make others, one who denies and defies, preferring to see the sky red by himself rather than blue with the mob."

Strindberg then pulled himself up with a smile. "It seems, *ma foi*, that since I've worked myself up in the course of writing I must be beginning to have a certain understanding of Gaugin's art. After all, a modern writer has been criticised for failing to depict real people and simply creating his own characters by himself. Simply! *Bon Voyage*, Master; but come back and look me up. Perhaps I shall have learned to understand your art better by that time so that I shall be able to write a true preface for a new catalogue in a new Hotel Drouot, because I too begin to feel a great need to become a savage and to create a new world."

Gauguin was delighted. "Your letter *is* a preface to my catalogue," he replied. "I had the idea of asking you to write a preface when I watched you the other day in my studio playing the guitar and singing, your blue Nordic eyes looking hard at the pictures on the walls. I had a presentiment of a revolt, of a clash between your civilisation and my barbarism, a civilisation that makes you suffer, a barbarism that rejuvenates me."

He took up Strindberg's comment on his Eve as a touchstone of his art. "Before the Eve of my choice whom I have painted in forms and harmonies from another world your memories have perhaps called up a painful past. The Eve of your civilised conception turns you and almost all of us into misogynists. The old Eve who frightened you in my studio might well smile on you less bitterly one day. This world which perhaps neither a Cuvier nor a botanist would ever be able to find would be a paradise which I alone shall have sketched out. From the sketch to the fulfilment of a dream is some distance. But what matter? To catch a glimpse of happiness, isn't that a foretaste of Nirvana? The Eve whom I paint (and she alone) may logically remain nude in front of our eyes. Yours in this simple condition could not walk without immodesty, and if too beautiful would evoke evil and sorrow. So that you can understand my thoughts thoroughly I will compare not these two women directly but the Maori language spoken by my Eve and the language spoken by yours, the flexible European language. In the languages of Oceania, with their *fundamental* elements preserved in their crudity, isolated or soldered with no regard for polish, everything is bare and primordial. While in the flexible languages the roots with which, as with all languages, they began, are disappearing in everyday intercourse which has worn down their outlines and their sharpness. It is an absolute mosaic where one ceases to see the joints of the stones, more or less clumsily fixed together, being too busy admiring the beautiful stone picture. Only a practised eye can discover the way it has been constructed. Excuse this long philological digression; I believe it is necessary to explain the 'savage' drawing which I had to use to decorate a Polynesian country and people."

Here was his catalogue preface, the reply and the answer; he printed both. But this was his one satisfaction. The sale was a failure, for which he was in part responsible. He offered forty-nine paintings; but with an unhappy return of business acumen at the last minute, he put a high price on many of the best in the name of fictitious collectors. The brisk bidding he expected (forgetting perhaps the change in his work since the previous Drouot sale) never occurred. Every one of these paintings was knocked down to him. For the rest, his friends bought about a dozen between them, Degas taking the copy of *Olympia*, and the *Manao Tupapau* fetched the highest genuine price—nine hundred francs. After his expenses had been deducted Gauguin's profit from the entire sale was just under five hundred francs.

Disgusted, he hurriedly prepared to leave the country. He would have to go alone once more; he had enough money left for the fare and a little over, but there was nothing to spare for Séguin or O'Conor. He spread his unsold canvases, his sculptures and pots between those dealers who offered to try to sell them. He gave to De Monfreid and the Molards practically everything in the studio that Anna had not been able to carry with her. He tried to persuade the Director of the Beaux Arts to redeem the promise to buy a Tahiti picture and grant him another "official mission". The Director who made the promise had been replaced by a man named Roujon—afterwards notorious for his refusal to decorate Cézanne. Roujon was a die-hard. "I don't understand your art," he told Gauguin. "It disgusts me and I shall do nothing to encourage it." He asked for written proof of the promise; Gauguin possessed nothing; he was given nothing.

He made one more effort to get government help. He set off to the Colonial Office in his blue frock-coat, beribboned hat, white gloves and startling stick. He sought a post as Resident in Oceania. But the Under Secretary for State did not see in this gaudily apparelled, arrogant and distinctly seedy figure a suitable Resident.

Only one detail remained—a letter to Mette. This was difficult to write. One would have thought that the recent plain speaking, whether face to face or by letter, had left little to say; but he was still bent on justifying himself and Mette was still after her pound of flesh. Had the sale been a success he would have written a triumphant note: see the man she had spurned, an acknowledged success. The sale was a failure, so he used it as an excuse for living their disagreements over again. But no words of his could disguise the facts; he had run through the legacy, his prospects were so poor that he could no longer talk seriously of making a home for her. Mette fastened on the facts. She demanded her six thousand francs, demolished every thought of living with him in Tahiti or anywhere else. As for him, he had better make the best of his own bad job.

He repeated the result of the sale—"I have 464 fr. 80 in my pocket!"—then tabulated his grievances.

"1. You write: 'You *must* shift for *yourself*.'
2. The children write: Nothing.
3. My leg has been broken, my health ruined; from my family not a word.

4. The winter has been terribly long, I have been alone in my studio trying uselessly to cure a chronic bronchitis; literally I can live only in the sun.

Under these conditions, surrounded by enemies which my painting has made, I have the right to take every precaution to prevent disaster. At 47 years of age I *must* not fall back into despair, but I'm very near to it; and once I am down *no one* in the world will help me up again. Your words 'you *must* shift for *yourself*' are very wise; I shall hold by them."

He ended, "I am your husband", but the marriage, even the pretence of it, was over and, though he still would not admit it, he knew it. He was bitter, angry, his pride affronted, his affection rebuffed once more. He had exaggerated his plight, as he always did to Mette, but he was unhappy.

Mette did not reply. He had friends (the good De Monfreid looked in often), but the stripped studio was melancholy, the bright yellow walls mocked him, the few parties he held on Thursdays were overshadowed by the forthcoming departure, every franc spent was so much the less for the future. He longed for Tahiti, but he feared it also; he remembered the loneliness, the absence of letters, the perpetual scramble for money. He became truly wretched.

In his wretchedness he destroyed himself. He picked up a prostitute on the boulevard Montparnasse and took her back to the deserted studio. At the end of February, just before he left for Tahiti, he told De Monfreid that "the previous month he had caught a sad infirmity". He had contracted syphilis.

Chapter Nineteen

THE FINAL YEARS

1895-1903

I

GAUGUIN still had eight years to live, he was to paint great pictures, to write an interesting book, to know moments of contentment, but he was a dying man in every sense when he left France for the last time. He was a strong man and difficult to kill, as he had often said, but his end, though long-drawn-out, was inevitable, and the growing sense of this inevitability darkened his final years in Polynesia. The record of these years is a record of suffering, disillusionment, of a courageous but hopeless fight by a man who more and more knew himself to be doomed. Even the legend of the romantic struggle (to those who can see it as such) against poverty was little more than a legend. Sooner or later the promiscuous man and woman meet their deserts. Gauguin was an exception only in the severity of his punishment—a punishment so dreadful that one can feel nothing but pity for him.

At first, as was to be expected, he began with a burst of high spirits. The voyage set him up, the sight of Tahiti filled him with hope, the sunshine poured down and promised new health. By July he was in Papeete exclaiming at the improvements: electric light! He told Molard, "Next month I shall be in La Dominique, a small and beautiful island in the Marquesas where one can live practically for nothing and where I won't always be seeing Europeans. There I shall be like a squire with my small fortune and my studio fitted up as I wish."

This idea was not new—he had talked when last in Tahiti of moving to the less spoiled Marquesas—but before he could carry it out he discovered an attractive plot of land at Punaria, a seaside village some ten miles from Papeete and rented it; "a superb aspect, in the shade, by the side of the road, and behind me an amazing mountain view". He had chosen one of the most fertile spots in the island, where the vegetation was thickest, the sun hottest, and where the rich scent of the flowering shrubs bordering his little estate drifted across in warm gusts. From the door of the hut which he built on the land he looked as before across lagoon and coral reef to the dramatic peaks of Moorea. In November, when he had just moved in, he described the hut to De Monfreid—he was later to put it into his *No Te Ana Se Rive*. "Imagine a large sparrowcage made of bamboo, divided in two by my old studio curtains and with a roof thatched with cocoanut leaves. One part is the bedroom with very little light so that it keeps cool. The other part has a big window to form a studio. On the floor are mats and my old Persian carpet. The whole is decorated with stuffs, curios and drawings." He made a stained-glass window for the studio and carved two of the island gods out of cocoanut tree trunks and put one on each side of the door. He had a horse and cart, kept in a small hut near by. His main "consolation" was the music he made with his guitar. Altogether "I'm not much to be pitied at the moment."

But he had not painted since he had reached the island four months earlier. This he put down, as before, to the lack of a vahine. As soon as he reached the island he had gone to Mataiea to look for Tehura. He found her married and could not persuade her to live with him again, but apart from that reservation she was not particular: "I have been obliged to make a cuckold of her husband." When his hut was built she came over to christen it with a week's "escapade".

Tehura gone, "my bed has been invaded every night by young hussies running wild; yesterday I had three". This was unsettling: "I want a serious woman for the house." He found her in Pahura, a girl of fourteen who lived with him and bore him two children. Pahura was beautiful as Tehura was not—how much so can be seen in *Les Seins aux Fleurs Rouges*—but "she is very debauched, but this isn't obvious since there's no such thing as virtue to compare it with". Perhaps for this reason she was not such an understanding or inspiring companion. Little is heard of her, but for a time she served her purpose. She looked after him and made an excellent model. He began to paint.

He had all the more need of a home and the suggestion of a wife because his hopes of Mette had become so remote. Her one or two notes—letters they could not be called—were concerned entirely with money. She employed as advocate the unhappy Schuff. His letters had never been lively or original; now they breathed wretchedness and a kind of spite. At Pont-Aven, after one of these long "painful" letters, Gauguin said, "I'm really afraid that one day he'll be taken away madly hypochondriac." Now he was simply annoyed that Schuff should complain about his lack of success as an artist when he spent more than half his time making money, and about the life his wife was leading him while criticising in the same breath De Monfreid for divorcing his wife and Gauguin for leaving his. Mette, he wrote, was furious that Gauguin had left France without telling her when he was going; he was "criminally selfish".

"One can see the mote in one's wife's eye," commented Gauguin "but not the beam in the eye of one's neighbour's wife." As for Mette: "So you see what I've done about the ménage at home," his letter to De Monfreid ended ironically, "I've sneaked off without warning. Let my family get themselves out of the soup, for if there is only me to help them . . .!!! I reckon to end my days here in my hut perfectly tranquil. Ah yes, I am a *great criminal*."

Unhappily his days were not to end in tranquillity. He had no sooner settled down to a regular domestic life with Pahura than the disease began to assert itself. His ankle would not heal. By April of the next year, 1896, he is crying to Molard, Morice and De Monfreid, his chief correspondents, of his misery. No money had come from Paris and "as always when I know I have money in my pocket and am feeling optimistic I spend without counting, confident in the future and in my talent, and quickly come to the end of my means". And "I'm not only at the end of my resources but the end of my strength. . . . My health gets worse every day. My broken foot makes me suffer terribly; I have two open wounds which the doctor can't manage to close up—in hot countries it's difficult. At night the violent throbbing keeps me awake."

The pain, the sense of disease getting a foothold in his body, roused the old animus: "My life is very cruel. I made unheard of efforts during my first stay in Tahiti, the result of which you saw at the rue Laffitte. What did they lead to? To a *complete defeat*. Plenty of enemies and that's all—bad luck pursues me all my life without a break; the more I struggle the further I fall. Perhaps I haven't much talent (all vanity put aside), but I don't believe that one begins an artistic movement however small without talent of some kind."

The disheartened pioneer was matched by the neglected friend. He was owed not only letters but cash from the men who had borrowed freely in the Vercingetorix days and the dealers who had taken his pictures with fair promises. He had not forgotten—he could and did write down in his letters to the patient De Monfreid all the names, all the amounts of money due. But no letters arrived, and no money.

2

This was to be the sum of Gauguin's life for the future; deceptive spurts of good health after a change of scene or activity or a spell in hospital, with an accompanying rise of hopes; and periods, always growing longer, of suffering and despair which culminated in his attempted suicide. It is necessary when reading his letters from now onwards—letters filled with complaints, recriminations, agonisings, and endless talk of money—to remember that they were almost all written in pain by a man dying slowly from a disease which does not stop short at the body but eats away nerves, will, confidence, and at last the very heart itself. Had he been an ordinary man Gauguin would have died years earlier and his heroism would be more easily recognised. But he was no ordinary man; he had a powerful body and a no less powerful will, he had a mission and was determined to carry it through. He lived on, writing letters that for the most part would be better forgotten.

But he did not only write letters. In his own way he tried to help the Tahitians—a people who, exploited and relentlessly Westernised by the French, and as relentlessly Christianised by the missionaries, were being butchered as effectively though not as mercifully as if they had been mown down out of hand.

He also worked—at his painting and his sculpture—whenever he could force himself to his feet. The wounds on his ankle never healed; they grew larger, they festered. Sores broke out on the injured leg, then spread to the other: the virulent eczema was followed by erysipelas—the first open sign of his disease. His sight began to weaken. He could not sleep without drugs and then only for an hour or two, tormented by ghastly dreams. Often he could not walk beyond his garden to collect food; for weeks he and

Pahura lived on rice and water; for two years they did little more than keep alive. He lost strength, but he worked on. He had to lie on his bed for hours until the swelling and the throbbing eased sufficiently to allow him to put his feet to the ground. He waited patiently, then went back to work, knowing that the pain would become agonising soon after he stood upright. He could not finish the paintings as he would have wished, he said regretfully, "but they contain so much agony and suffering that this may compensate for the lack of skill in execution". To the onlooker today the miracle is that they were ever painted at all.

One would not expect to find his finest work done under such conditions, and in general it was not. But there were exceptions. This same year of 1896, after being driven into hospital for a month by the pain in his leg, he painted his *Te Arii Vahine*. He claimed that it was "better than anything I have done so far"—a claim which showed that his enthusiasm survived every assault on it. "A nude woman lies on a green carpet, a servant gathers fruit, two old men by a large tree discuss the tree of knowledge, the sea forms a background, the trees are in flower, a dog watches, two doves coo on the right. As far as colour is concerned I don't think I have ever made anything with such great and sonorous depth. But why send such a canvas home when there are so many others there that don't sell and merely cause a rumpus? This would cause an even bigger fuss."

He sent it to De Monfreid, nevertheless, together with three others—*Poèmes Barbares*, a dazzling flowerpiece and a still life. Difficult indeed when looking at these radiant canvases to believe that they were painted by a stricken man. But when he was at work on them Gauguin forgot his doom; or rather, since pain does not disappear but merely ceases to possess the mind as well as the body, he became for the time the man offered an opportunity given to no other.

For a few months after hospital treatment, which arrested the disease, Gauguin worked furiously from six in the morning to midday before pain drove him to his bed. He had received no money, letters were few and far between, he was sunk in debt, he had no cause for hope but, at work or contemplating his work, he hoped on. He painted his canvases and made his beloved sculptures, placing them in the grass which grew thick about the hut—"at

Coll. Mr. W. Church-Osborne *Photo: Vizzavona*

LES SEINS AUX FLEURS ROUGES. 1899

(Pahura on the left)

Private coll. *Photo: Vizzavona*

CONVERSATION A TAHITI. 1900

Louvre (Former coll. Mme. A. Joly-Segalen) *Photo: Vizzavona*

VILLAGE BRETON SOUS LA NEIGE. 1903
The last, unfinished canvas

first a nude woman, then a superbly whimsical lion playing with its cub; the islanders, who had never heard of these ferocious beasts, are all amazed". This led to a quarrel with the Protestant pastor who, ignoring the lion, fastened horrified eyes on the nude: "he's done everything he can to make me put her further back, out of sight of the villagers"—even to applying to the magistrate for an order. In this, his first open brush with the missionaries, Gauguin (who had not yet opened fire on the civil authorities) came off victorious; the magistrate "laughed at him up his nose" and the nude stayed where she was, unregarded by the Tahitians who were too busy slipping off their own scanty clothes whenever the pastor was not looking.

This little success cheered Gauguin enormously; his vahine was about to give birth to a "demi-jaune"; his work went with a swing. This was enough to send his spirits soaring. "Ah, if only I were given my due my life would be extraordinarily calm and happy." He believed this against all the evidence and urged De Monfreid to join him and be calm and happy too. De Monfreid, who was just moving from Paris to the country, was not tempted to follow his master, but he approved absolutely of Gauguin's return to Tahiti, he believed in his future triumph and he tried unceasingly to hasten its coming. For the rest he could only consider the bevy of plans that Gauguin poured out—plans for changing dealers, for establishing a pool of Gauguin purchasers, plans without end—and counsel patience. There were signs of a trend in Gauguin's favour, he reported, signs that even his Tahiti work would be accepted, then treasured, but they were signs only and not to be hastened. Have patience.

Patience! To Gauguin, chronically short of money, recalling the neglect of his first Tahiti years, feeling ill and old as soon as he stopped work, the word was a mockery. After all, how many great artists had been recognised in their lifetime, had profited by their work? "If I don't die first of hunger I shall die of goodwill—that seems to be my fate."

Early in the new year of 1897 one of the Paris dealers, Chaudet, sent him some money—the first he had received since arriving in Tahiti eighteen months earlier. He paid off debts and went back to the hospital for more treatment, agreed to pay five francs a day and was given a card marked "Pauper"—he was assigned to the ward with the white dregs of Papeete. He refused to go into "this mêlée of soldiers and servants . . . you understand that I speak of the Europeans . . . I always respect the islanders", tore up his card and, such is the power of indignation, returned home to paint several pictures before he again collapsed. One of these was *Nevermore*, a study of Pahura lying on the bed—a companion piece to *Manao Tupapau*. As Manet had illustrated Poe's poem, he felt it necessary to explain the unusual title: "It's not at all the raven of Edgar Poe but the bird of the devil who watches. It is badly painted (I'm nervy and work in jerks), but all the same I believe that it is a good canvas. . . . I wanted to suggest by a simple nude a certain barbarian luxury of past years. The whole thing is flooded in colours deliberately sombre and sad; it isn't the silk, the velvet, the cambric or the gold that gives this impression of luxury but purely the material, that becomes rich under the hand of the artist . . . the play of man's imagination alone has enriched this house."

3

He had no sooner finished and sent off this and a few other canvases when, in April 1897, he had a shock that sent him to his bed. Mette's complaints that she did not know how to make ends meet—the sole subject of her notes—had been proved untrue by De Monfreid and Morice. They told Gauguin that she had sold more pictures in Denmark and that, helped by Schuff, she was claiming as hers any new ones that arrived from Tahiti. Nevertheless, Gauguin at first told De Monfreid to send certain canvases to her with the hopeless injunction that if she sold them one-third was to be passed on to him. How hopeless this was (and how blind he could be even at this late hour) is shown by Mette's remark to Schuff: "Yes, Paul and his ferocious selfishness pass all human thought, and what irritates me is that he considers himself 'a martyr to his art'. . . . If, then, you are able to send some of his pictures to me I shall try to sell them, and I certainly shan't send the money to Paul."

This incurable hostility finally killed Gauguin's hopes that a reconciliation might be arranged before he died. Perhaps Schuff, trying to serve two masters, revealed more than he intended. Perhaps Mette demanded money once too often. At any rate Gauguin in early spring lost patience: "If you can only write letters like the ones you have sent me since I came here I must ask you not to write at all. I haven't finished my work yet and I must live; think of that and stop your perpetual complaints that do you no good and me a lot of harm. I could write to you if you had a heart that would understand anyone but your children."

There was silence. He heard no more. He thought of his children: did he hope still that they, and of them specially his best-loved Aline, might live with him later and take care of him? It is not impossible. He still scribbled his injunctions and exclamations into the *Cahier Pour Aline* which in odd moments he had decorated with tropical fishes, a Corot mandoline player and cutting after cutting from the Paris newspapers. One day she should read what men had thought of the father who was not mentioned in the Copenhagen home.

Then, in April 1897, came a letter from Mette, "very short and very terrible. She tells me brutally that my daughter has died of pneumonia."

For a time he was stunned. "Why reply? I endured feelings of passion, of rage, of something like the delirium of a patient who is being tortured and who demands new sufferings. Since my childhood bad luck has fastened on me. Never a chance, never a pleasure. Everything always against me and I cry to myself: 'My God if you exist I accuse you of injustice, of wickedness.' Yes, at the news of the death of poor Aline I doubted everything, I even laughed in defiance. What good was virtue, work, courage, intelligence? Crime alone is logical and makes sense. Then the force of my feelings diminished, my great anger wasn't stimulated any more and I began to think. Ah those long nights without sleep when one is growing old! And that's how I now feel the sadness of Aline's death; the numbness is over. My own disease takes its place."

To Mette at first he said simply, "I've just lost my daughter, I don't love God any more. She was called Aline after my mother. Each loves after his fashion. For some love is roused at the coffin, for others . . . I don't know. Her tomb is there with its flowers—an illusion, all that, her tomb is here, close to me, and my tears are living flowers."

His forty-ninth birthday came and went, unacknowledged. Even then, after the loss of Aline, Mette's heart had not softened. His smouldering fury burst out in a last letter: "Madame," he wrote, "I asked you to let my children write to me on the 7th June, my birthday, 'My dear Papa' and their signature. You replied, 'Don't count on it; you haven't any money.' I won't say to you, 'God help you,' but less fabulously 'may your conscience sleep so that you won't long for death as a deliverance'."

This was the end of the relationship between Mette and Gauguin.

An event nearer home, disaster though it seemed at first, took him out of himself. The owner of his land died and Gauguin was told by the new owner to pull down his hut and go. He found another strip of land near by—a promising piece with a hundred cocoanut trees—and rebuilt his hut on it. Reacting violently to injustice, he did more than rebuild, he enlarged the hut to a length of sixty feet and a depth of more than twenty—divided as before into living-room and studio. He decorated it with sculptures in wood and planted the garden with vanilla, reputed profitable. The hut and garden cost him a thousand francs, which he managed to borrow from the local bank. The work distracted him from his grief and pain, but was far too heavy for a sick man; in July, when all was done, he collapsed; he had several fainting fits, he went down with one attack of fever after another.

The record of his existence to the end of the year is deplorable. He talked for the first time of suicide. His mind began to be affected by the disease; he could no longer grasp realities; he saw his position as even worse than it was; he was haunted by his debts, embittered by the seeming desertion of most of his friends, convinced that all the dealers were tricking him, certain that fame and success would elude him. When money arrived (and he had several remittances), he complained that it was never as much as he had expected—for he spent it, as always, almost at once. He could not leave his bed or chair long enough to work, he could not even read for many minutes together, his eyes were too painful. The more inactivity was forced on him the more intolerable his restlessness grew; he talked of leaving the home he had just built and of going to the Marquesas.

Then he was overcome by fits of suffocation, he vomited blood every day. This was surely the beginning of the end: "the body still holds out, but it's bound to crack", he wrote with relief;

"nature will take care of it after all. It will take longer, which is a terrible thought, but I feel in duty bound not to try to anticipate my fate."

4

He did not die; his body, it seemed, was not going to crack after all. Foreseeing years of living death, his resolve weakened. What had he to live for? His daughter was dead; his wife was dead to him; his other children he would never see; his friends were far away. He would live for his work, but soon he might be unable to work. By the end of the year he made up his mind to kill himself. First, however, he determined to paint a picture which would embody all his philosophy and display all his genius. With a great effort he forced himself to his feet; he worked at the new painting day and night for a month. It was large—nearly fifteen feet by five—so large that, as he had no canvas big enough, he used sackcloth full of knots: "It looks horribly rough . . . but by God it is not a canvas made like a Puvis de Chavannes, studies from nature, preliminary sketches and so on . . . it is all boldly done directly with the brush. . . . It does not smell of the model, of the profession, or of so-called rules. . . . I put into it, before dying, all my energy."

He called it *Où Venons-Nous? Que Sommes-Nous? Où Allons-Nous?* and he described it fully to De Monfreid: "The two top corners are chrome yellow with the title on the left and my signature on the right like a fresco damaged at the corners and painted on a gold wall. At the bottom on the right a baby sleeps, then three women crouch. Two figures dressed in purple are confiding their thoughts to each other; an enormous figure deliberately and in spite of the perspective squatting, raises arms in the air and looks, astonished, at the two who dare to think of their destiny. A figure in the centre picks a fruit. Two cats near a child. A white she-goat. The idol with arms raised mysteriously and rhythmically seems to indicate the hereafter. A crouching figure seems to listen to the idol. Finally an old woman close to death who seems to accept and resign herself to her thoughts, finishes the legend; at her feet a strange white bird holding a lizard between its claws represents the futility of vain words. The scene is placed in a wood beside a stream. In the background the sea, then the mountains of a neighbouring island. In spite of changes of tone, the landscape is continuously blue and Veronese green from end to end. All the nude figures stand out from it in a bold orange. If one said to the pupils of the Beaux Arts for the Prix de Rome, 'The picture you have to make represents Whence do we come, what are we, whither do we go?' what would they do? I have finished a philosophical work on this theme which can be compared with the Gospel."

The painting, like his *Manao Tupapau*, stimulated him to many words, first in defence then as an explanation of his work as a whole. Much of this was said to the critic, André Fontainas, who had commented unfavourably in the *Mercure de France* on his "violence, his arbitrary use of colours, the monotony of his tones". Gauguin usually disdained a reply to criticism, but a hint of sympathy in the Fontainas article drew a long letter from him. He was, after all, thousands of miles from anyone who could understand him; he never spoke or heard one intellectual word from one year's end to another; the longing to communicate overcame even the strong-minded Gauguin from time to time. "These repetitions of tones in monotonous agreement with the musical sense of the colour, can't an analogy be found for them in the oriental chants sung in a harsh voice accompanied by vibrant notes in a neighbouring key which enrich them by opposition? Beethoven uses this method often (if I understand it rightly) in the Pathétique Sonata, for instance. Delacroix with his repeated accord of maroon and dull violets makes a sombre cloak suggesting drama. . . . You write of certain pictures which I consider of little value, 'Ah, if Gauguin were always like this!' But I don't want to be always like that."

How he wanted to be, he explained, could best be seen in the great new canvas. If Fontainas looked for an obvious allegory he would be disappointed. Gauguin preferred to think of it as a musical poem without words. He quoted Mallarmé's "the essence of a work consists precisely in what is not expressed; it is not materially constituted, it is implicit in the arrangement of the lines, without colour or words", and declared: "I act consciously according to my intellectual nature, I act a little like the Bible in which the doctrine (especially concerning Christ) is expressed *symbolically*—first by materialising the pure Idea to make it perceptible . . . then by giving its Spirit, the explicit meaning."

Fontainas, possibly befogged by this cloudy language so far removed from Gauguin's work, scandalised the painter by saying that he preferred the method of Puvis de Chavannes. Gauguin, shocked, put the matter to Morice. "Fontainas reproaches me for being unable to make my idea understood—its title and its not being explained on the canvas in concrete forms, etc.; and he cites Puvis de Chavannes, always understandable, always knowing how to explain his idea." Up to a point he agreed, taking as example a picture he thought highly of—a photograph of it was pinned up in his hut alongside the masters. "Puvis explains his idea—yes, but he doesn't paint it. He is a Grecian while I am a savage, a wild wolf in a wood. Puvis calls a picture *Purity* and explains it by painting a young virgin with a lily in her hand. That's a known symbol—it's understood. Gauguin, to convey Purity, would paint a landscape with limpid water; no civilised man to blemish it, perhaps one figure. Without going into details there is a world between Puvis and me. As a painter Puvis is a lettered man but not a man of letters, while I am not lettered but am perhaps a man of letters."

He could not stop looking at the new painting, he told De Monfreid: "I admit to you, I admire it. The more I see it the more I realise the *vast mathematical faults* that I don't want to alter at any price—it must stay as it is, like a sketch if you want to call it so. But this question poses itself and perplexes me—where does the execution of a painting begin and where does it end? When extreme feelings blend together in the depths of one's being, when they break forth and all thought comes out like lava from a volcano, isn't that the hatching of a work suddenly created, brutal if you like but great and with a superhuman appearance? The cold calculations of the reason haven't presided at this birth, but who can say when the work has really taken shape in the depths of one's being; subconsciously perhaps? Have you noticed that when you copy a drawing done in a moment, a second of inspiration, a drawing with which you are satisfied, you only make an inferior copy?"

The question has been asked many times and does not call for an answer here. But with Gauguin the reason, even when he affects to despise it, was never very far away, guiding, controlling. His compositions were primarily a result of conscious thought—he explains them precisely a dozen times. Before leaving France he had written to De Monfreid, "Adieu painting except as a distraction;

my house will be of sculptured wood." If he meant that he was abandoning painting for sculpture he did not keep to his word, but it seems more probable that he foresaw that his paintings would become more and more like sculptures. He speaks of his enormous painting as a fresco, and it is of frescoes, murals, bas-reliefs that one thinks when regarding much of the later Tahiti work. This was deliberate or, one could say, it was his inevitable interpretation, as he had told Fontainas, of an ancient civilisation. He had before him as he made his studies photographs of Greek, Roman and Javanese bas-reliefs and of an Egyptian fresco (these photographs still exist) and all but the first he followed meticulously. "Have always in your mind's eye," he said, "the Persians, the Cambodians and a little of the Egyptian. The Greek is the great error, beautiful though it is."

He put this precept into practice as early as 1892, when he painted Tehura in *Te Aa No Areois*, but it was after his return to Tahiti that the process can be seen expanding through the *Poèmes Barbares* to his *Ta Ma Tete* with the five Tahitian girls seated in a row, bodies stiffly posed, arms bent at right angles after the manner of the Egyptian sculptors. This was cerebral painting indeed, but Gauguin persuaded himself that he saw beyond the mechanics: "Animal figures with a statuesque rigidity, I don't know how old, how august and religious in the rhythm of their gestures, in their rare immobility. In the dreaming eyes the surface is troubled by an insoluble enigma."

5

Something of this he believed that he had put into his last great work. That done and sent to France early in 1898, he dragged himself into the mountains and, on the night of February 11, took a large dose of arsenic which he had collected from the ointment for his legs. But he did not die—the dose was too strong, he afterwards believed. He was violently sick, and the next day crawled home weak and ashamed. It was the one completely uncharacteristic act of his life and he excused himself uneasily: "If you only knew what a state my mind has got into after these three years of suffering!" he pleaded to the reproachful De Monfreid. "Perhaps I may never paint again, and that's all I have to love—neither wife nor child. My heart is empty." But he felt guilty—"I am disgusted with myself"—and never again, though tempted even more sorely, tried to escape his fate.

He paid dearly for the lapse; until April he lay in his bed unable to eat, perpetually sick and with a crushing headache. Then, abruptly, he went into Papeete—"I am going to swallow my pride"—"prostrated" himself before the authorities and was given a small job at six francs a day in the office of Public Works. He drew plans and copied specifications. He took the job to save money—he was still in debt—and to be near the hospital. He was often too ill to walk as far as his office, but except for a break of three weeks in hospital in October he stuck to the unlovely work—under the orders of an artillery soldier—for nine months.

The hospital treatment, which he took fully and paid several hundred francs for, was unexpectedly satisfactory. In January of the new year, 1899, he felt fit enough to go back to his hut and fetch his vahine and children from her family. He even believed for a while that he might be cured. He had done no painting for a year, but he asked De Monfreid to arrange an exhibition of his latest work—the "Sérusier-Denis band" not to be invited. In June he refused an invitation from Denis to be represented in an exhibition of "Symbolists, Pointillistes and *Rose Croix*" on the tenth anniversary of the Volpini show.

This invitation was unhappily timed. Gauguin had no sooner gone off to Tahiti than Bernard at last came out into the open; he wrote an article for the *Mercure de France* explaining how the Ecole de Pont-Aven had come into being. The article caused a sensation, as he meant it to do. Was Gauguin a thief?—every café in Montparnasse was asking the question.

Had he been content with his version of events in Brittany, Bernard might have been justified. He had reason for anger when he found all his work regarded as childish imitations of Gauguin. But he was not content. Perhaps the death of Madeleine removed a restraining influence. In any event, between his travels (he spent years in Italy and Egypt) he occupied himself by claiming as his own in all but the actual execution practically every work made by Gauguin in Brittany.

In Tahiti, when the news reached him, Gauguin burned with helpless rage. All he could do was to write scathingly to De Monfreid and to scribble in the *Cahier Pour Aline* (now never to reach his daughter) the untranslatable summing up: "J'ai recontré durant mon existence bien des merdeux. Mais pas un comme le petit Bernard: partout où vous allez vous êtes sûr de mettre votre pied dans une de ses ordures. Il chie dans tous les coins."

And now Denis had the audacity to ask him to exhibit with the libeller! He replied sarcastically "my personality is of no further interest today. Ten years ago I wanted to dare everything and in some way to *liberate* the coming generation, then to work in order to acquire a little talent. The first part of my programme has borne fruit; today you are all daring everything and what is more, no one is surprised. The second part, alas, has been less happy. I am an old man, the pupil of many in your exhibition; *in my absence* this has become very evident. Much has been written on this subject and the whole world knows that I have actually stolen from my Master Emile Bernard! paintings and sculpture of which (has he not said so in print?) he has no more left! Don't believe that the thirty or so canvases which I have given him and which he has sold to Vollard were mine; they are a shocking plagiarism of Bernard!"

The reply was inevitable, but Gauguin's attitude was expressed more characteristically in his "I want simply *silence*, *silence* and again *silence*" to De Monfreid. "Let me die in peace, *forgotten* or, if I must live, let me be left in peace and *forgotten*. What does it matter if I'm the pupil of Bernard or Sérusier! If I have made good things nothing will blemish them; if I've made rubbish, why try to gild it and deceive people about the quality of the goods? In any case Society can't reproach me for taking lots of money out of its pocket by means of lies. If I added up the canvases placed, the number I've *given* away is greater than the number sold. And I don't regret it—on the contrary."

To Denis he had said, "My work is done," but he had several pictures left in him and one great one; *Les Seins aux Fleurs Rouges* of this year, 1899. Much has been written about this picture; here, three points will suffice, all characteristic of Gauguin at his greatest. First, there is the absence of sexuality in a picture which by almost any other hand would be full of it. Secondly, in place of the conventional beauty of feature we are given that other beauty, the grave serenity of soul which shines unforgettably out of both faces. Thirdly, there is the effect of grace that he gives to these women as to most of his Tahiti models in spite of their wide shoulders and thick necks. He had seized on and exploited the fact that their bodies were well-proportioned—the true secret of grace. "What distinguishes the Maori woman from all others and often causes one to mistake her for a man, is the proportions of the body. She is a Diana with wide shoulders and narrow hips. However thin one of her arms, the bony structure never obtrudes, its line is supple and beautiful. Have you ever noticed the young girls of the Occident at a dance, their thin arms gloved to the elbow, a sharp, excessively sharp elbow—ugly, in a word—and with the forearm longer than the upper arm? . . . The arm of the Maori woman is like that of all Oriental women, though larger. Have you also noticed, at the theatre, the legs of the dancers, those enormous thighs, the vast turned in knees? . . . In the Oriental, and especially the Maori woman, the leg from hip to foot gives a single straight and beautiful line. The thigh is heavy but not wide, which gives it roundness and avoids the spreading effect which makes so many women in our country look like a pair of tongs."

6

With this perceptive comment one can fittingly take leave of Gauguin the painter. But the man lived on. Unable to paint more (for the effect of the hospital treatment was wearing off) he began to write. His friend the trader, now a merchant, prodded by Gauguin, started a monthly newspaper, *Les Guêpes*, in Papeete. The paper was anti-church, anti-government, with a slogan of "Right is Might", just what Gauguin needed. He began to contribute. He printed in it an open letter to the magistrate of his district who had declined to take action about thefts from his hut and garden. The letter was "very violent" and slanderous; Gauguin invited the magistrate either to fight a duel or to go back to France to learn law: "You have no powers, Sir, you have only duties."

Expecting—indeed, hoping—to face a libel action, he prepared his defence; it ran to seven full pages. To his annoyance it was not needed; the magistrate ignored the letter. However, it caused a stir in Papeete and set Gauguin off on his government-baiting track.

In the same issue of this paper he published an article which explained, ironically but effectively, why he championed the islanders. "To colonise," he wrote, "is to cultivate a country, to make an undeveloped area produce things which are useful, first of all, to those who live there. That is a noble cause. But to conquer that area and erect a flag, to put in a parasitical administration kept going at enormous cost by and for the sole glory of the conquering power is an uncivilised and shameful stupidity." He compared the activities of two Frenchmen. First, Rimbaud, "a poet and in consequence considered by a section of society as a useless being", who in Abyssinia, "without any other help than the modest manners of a gentleman, successfully made himself respected and even adored by savage races". Rimbaud was regarded in French colonial circles as a waster. The swashbuckling Captain Marchand who raided the Sudan and provoked an incident at Fashoda which almost led to a Franco-English war was regarded as a hero. "The welfare of the Sudanese was not considered." "One might have thought," Gauguin concluded, "that with the means at his disposal the officer should have carried out the greater civilising mission and not the confounded poet."

This article was his only obviously serious contribution; he concentrated chiefly on digs at local institutions and people of whom he disapproved. These were legion. His attack on a Papeete advocate who wrote in the papers under the name of Jean de Pare is typical of his pleasanter vein. This man was accustomed to report his own speeches—dealing usually with sexual offences by the islanders—in high-flown terms. Gauguin used the old satiric models. "Ah, Monsieur Jean de Pare! Qu'en termes galants vous dites de ces choses, de ces choses!!! Vous douteriez-vous, naïf enfant aux cheveux frisés, de l'importance de votre nom. Le premier du nom s'appelait tout simplement Isidore Crouton et était mitron du Roi Dagobert!" In cruder manner he dealt with the Governor. "Notre gros functionnaire continue à promener sa belle corpulence et son visage stupide dans la rue." But, pleasant or unpleasant, his jibes were taken in annoyingly good part and, having tasted blood, he launched his own paper in an effort to do the job thoroughly and to make some money by the way—for his plain speaking had caused much comment in Papeete. The first number appeared in August. "With so much time on my hands," his editorial explained, "and with so many ideas in my mind, eccentric ones perhaps but dear to me, I have founded *Le Sourire*. Although shapeless at first sight, what I write will form a pattern if examined closely and considered—that is, if you choose to regard it so. I shall not tell the truth—everyone prides himself on telling it. I shall show my thoughts by fable only—that is if dreaming is thinking."

The paper consisted of four pages and had as title a woodcut made afresh by Gauguin for each number. Its sub-title "Journal Sérieux" was soon changed to the more appropriate "Journal Méchant"—"laughing wickedly it has made many people turn pale—wicked people. . . . Trivial at times but pungent, it was necessary". Certainly it was pungent. Of its twenty contributors, nineteen were Gauguin masquerading under various lively pen-names crowned by the obscene Tahitian "Tit-Oil". Like his grandmother, Flora Tristan, he had discovered the joys of polemical writing and, his disease forgotten for the time being, he flung himself into the battle with similar abandon. Apparently there was no limit to what he could say: venomous articles, scurrilous reports, ironical versions of law court cases, sarcastic rewritings of government and church pronouncements followed one another in a violent stream, strengthened by savage cartoons. As in *Les Guêpes*, his targets were the Governor ("that ferocious despot"), the Chief Justice ("Saint Platitude"), the *Conseil Général* ("the administration is the enemy of colonisation") and the Protestant missionaries ("meddling, sexless, cowardly, they poison our country"). Sometimes he was merely silly, sometimes moving and often convincing. His indignation led him into absurdities but it had a nobility too and the kind of reckless courage that his profile always suggested. But although it struggled on until April of the next year, 1900, *Le Sourire* had none of the effects he intended. He never sold more than twenty or thirty copies; each copy, he complained, "is passed from hand to hand". Its influence on the politicians, lawyers and missionaries was nil. The French residents, who Gauguin believed hopefully would be driven to investigate his charges and to protest against the treatment of the islanders, merely sniggered at this latest absurdity of the mad painter who had gone native. They read with pleasure but did nothing.

Before *Le Sourire* came to an end Gauguin's finances—which for at least a year had been more promising than he would admit—were set on a reasonably firm footing. De Monfreid was a good friend to him, seeking out purchasers for his pictures, keeping a firm eye on the dealers. At the beginning of 1900 he persuaded

Ambroise Vollard, the most enterprising dealer in Paris, to pay three hundred francs each month for a total of twenty-five canvases a year—an offer that Vollard improved a few months later to a fixed price of two hundred and fifty francs per canvas. As De Monfreid already held many recent Tahiti canvases, this meant that Gauguin would have a settled income for several years to come. The good news—though Gauguin suspected with some justice that Vollard would make an excessive profit—was followed by money from other dealers, from De Monfreid and finally, at the end of the year, from a rich collector who bought two canvases for twelve hundred francs. This man had noticed a Gauguin painting in his dentist's waiting-room—a painting handed over by Gauguin in Paris years earlier when he had no other means of settling the bill.

All in all, Gauguin had never before been in such a comfortable position; and it was becoming evident, by what he heard from De Monfreid, Morice and Denis, that a demand for his work (based partly on the growing legend of the solitary painter of the tropics) was at last showing itself. But showing itself too late; the money could not give him health enough to take up work with his old vigour, it could not even preserve him from anxiety—for his tastes, the greater his pain and restlessness became, inclined more and more to European delicacies, to wines, spirits, tinned foods. The money melted—the cost of imports was shooting up—and he was for ever worrying about the possibility of Vollard going back on his agreement, of a mail not arriving to time, and of once again finding himself at starvation point.

The year, for all its good news, was therefore a failure. Gauguin was unable to paint more than one or two still lives, he did not make a single sculpture. He wrote *Le Sourire* during the early months, he read books when his eyes allowed, he looked after his garden when his legs would bear him. An influenza epidemic which ran over the islands killing hundreds prostrated him for weeks.

One shock, however, he was saved. In April his son Clovis died of septicaemia. He was twenty-one. Mette asked Schuff for Gauguin's address: "It seems necessary to write to him although it costs me much to do it because his ferocious selfishness revolts me every time I think of it." One would have thought that it would have been kinder to leave Gauguin in ignorance, but Mette persuaded herself that it was her duty to tell him: she had the sort of mentality that gathers every relative about the bedside of the dying. And to tell him that his second favourite child had died was her pleasure. Clovis had died because of the hardships he had undergone as a child in Paris—so she believed and was to repeat to the end of her life. Let the man suffer for his sins: "I have borne all the heavy loads, I have suffered all the sorrows, all the worries *alone*." But Schuff, who had at last divorced his wife, no longer listened with patience. He had done with these Gauguins—the one complaining incessantly about her lot, the other replying rudely to his own complaints. He did not answer Mette's letter, and Gauguin went to his grave without knowing that Clovis had gone before him.

When he was strong enough to move, at the beginning of 1901, he went into hospital again. In a month, as before, he was out, hopeful of a cure. He began work on his sculpture, he took up his palette again, but was thwarted almost at once. Two more bouts of influenza undid much of the good that the hospital treatment had done, prices soared when incoming ships were put in quarantine because of an outbreak of plague in San Francisco, and his attempt to resume painting was badly hindered when the islanders began to fight shy of sitting for him—the Protestant Mission was taking its revenge for *Le Sourire*.

He decided to move to the Marquesas. He had enough money to go, he felt restless and ill. "I'm brought low," he told Morice, who had written to him about the publication of *Noa-Noa*; "vanquished by wretchedness and above all by the disease which has driven me into old age before my time. Shall I be given a respite to finish my work? I dare to hope so; in any case I'm going to make one last effort and shall next month install myself in Fatu-Iva, one of the Marquesan islands which still remains almost cannibalistic. I believe that the completely savage element and the absolute solitude will rouse in me before I die a final fire of enthusiasm and bring my talent to a fitting end."

He sold his hut and land at a handsome profit, getting five thousand francs for them—the one successful business deal he had made since leaving the Bourse—and in August 1901 said good-bye to Pahura and her children and sailed off. He went, after all, not to

Fatu-Iva but to the island of Hiva-Oa, the largest of the group, called by the French La Dominique when they took over the Marquesas in the middle of the century.

7

Gauguin arrived too late in Hiva-Oa as he had arrived too late in Tahiti. The Marquesans had been a wild people, very different from the peaceable Tahitians, but they had shared the same fate. Westernisation and Christianisation had taken the life out of them; enfeebled by the clothes which the missionaries forced them to wear, the shoes that made their feet too tender to gather food in the mountains, they could not survive the artificial foods and the diseases brought by the French, they perished by the thousand of measles, small-pox, consumption, syphilis. One by one the smaller islands were abandoned as the population shrank, and on the larger islands the people died like flies. The sixty thousand Marquesans in the middle of the nineteenth century had been reduced to less than one-twelfth, a total of some four thousand, when Gauguin landed on Hiva-Oa in the autumn of 1901.

Gauguin also arrived too late in another sense; he was a dying man, his powers declining, and he cut his life still shorter by living on an island where there was no hospital and no regular doctor. All this he knew, yet he felt excited and confident as he got off the boat at the village of Atuona. The voyage, the change, had given him an illusion of well-being. The country struck him at once as wonderful material for a painter. The people might have lost their wildness (although they still wore barbaric tattoo-marks under the missionary clothes and old men talked wistfully of the glorious taste of human flesh), but the islands remained savage, with great bare jagged peaks, inaccessible forests in which lay buried the ancient tombs and enormous stone statues of their kings, and long narrow valleys with vast stone walls falling sheer to a violent torrent. Superimposed on this savagery of scene was a dense and vivid vegetation compared with which the colours of Tahiti seemed almost mild—everything, bird, animal, insect, added to this cacophony of gorgeous, stupefying colour. Gauguin was a contented man as he leaned, staring, over the side of the schooner.

On shore he found that all the good land in the Atuona valley

Mme. A. Joly-Segalen

GAUGUIN'S STUDIO AT ATUANA

With his last 'Vahine', 1903

(On wall in background, photographs of – top left – Degas 'Arlequin' – bottom left – Holbein 'Portrait of his Wife and Children' – top right – Puvis de Chavannes 'l'Espérance' – bottom right – idol reflected in mirror)

THE LAST SELF-PORTRAIT 1903

Mme. A. Joly-Segalen

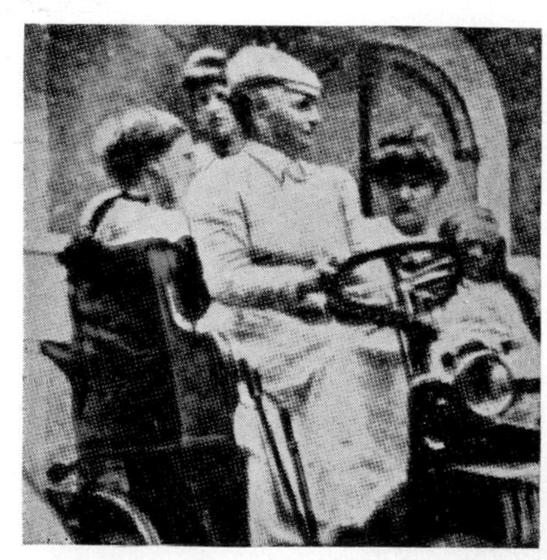

METTE IN 1905

Mme. Huc de Monfreid

belonged to the Catholic Mission. This Mission, like the Protestant Mission in Tahiti, had a firm grip on the people—their land, their morals, their life from rising up in the morning to lying down at night. Gauguin, furious, realised that he would have to ask the Bishop's permission to buy a strip of land. The Bishop was away for a month. Leaving his stores on the beach and getting a bed each night, Gauguin began to qualify himself; he attended church regularly, groaning inwardly as he watched the spiritless islanders crowding in incongruously clothed, and almost stifled by the cheap European scent they flooded themselves with as some sort of compensation for the clothes. He looked at the fierce striped faces of some of the older men, caught glimpses beneath their shirts of tattoo marks and mutilations perpetuating some long past feat of arms. Yes, they had been savages, proud of their strength, their cunning, their gleaming bodies, their prowess in hunting food and enemies, their skill in making the great stone idols, the figure. curiously carved in wood, bone and mother of pearl, the mats decorated with glowing patterns. How had the mighty fallen—their statues banned as idolatrous, their ornaments forbidden as fetishism, their bodies denounced as a shameful snare and draped in hideous clothes, their simple pleasures stopped as evil! Now they created nothing, they crowded meekly into church, they lived in perpetual fear of breaking the white man's inexplicable laws, they grew feeble, they died early. But he, Gauguin, would show them—in him lived a savage that no Bishop, no Mission could civilise!

His reputation had not followed him across the hundreds of miles of sea from Tahiti. His churchgoing recommended him. The Bishop allowed him to buy a small plot of land—at seven hundred francs. First the church, then overcharging! Very well, there would be a reckoning. But it was difficult to think of reckonings while his hut was being built. The land was superbly placed: "I am in the middle of the village, but no one can see my house because it is surrounded by trees. No need to worry about provisions; my neighbour is an American, a charming boy, who has a very well stocked shop where I can get everything I need. I become more and more happy with my choice and I assure you that from the point of view of a painter it is *adorable*. What models!!! Marvellous! I have already begun to work." He felt extraordinarily well; the change, the excitement of building a new home, the thought of the paintings to be made with such colours, such vegetation, such women (for the Marquesans were more beautiful than the Tahitians)—all this drove pain away, and tiredness and the illusion of old age. What was fifty-three? He helped to build the hut, driving in the long piles on which it stood, fixing the plank floor, laying the walls, thatching the roof. He looked at it with pride: "A great studio with a small corner for my bed; everything to hand, laid on shelves, the whole thing two metres from the ground. Here I eat, do my carpentry, do my cooking. A hammock for my siesta is slung up sheltered from the sun but refreshed by the breezes from the sea three hundred metres away which blow gently, broken by the cocoanut trees all above me."

By November he was living in the hut. His pictures were fixed to the walls—his Manet, Degas, Puvis de Chavannes, Rembrandt, Botticelli, his photographs of Mette and the children—his easels were up, he was at work. But he did not forget the Bishop. The hut had still to be decorated; with the decorations he could say without a word what he thought of the Bishop and the entire Mission. He carved two lifesize nude women on panels which he coloured and placed on each side of the central doorway. Under one was the inscription *Soyez Amoureuses, Vous Serez Heureuses*, the other *Soyez Mystérieuses, Vous Serez Heureuses*. Above the door he fixed a large plaque on which he had carved *La Maison du Jouir*. Then came his masterstroke. In the Bishop's household was a Marquesan girl named Thérèse, a favourite ward of his, married off to the verger of the church but, the entire village insisted, remaining the Bishop's mistress. Gauguin now carved two large figures in rosewood: one was a devil in the garments of a priest, the other was a nude girl garlanded with flowers and named Thérèse. These figures he placed against large canvases of Marquesan scenery and people, fixed to each side of the hut. In the garden before the hut he made a statuette of the island god Atua which he placed reverently in a kiosk specially built for it. And, final gesture, he filled one corner of the hut with indecent postcards he had bought at Port Said. He then sat back happily, waiting for trouble.

The villagers and the foreign residents were encouraged to visit his garden, look over his hut. The French colony did not come twice, but gossiped happily about this scandalous impiety. The islanders crowded into his hut emboldened by his defiance; the village buzzed with stories. The Bishop, sensing the laughter, seeing the furtive glances, hearing reports of indecencies, was angry and curious, but neither he nor his priests were allowed inside Gauguin's garden. For the moment there was nothing he could do except to protest—ineffectually—against the horde of girls who were visiting the painter at night. He bided his time. He had been tricked into giving this blasphemous rake a foothold in the village; one day Gauguin would overreach himself.

Gauguin was not worrying. He was painting, painting. "In my isolation here one has everything necessary to strengthen oneself. The poetry alone frees one and it is enough to let oneself sink into a dream and paint as it suggests. I ask only two years of health and not much trouble about money, which has taken an excessive grip on my nerves, to arrive at a certain maturity in my art."

He added, warned perhaps even in the midst of his eagerness by some memory of the past, some premonition of the future: "I know that in art *I am right*, but have I the strength to express it affirmatively? In any case I shall have done my duty, and if my work doesn't last there will last for ever the memory of an artist who freed painting from many of the academic faults of the past and from the faults of the symbolists (another kind of sentimentalism)."

8

It was as well that he felt that he had done his work. For a time it seemed that some miracle had occurred; by April of the next year, 1902, he had painted and sent off to Vollard twenty canvases; they were not the equal of some earlier work, but they showed how he had grasped the chance to put the Marquesan colour on to canvas. But he was not to have his two years. The revival of health was longer than hitherto because the change of life was greater, but it merely delayed the inevitable.

By August eczema had spread up both legs, his broken ankle was raw, his feet so swollen that the slightest movement was acutely painful. By November he had to abandon for a time all effort to paint and the village missed the sight of the big man limping along barefoot to some lonely part of the valley, traps slung over the broad back, the astonishing green beret with its silver tassel pushed over one eye, white cotton slip strained across the broad chest, coloured pareu round the spreading waist, and legs huge and ungainly with their rolls and rolls of bandage. The islanders could not make him out; he was short of speech, rather terrifying with the huge nose thrusting out of a ravaged face, the sunken eyes, the powerful wreck of a body. But he was the only European who never tried to exploit them, never treated them as inferiors; he encouraged them to tell him their grievances, and his anger was all against the French. They missed him.

After a time he was not even to be seen pottering about in his garden. Sometimes the bulky form could be made out through the trees swinging slowly in the hammock, moaning, cursing. Then he disappeared and they had not the courage to follow. The village girls stopped dropping in at night, and his last vahine slipped away whenever she could: what was the use of a man who lay on the bed almost all the day and night twisted up in pain? He rarely left his bed. At last he understood that without constant medical attention there was no hope for him; he told De Monfreid that he would have to abandon the Marquesas and come back to France, or perhaps to Spain, where the fierce colours might compensate a little for those he would have to leave.

De Monfreid again discouraged him. He had no idea how ill Gauguin was—six years of complaints had inevitably led him to think of the writer as a hypochondriac. The Gauguin legend was spreading, he assured him, the legend of a man who had discovered in the primitive a new source of art, who lived like a savage in a land of wondrous beauty. In a few more years his paintings would fetch the kind of price they deserved.

A few more years! Gauguin knew now that he would not see those years. He was already too ill to move and he was spending on tobacco, drink, food, medicines, all the money that might have taken him home. He resigned himself to the inevitable. But idle he could not be; if he could not paint he would write. His eyes were failing rapidly but he wrote on slowly, between long pauses. First he wrote an article for the *Mercure de France*. *Racontars d'un Rapin*, he called it, and he told De Monfreid to look out for it. For years, he said, he had kept silent, he had worked and left the talking to others even when his good name had been taken away—"the heartless man who abandons his children, etc."—his art maligned and all credit for his innovations stolen by others. Now he felt that it was time to speak: "I'm trying to prove that the painter *never* needs the support or the instruction of the literary man. I'm trying also to fight against the groups who set themselves up in every age and preach dogmas and who lead astray not only the painters but the art-loving public." He preached liberty in art. "When will men understand the meaning of that word?"

He had a good claim to his rôle as champion of the painters: "You have known for a long time that I have wanted to establish '*the right* to dare all'. My gifts have not brought any big result (the difficulties of earning enough money to live have been too great for such a task), but nevertheless the boat has been launched. The public owe me nothing because my work is only relatively good, but the painters who are profiting from this liberty today do owe something to me."

He sent the manuscript to Fontainas. It was refused. By that time he was already at work on another and longer work, his *Avant et Après*, into which, he declared, he would incorporate the rejected article. He sent the new manuscript to Fontainas; it contained "memories of my childhood, the explanation of my instincts, of my intellectual growth; also what I have seen and heard (criticisms on the subject of men and things), my art and the art of others, my likes and dislikes. It is certainly not a literary work in a form chosen by others, it is something else, a mixture of the civilised and the barbarous. In it *the style must harmonise*, like a man stripped, often shocking. This comes easily to me, but for the rest—I am no writer."

He told De Monfreid that he had sent off the manuscript: "During my long sleepless nights I wrote down a record of what I have seen, heard and thought in my life; there are *some terrible things* in it—especially for the benefit of my wife and the Danes."

The realisation that Mette's refusal to live with him was final, far from silencing him, drove him to speech. He and she might be finished as husband and wife, but the subject of their marriage was not. Hence the sarcastic references, in letter after letter to De Monfreid, of himself as the man who "of course" had been cad enough to desert his wife and children. These references have been commonly ascribed to guilt feelings, but they were just as much due to disappointment. His vision when he proposed to her thirty years earlier—of himself surrounded by loving wife and adoring children—had never wholly left him. He, regarded everywhere as a libertine, believed in marriage, needed it and never gave a serious thought to any other woman but Mette for the rest of his life. Was this love? Let some wiser and bolder man decide. His feeling for her explains many of his actions; if he is to be understood, this feeling—absurd, pathetic, selfish, noble, what you will—must be allowed to him. Because of it, he was drawn to her all the more as the one woman in the world who had refused him. He never forgot, never forgave; realising that he was a dying man, his bitterness flowed over into passages of irony, sarcasm, invective. To him these were "terrible"; how little terrible they are is a measure of the innate goodness of the man who wrote them; the worst he could find to say of Mette was to call her "that other 'Enemy of the People', the wife who not *only* did not follow her husband, but actually brought up her children so well that they don't know their father."

Gauguin never pretended to be a writer. *Avant et Après* has no form, it is a medley of snippets: random recollections and opinions jotted down as they came into his mind, quotations from reviews, letters, books. "It is not a book," he declared repeatedly. In a sense it is not; nevertheless *Avant et Après* has importance because it is characteristic. It has been for the last thirty years the bedside book, with Blake and Shakespeare, of one of the most distinguished of living men. The reasons given for this choice are that it is unique—no other man could have written it—and is the work of a great man. The whole of Gauguin is here, with his sudden profundities, his childish attempts to shock, his passion for painting, his interest in theology, metaphysics, sex, sport, travel and people—most of his personality expressed, as in his painting, simply and strongly. One may not like the book—but that is simply to say that one does not like Gauguin. Some of what he wrote is no more than confused thinking—he was not a theologian or a metaphysician—but even such passages are redeemed by his strong feelings; he really cared about these things even when he could not fully understand them. It is this feeling which gives the book its value; all that he wrote—the pithy comments as the naïve and turgid explanations—is Gauguin, plainspoken, pungent, deeply concerned. The book has a peculiar charm—the charm of an honest, passionate man.

Ostensibly *Avant et Après* was supposed to be the book of a man looking back, as so many look back in their fifties, and in solitude, to the days of their youth. But, being Gauguin, he could not stop there; *Avant et Après* had to contain all his thought, all his experience, so that he also wrote in it what was uppermost in his mind at the time—page after page is filled with examples of the tyranny of the Church and colonial rulers.

Before the book was written he had tried, less offensively than by the decorations of his hut but as hopelessly, to convince the Bishop of error. He wrote a long essay on "The Modern Spirit and Catholicism". He listed the similarities between the teaching of the New Testament and modern scientific thought. Having shown to his satisfaction that man was living outside the Church but in the spirit of the Gospels, he demonstrated how the interpretation of them by the Church had departed from their true meaning. His knowledge of the subject was not surprising—France had been rent for years by the question of separating Church and State—and his familiarity with the Bible made him an uncomfortable critic. Claiming that he had uncovered the reason for the dislike and distrust of the Church by the educated class, he sent his essay by devious means to the Bishop. By equally devious means he received in return a large and handsome book by "twelve venerable men" containing the full "history and achievements" of the Catholic Church.

Gauguin read the book minutely and returned it heavily annotated. He did not spare the Church; he used plain words; he was enjoying himself, but he was also in earnest. The Bishop saw only the enjoyment; the courtesies came to an end.

9

Everything, it seemed, had come to an end. In February of the new year, 1903, Gauguin had finished and sent off *Avant et Après*. His mind was strung up by what he had written. He was alone. The European colony had long since shunned him as a heretic, an evil-liver, a traitor. The villagers, cowed by the priests and gendarmes, no longer dared to come near his hut for fear of punishment. His vahine had gone for good. A boy came in for an hour or two to clear up and make a meal. One old islander, Tioka, secretly revered as a witch doctor, refused to be scared away. He had been imprisoned for cannibalism, Gauguin interceded, had his sentence shortened, and from that moment the white painter was a god to him; he praised him throughout the village and put on him and his possessions the sacred *tabu* which gave him a privileged position on the island—the one European to receive such an honour. The Bishop, who had banned the *tabu*, was furious but helpless, and Tioka continued to call in for a screw of tobacco, bite his way through a tin of sardines (he disdained the new-fangled opener) and depart with his blessing—a queer, ominous figure horribly disfigured by tattooing. The only other visitor to the hut was Vernier, the Protestant pastor, who acted as village doctor. Gauguin was forced to call him in from time to time. Vernier did not like him or approve of his way of life—"he lived like a savage" he said—but he attended to him because he believed it to be his duty.

Apart from Vernier, Tioka and the boy, Gauguin saw no one. He was crippled and in constant pain. He made a supreme effort, after sending off *Avant et Après*, to paint once more; he managed to finish and send off three canvases, and practically finished a fourth, then he collapsed. He could not read. He lay on his bed brooding over the wrongs of the islanders—wrongs still fresh in his mind from the writing of his book: gendarmes spying on the village girls bathing, then arresting them for indecency; a girl appealing for protection against rape being raped in turn by the magistrate who dismissed the case; gendarmes calling the islanders a filthy name and they, not understanding, shouting it back laughingly, and being thrown into prison; he, Gauguin, threatened with expulsion from the island when he tried to intervene.

Before *Avant et Après* was finished, the governor from Tahiti arrived in his yacht escorted by a French warship. Gauguin watched him leaning over the side of the yacht taking photographs of the romantically situated village, watched the foreign colony giving him a festive welcome, watched the Marquesan girls, dressed up for the occasion, showering flowers before him as he landed. He heard of the festivities in the village—the processions, the banquets; heard too that the islanders had not been allowed to present him with a petition of their grievances—and watched the governor sail away as ignorant of the truth as he was when he arrived.

He at once sent a long memorandum after him to Papeete—long and sarcastic. "When you look at those superb photographs you have taken, it will be evident to you that this is a delightful country where beauty, *joie de vivre* and a luxuriant vegetation conspire to make everyone happy." But he reminded the governor that if he had used his own eyes instead of the camera's he would have seen the effect of injustice in every native hut—in living misery and an early death. He proceeded to open the governor's eyes—but so bitterly that the memorandum was ignored. A copy which he sent to the *Mercure de France* was put on one side because "it would not interest our readers".

His indignation flowed into *Avant et Après*, but, the book finished, he could not rest. He thought he would go mad with rage; somehow he must tell the world, get justice done. In *Avant et Après* he had written down one or two of the worst examples, but would the book be printed, and if printed, what effect would it have? He could not wait; time was short; he must attack the evil at its source.

That same month his opportunity came, as he in his simplicity believed. Two colonial inspectors arrived from Tahiti accompanied by a magistrate. The magistrate came to try cases which had accumulated since his last visit; the inspectors were making one of their periodical calls at the Marquesas to consider grievances—not from the islanders but from the Europeans. This significant fact might have warned Gauguin, but he was in no mood for warnings. He laboriously wrote out another long memorandum giving precise details of the manner in which the islanders were intimidated, ill treated, denied elementary justice. He sent the memorandum to the inspectors and a copy to Morice begging him to persuade a Paris newspaper to print it quickly: "Monstrous things are happening here." For good measure he wrote another, shorter memorandum to the magistrate, giving evidence in favour of an islander who was to be tried for murder; the man, he said, was not guilty and the police had acted mistakenly in accusing him and wrongly in keeping him in prison. Then he lay back, contented.

He might have known from the reaction of Vernier, to whom he sent a copy, what the official view would be: "I am astonished that you should have sent it to me. You ought to have realised that I should decidedly disapprove of it. I prefer to think that it got in amongst the other papers by mistake." That was the attitude of a minister of the Church, who had no sympathy with the Catholics and little with the government. But Gauguin was a child to the end; he refused to be warned; justice would be done.

Justice was not done; there was no possibility that it would be done; the authority of the gendarmerie had to be upheld, as had the work of the Church and the pre-eminent position of the white population. Who would believe Gauguin—a confessed enemy of civil and religious authority, a man who had blatantly rejected his fellow-countrymen and tried to rouse the subject people, a man openly immoral and who had written an impertinent screed of lies to the governor? His word was considered worthless; he had no proof of his statements; the islanders were too terrified to testify. All the Europeans who were called testified against him. The memoranda were enough to damn him.

He had delivered himself into the hands of his enemies. Now was the chance for which all had been waiting, to put this nuisance out of the way. His statements were declared by the inspectors to be not only untrue but libellous. They instituted proceedings against him. The magistrate, conveniently on the spot to finish the matter off, tried him and on March 23, condemned him to three months' imprisonment and a fine of a thousand francs.

He was stunned. "I've been the victim of a horrible plot," he told De Monfreid. "This will be my ruin and will completely destroy my health."

Even then he rallied. He would not be beaten. He appealed to the court at Papeete. He wrote to Morice: "I'm down but I'm not yet vanquished. The Indian who laughs under the torture—is he vanquished? Decidedly the savage is better than we are. You were mistaken when you said that I was wrong to say: 'I am a savage.' But it is true; I am a savage. And civilised people sense it because in my work there is nothing that surprises or baffles except this 'savage-in-spite-of-me'. That is why it can't be imitated. The work of a man is the explanation of that man. There are two kinds of beauty, the one that comes from instinct, the other from study. Clearly the combination of both with the modifications this involves produces a great and very complicated richness which it is the duty of the art critic to busy himself in detecting.

"You are an art critic today; allow me, not to guide you but to advise you, to open your eyes on what I have just told you a little mysteriously. The great science of Raphael doesn't puzzle me and doesn't hinder me for one moment from feeling, seeing and understanding his primordial element which is the instinct of a noble man. Raphael was born noble. Everything else, with him, is only a modification. Art has been going through a very long period of aberration caused by physics, chemistry, mechanics and the study of nature. The artists, having lost all their savageness, having no more instinct, one could even say imagination, are straying in every direction trying to find productive elements which they hadn't the strength to create. In consequence they no longer act except in disorderly mobs, becoming timid and like lost souls the moment they are alone. That's why it's not possible to advise solitude for everyone because one must be strong enough to endure it and to work alone. All that I have learned from others has hampered me. I can therefore say: nobody has taught me anything. It's true I know very little! But I prefer this little that comes from myself. And who knows whether this little, worked on by others, won't become something great? How many centuries are needed to create an *appearance* of progress!"

This defiant and prophetic note was the end. There was no possibility of his being able to make the journey to Papeete. Early in April he realised that his situation was hopeless: "These preoccupations are killing me," he cried to De Monfreid. That was the final sentence of his last letter to this good friend.

A few days later Tioka brought a note to Vernier: "Would it be troubling you to come to visit me? My eyesight is going. I'm ill. I can't walk."

Vernier walked over. Gauguin was in great pain. He applied a dressing that Vernier gave him for his legs. He seemed anxious to talk—of the injustice that had been done to him, of course, but even more of his work and of his friends who believed in it. He gave the pastor a copy of his etching of Mallarmé and insisted on his taking away some books, including Mallarmé's copy of *L'Après-Midi d'un Faune*.

Ten days later, in the first week of May, Tioka came again to Vernier's hut. This time he brought no note. Gauguin was very ill, he said.

Vernier hurried across. Gauguin lay on his bed groaning. There was little that Vernier could do, but he saw that Gauguin wanted to talk. He talked again of his painting, and Vernier noticed that even at that late stage the pain seemed to disappear when Gauguin's mind ran on this subject. He began to feel unwilling admiration.

On May 8, early in the morning, Tioka came again. Vernier found Gauguin alone, blind and in terrible agony. He had had two heart attacks, his whole body was convulsed with pain. He had no idea of the time, the day. He felt that he was about to die.

Vernier comforted him as well as he could, and encouraged him to talk. Again he talked of his work and of books. Vernier remembered that he discussed *Salammbo*. When he seemed calmer, Vernier went away.

A few hours later, at eleven o'clock, Gauguin's boy ran over. The master was dead. Tioka had found him alone in the hut, one swollen leg thrown outside the bed as if he had tried to get up.

Again Vernier hurried across, but the Bishop and his priests were before him, surrounding the still warm body. Tioka wept in a corner of the hut and cried "Gauguin is dead: we are lost!" Behind the dead man, on his easel, was the last picture he had painted—a snow scene in Brittany.

The Bishop made short work of his adversary. Despite Vernier's protests, he buried him the next day in the Catholic cemetery. Everything in the hut that was considered indelicate or sacrilegious was destroyed, including the famous walking-stick. Gauguin's papers were sent back to France. The rest of his belongings—furniture, pictures, books, sculptures—were sold by auction in Papeete to pay the fine of a thousand francs. They did not fetch that figure. The auctioneer, in jovial mood, held Gauguin's last canvas upside down and sold it for seven francs as "The Niagara Falls". This sally met with roars of laughter; the auctioneer had correctly judged the mood of the saleroom; the islands were well rid of a nuisance; but the nuisance, now that he was dead, was seen to have been rather a joke. There was particular amusement when large stocks of wine and luxury tinned foods went under the hammer; this poverty-stricken artist had done himself pretty well!

Gauguin's hut was bought and changed out of recognition by the American trader. In a few weeks all that remained of the troublesome painter was his grave in an inconspicuous corner of the cemetery and his green and silver beret on the proud and defiant old head of Tioka.

EPILOGUE

To Mette his death was as great an outrage as his life: neglect of her and the children—that was what both amounted to. Her rancour lived long: in the summer of 1905 she was still complaining, at a luncheon party of acquaintances, of his scandalous behaviour and no less scandalous escape from all responsibility at the comparatively early age of fifty-four. She continued to do her duty.

As time went on, however, her murmurs grew fainter until at last—except when she forgot herself for a moment—they were hushed altogether. In death the good-for-nothing husband proved himself to be a better bread-winner than in life. His end was his beginning. At first his life and death in Polynesia merged into a highly coloured legend that made him and his work one of the most sustained sensations known in Paris for many years. The prices of his canvases, sculpture in wood and pottery began to rise; Mette prospered, as did Schuff, Madame Caron, the *patron* of the Café des Variéties, the many to whom Gauguin had given canvases and with whom he had exchanged them, and the fortunate dealers holding stocks.

The sensation died down, but the prices of his work continued to rise. Mette was astonished and perhaps a little irritated—could she have imagined such an eventuality she might have held her hand—but on the whole she was gratified. It began to appear, largely through a change in the general attitude towards her, that her dead husband was a famous man—not solely, possibly not mainly, because of his extraordinary life beyond France, but by reason of his painting. She heard and she was assured that he was revered by all the younger painters as, with Cézanne and Vincent van Gogh, one of the masters of his age; the big men of the Nabis and Fauves—Bonnard, Vuillard, Matisse, Picasso, to name the most renowned—all admitted their debt to him; the development of modern painting could be traced largely to his lead.

To Gauguin this vindication of his struggles would have given enormous pleasure but little surprise. His own high status might have produced some sharp comment, the extent of his influence not a word—he had said again and again and he believed that painters must go his way. To his widow, basking under this glow of admiration by proxy, amazement gradually gave place to a dignified awareness. She had been justified in marrying him, justified in her sufferings; she began in mellowed mood to recount the early years of their life together, admitting her blindness ("I had *no idea* that he had a leaning towards the arts") but proving her later acumen by recalling her demands that he send all his paintings from the islands where he had so strangely insisted on living and to which he had even more strangely believed that she and the children would follow him.

Before she died it could be said of Mette that, noting her children's pride in their father and their name and by putting two and two together, she was prepared to acknowledge in her husband a great painter. Whether she really believed as much will never be known; certainly she accepted the inevitable with stern graciousness. But to her dying day it apparently never once occurred to her that he might also be a great man, nor does it seem likely that the thought would have struck her if she had read the statement of faith scribbled in the *Cahier pour Aline* long after his daughter's death. Some readers may, however, feel otherwise; for them these revealing words are now printed—perhaps the most suitable finale of an account of the man and the painter.

"Je crois en la sainteté de l'esprit et en la vérité de l'art un et indivisible . . . je crois que cet art est de source divine et qu'il vit dans le cœur de tous les hommes illuminés par la lumière céleste; je crois qu'après avoir goûté les sublimes délices de ce grand art, on lui est fatalement et pour jamais voué, on ne peut le renier; je crois que tous, par son entremise, peuvent parvenir à la béatitude.

"Je crois en un jugement dernier, où seront condamnés a des peines terribles tous ceux qui, en ce monde, auront osé trafiquer de l'art sublime et chaste, tous ceux qui l'auront souillé et dégradé par la bassesse de leurs sentiments, par leur vile convoitise pour les jouissances materielles. Je crois qu'en revanche les disciples fidèles du grand art seront glorifiés, et qu'enveloppés d'un céleste tissu de rayon de parfums, d'accords mélodieux, ils retourneront se perdre, pour l'éternité, au sein de la divine source de toute harmonie."

BIBLIOGRAPHY

Manuscripts

Letters of Gauguin to De Monfreid	Coll. Mme A. Joly-Segalen Bibliothèque d'Art et d'Archéologie
Letters of Gauguin to his wife	Bibliothèque d'Art et d'Archéologie
Letters of Gauguin to Madame Heegaard	Bibliothèque d'Art et d'Archéologie
Letters of Gauguin to Emile Bernard	Coll. Mme Emile Bernard Coll. M. Roland de Margerie
Letters of Gauguin to Emile Schuffenecker	Coll. Mme Jeanne Schuffenecker
Letters of Gauguin to Maurice Denis	Coll. M. Dominique Denis
Letters of Gauguin to Charles Morice	Coll. M. Alfred Dupont
Letters of Gauguin to Arsène Alexandre	Coll. M. Alfred Dupont
Letter of Gauguin to the colonial inspectors	Coll. M. Alfred Dupont
Letters of Gauguin to William Molard	Coll. Mme Judith Gérard
Letters of Gauguin to André Fontainas	Coll. M. André Fontainas
Letters of Gauguin to Félix Bracquemond	Bibliothèque Nationale
Letters of Gauguin to Messrs. Dillies of Roubaix	Coll. Mme Jeanne Schuffenecker
Letters of Gauguin to Odilon Redon	Coll. Mme Emile Bernard
Letters of Gauguin to Pastor Vernier	Coll. Mme A. Joly-Segalen
Letter of Gauguin to Gustave Fayet	Coll. Mme A. Joly-Segalen
Letters of Mette Gauguin to her husband	Bibliothèque d'Art et d'Archéologie
Letters of Mette Gauguin to De Monfreid	Coll. Mme A. Joly-Segalen
Letters of Mette Gauguin to Emile Schuffenecker	Coll. Mme Jeanne Schuffenecker
Letters of De Monfreid to Gauguin	Coll. Mme A. Joly-Segalen
Letter of Pastor Vernier to Gauguin	Coll. Mme A. Joly-Segalen
Letters of Charles Morice to Gauguin	Coll. Mme A. Joly-Segalen
Letters of Vincent van Gogh to Gauguin	Coll. Ir. V. W. van Gogh Coll. Mme Jeanne Schuffenecker
Letter of Gustave Fayet to Gauguin	Coll. Mme A. Joly-Segalen
Letters of Vincent van Gogh to Emile Bernard	Coll. Comtesse de Goldschmidt-Rothschild Coll. Ir. V. W. van Gogh

Letters of Odilon Redon to Emile Bernard	Coll. Mme Emile Bernard
Letters of Vincent van Gogh to his brother	Coll. Ir. V. W. van Gogh
Letter of M. de Haan to Theo van Gogh	Coll. Ir. V. W. van Gogh
Letter of Marie Uribe to Victor Segalen	Coll. Mme A. Joly-Segalen
Letters of St Pol Roux to Victor Segalen	Coll. Mme A. Joly-Segalen
Letter of Paul Sérusier to De Monfreid	Coll. Mme A. Joly-Segalen
Letters of Ambroise Vollard to De Monfreid	Coll. Mme A. Joly-Segalen
Notebooks of G. D. de Monfreid	Coll. Mme Huc de Monfreid

Works of Gauguin—Manuscripts

Notes Synthétiques	1890	The Louvre
Cahier pour Aline	1892–6	Bibliothèque d'Art et d'Archéologie
Noa-Noa	1893	The Louvre
Diverses Choses	1897	The Louvre
Racontars d'un Rapin	1902	The Louvre
Avant et Après	1903	In private hands

Works and Letters of Gauguin Printed Editions

Notes Synthétiques	in *Vers et Proses*, Paris 1910
Noa-Noa	in *La Revue Blanche*, Paris 1897
	Ed. Morice, Paris 1901
	Facsimile edn. Ed. Meier-Graefe
	Ed. De Monfreid, Paris 1929
	Facsimile edn. Ed. Forlag, Stockholm 1947
Preface	to an exhibition of Armand Séguin, Paris 1895
Les Guêpes	Coll. Mme A. Joly-Segalen. Facsimile edn. Ed. Bouge, Paris 1952
Le Sourire	Coll. Mme A. Joly-Segalen. Facsimile edn. Ed. Bouge, Paris 1952
Racontars d'un Rapin	Paris, 1951
Avant et Après	Facsimile edn. Leipzig and Paris 1910
	Paris 1923
	Translated as *The Intimate Journals of Paul Gauguin*, New York 1921

Lettre au peintre danois Willemsen	*Les Marges*, Paris 1918
Lettres à Daniel de Monfreid	With 'Hommage' by Victor Segalen, Paris 1919
	Ed. Joly-Segalen, Paris 1950
Lettres à André Fontainas	Paris 1921. English trans. with letters to A. Vollard, San Francisco 1943
Lettres à Emile Bernard	Paris 1926, Brussels 1942
Lettres à Alfred Vallette	*Mercure de France*, Paris 1940–6
Lettre à Charles Morice	*Arts*, Paris 1946
Lettres à sa femme et à ses amis	Ed. Malingue, Paris 1946
Le Carnet de Paul Gauguin	Ed. René Huyghe, Paris 1952

Books on Gauguin

Jean de Rotonchamp	*Paul Gauguin*, Weimar 1906, Paris 1925
Maurice Denis	*Théories* 1890–1910, Paris 1912
Charles Morice	*Paul Gauguin*, Paris 1920
Charles Chassé	*Gauguin et le Groupe de Pont-Aven*, Paris 1921
Robert Rey	*Gauguin*, Paris 1923
Jean Dorsenne	*La Vie Sentimentale de Paul Gauguin*, Paris 1927
Arsène Alexandre	*Paul Gauguin*, Paris 1930
Pola Gauguin	*My Father, Paul Gauguin*, London 1937
Maurice Malingue	*Gauguin*, Paris 1948

Articles and Chapters on Gauguin

Albert Aurier	*Le Symbolisme en Peinture*, Mercure de France, 1891
	Paul Gauguin, La Plume, 1892
	Gauguin, Revue Encyclopédique, 1892
	Oeuvres Posthumes, Mercure de France, 1893
	Emile Bernard contre Paul Gauguin, Mercure de France, 1895
	Gauguin, Revue Universelle, 1903
Emile Bernard	*Gauguin*, Mercure de France, 1895
	Notes sur l'Ecole dite de Pont-Aven, Mercure de France, 1903

Emile Bernard—*continued* — *Gauguin*, Mercure de France, 1908
Gauguin et Emile Bernard, Le Point, 1937
Souvenirs inédits sur l'artiste Paul Gauguin et ses compagnons, Lorient, 1939

Jacques-Emile Blanche — *Gauguin*, Revue de Paris, 1920

Charles Chassé — *Gauguin et Mallarmé*, l'Amour de l'Art, 1922
De quand date le synthétisme de Gauguin?, L'Amour de l'Art, 1938
Gauguin, L'Amour de l'Art, 1938
Les Démêlés de Gauguin avec les gendarmes et l'évêque des Marquises, L'Amour de l'Art, 1938
Importance pour la Bretagne de l'Ecole de Pont-Aven, Nouvelle Revue de Bretagne, 1946
Le Mouvement Symboliste dans l'art du XIXe siècle, Paris 1946

Maurice Denis — *Notes d'Art*, Art et Critique (Louis Picose), 1890
L'Influence de Paul Gauguin, Mercure de France, 1904
De Gauguin et de Van Gogh au classicisme, L'Occident, 1910
Un homme a consacré sa vie à l'amitié de Gauguin, Beaux-Arts, 1938

Félix Fénéon — *Les Impressionistes en* 1886, Paris 1886
Autre Groupe Impressioniste, La Cravache, 1888

André Fontainas — *Histoire de la peinture française au XIXe Siècle*, Mercure de France, 1906
Histoire générale de l'art français, Paris 1922

Marcel Guérin — *L'œuvre gravée de Paul Gauguin*, Paris, 2 vols., 1927

J. K. Huysmans — *L'Art Moderne*, Paris 1883, 1903, 1929

Jean Loize — *Gauguin écrivain*, Paris 1949

Roger Marx — *A propos des œuvres céramiques de Gauguin*, Revue Encyclopédique, 1891
Gauguin, Le Voltaire, 1891
Maîtres d'hier et d'Aujourd'hui, Paris 1914

Octave Mirbeau — *Chronique*, Echo de Paris, 1891
Gauguin, Revue Universelle, 1903
Des artistes, Paris 1922

G. D. de Monfreid — *Gauguin*, La Dépêche de Toulouse, 1903
Gauguin, L'Hermitage, 1908

Charles Morice — *Preface* to Gauguin Exhibition Catalogue, Durand-Ruel, 1893
Gauguin, Mercure de France, 1903

Charles Morice—*continued*
Quelques opinions sur Paul Gauguin, Mercure de France, 1903
Les Gauguins du Petit-Palais et de la rue Laffitte, Mercure de France, 1904
Gauguin, L'Art Moderne, 1909

Victor Segalen
Gauguin dans son dernier décor, Mercure de France, 1904

Armand Séguin
Gauguin, L'Occident, 1903

Paul Sérusier
A.B.C. de la Peinture. New edn. with study of the man and his work by Maurice Denis, Paris 1942

August Strindberg
Letter printed in catalogue of Gauguin sale, Hôtel Drouot, 1895

Bernard Villaret
Les dernières années de Gauguin, Revue de Paris, 1953

Miscellaneous

Paul Cézanne
Letters, London 1941

Edgar Degas
Lettres, Paris 1931, 1945; Eng. trans. 1947
Mon oncle Degas, Jeanne Fevre, Paris 1949

Theodore Duret
Manet and the French Impressionists, 1910

André Gide
Si le graine ne meurt, Paris 1928; Eng. trans. 1951
Journals, 1947–9

Stéphane Mallarmé
Vie de Mallarmé, Henri Mondor, Paris 1941

Edouard Manet
Letters by and to. Bibliothèque d'Art et d'Archéologie
Manet raconté par lui-même, E. Moreau-Nélation, Paris 1926
Manet, E. Bazire, Paris 1884

Maxime Maufra
Maxime Maufra, Arsène Alexandre, Paris 1926

Claude Monet
Lettres, Paris 1934
La Vie de Claude Monet, M. de Fels, Paris 1929

G. D. de Monfreid
Les Amitiés de Monfreid et ses reliques de Gauguin, Jean Loize, Paris 1951

George Moore
Confessions of a Young Man, 1886

Charles Morice
Notes Quotidiennes, Paris 1917

Camille Pissarro
Letters of Camille Pissarro to his son Lucien, London 1945

Paul Signac
D'Eugène Delacroix au Néo-Impressionisme, Paris 1899

August Strindberg
Letters, Stockholm 1932, 1946, 1948

Flora Tristan
La vie et l'œuvre de Flora Tristan, Jules L. Puech, Paris 1925

Vincent van Gogh — *Lettres à Emile Bernard*, Paris 1911; Eng. trans. 1938
Verzamelde Brieven van Vincent van Gogh, 3rd edn. Amsterdam 1952-4; Eng. trans. of 1st edn. 1928-9

Ambroise Vollard — *Cézanne*, Paris 1914; Eng. trans. 1924
Degas, Zurich 1919
Renoir, Paris 1919
En Ecoutant Cézanne, Degas, Renoir, Paris 1938
Souvenirs d'un marchand de tableaux, Paris 1937; Eng. trans. 1936

Emile Zola — *Mes Haines*, Paris 1880

Note.—This Bibliography is in no way comprehensive. It consists only of the works used by us—restricted almost completely to Gauguin and the men who knew him—and which we consider essential to a study of the subject. Even so, readers would be well advised to treat with care items listed under *Bernard*, *Rotonchamp* and *Vollard*. We are unable to recommend books in English. In French, Charles Kunstler has written interestingly on Gauguin.

Some Gauguin Paintings in European Galleries

Amsterdam, Gemeente Museum	Vincent Painting Sunflowers (Coll. Ir. V. W. van Gogh)	1888
Birmingham, Barber Institute	Paysage à Pont-Aven	1888
	Baigneuses à Tahiti	1897
Brussels, Musée Royal	Le Calvaire, Bretagne	1889
	Portrait de Miss Cambridge	1891
Copenhagen, Carlsberg Glyptoteck	Jardin sous la Neige (2)	1879
	Etude de Nu	1880
	Le Pot de Bierre	1880
	La Famille de Paul Gauguin	1880
	Fleurs dans un Vase	1882
	Paysage de Banlieue	1883
	Baigneuses à Dieppe	1885
	La Martinique	1887
	Paysage de Bretagne	1888
	Paysage Tahitien avec Personnages	1892
	Arearea No Varua Ino	1894
	Fleurs et Chats	1899
Copenhagen, Ordrupgaard	Femme à la Vague	1889
Edinburgh, National Gallery	La Vision Après le Sermon	1888
Essen, Folkwang Museum	Tangsammler	1889
	Reiter am Strande	1892
	Das Mädchen mit dem Fächer	1902
	Contes Barbares	1902
Glasgow, Art Gallery	Jeune Bretonne	1889
Grenoble, Musée d'Art Moderne	Portrait de Madeleine Bernard	1888
	Portrait de Femme Accoudée	1890
London, Tate Gallery	Harvest in Brittany	1888
	Nevermore	1897
	Faa Iheihe	1898
	Flower Piece	1899
	Tahitian Study	1899
	Two Tahitian Women	1900
Lyons, Musée des Beaux-Arts	Nave Nave Mahana (Jours Délicieux)	1896
Moscow, Musée d'Art Occidental	Te Tiare Farani	1891
	Pastorales Tahitiennes	1892
Prague, Musée d'Art Moderne	Bonjour Monsieur Gauguin	1889

Paris, Louvre	La Seine au Pont d'Iéna	1875
	Nature morte aux Oranges	1878
Paris, Louvre—*continued*	Nature morte (avec fenêtre)	1880
	Nature morte — vase, fleurs, mandoline	1885
	Fenaison en Bretagne	1888
	Paysage d'Arles près des Alyscamps	1888
	La Belle Angèle	1889
	Femmes de Tahiti	1891
	Le Cheval Blanc	1898
	Et l'or de leur corps	1901
	Village Breton sous la Neige	1903
Paris, Musée d'Art Moderne	Te Arii Vahine (La Femme aux Mangos)	1896
Paris, Petit Palais	Le Sculpteur Aubé	1882
	Le Fils du Sculpteur Aubé	1882
	Le Vieillard au Bâton	1893
Stockholm, National Museum	Paysage Décoratif	1888
	Paysage d'Arles	1888
	Paysage de Bretagne	1889
Zürich, Kunsthaus	Aita Parari (Anna la Javanaise)	1893

INDEX

Anna la Javanaise, 240, 242-5, 250
Anquetin, Louis, 86, 93, 110, 112-14, 131, 163
Arosa, Gustave, 31, 32, 37, 40, 41, 43, 44, 84, 87
Aubé, 49, 95
Aubé, Mme, 15, 38
Aurier, Albert, 164, 182, 183, 191, 198, 201, 202, 228

Balzac, 38, 187
Barrès, Maurice, 198
Bauchy, 181
Baudelaire, 133, 134, 206
Beethoven, 216, 262
Bellini, 198
Bernard, Emile, Infant prodigy of Ecole Cormon—dabbling in *pointillisme*, 86; meets Gauguin at Pont-Aven, 92; his background, 93-4; talks much of Vincent van Gogh, 94; admires Gauguin, 94-5; doyen of little group that welcomes Gauguin back from Martinique, 109; introduced to Japanese prints by Vincent, 113; shows at Café du Tambourin and Père Tanguy's, 114; joins Gauguin at Pont-Aven, bringing his sister Madeleine with him, 130; Gauguin impressed by his work, 130-1; preaches synthetic art, paints *Bretonnes dans la Prairie* and inspires Gauguin to paint *Vision Après le Sermon*, 132-3; vainly offers *Vision* to churches, 170; preaches symbolism —effect on Gauguin, 134-5; Vincent's criticism of his olive trees, 135; preaches *cloissonisme* (influenced by study of windows of St Brieuc cathedral) and a movement back to ancient art, 135-6; introduces Paul Sérusier to Gauguin, 137; writes ecstatic letters to Gauguin after forced return to Paris, and tells Vincent (at Arles) heartrending tales of Gauguin's poverty, 138-9, but looks coolly on Gauguin's winter-in-Brittany plan, 140; friction with father, 140-1; he and Laval on shadows, 147; invited by Gauguin to Arles, 149; ordered by Gauguin to arrange exhibition in Paris "for little group of pals", 150; as poet, 134, 153; begins lithography with Gauguin but tires quickly, 162; a brainwave leads to the Volpini exhibition, 162; the mysterious Ludovic Nemo, 163; urged by Gauguin to visit Javanese village, 166; plays with idea of industrial art, 166; his description of Redon, 167; shilly-shallies when Gauguin tries to tie him down to Madagascar plan, 167-70; forbidden by father to join Gauguin in Brittany, 173; writes and encourages Gauguin to do likewise, 173; hears Gauguin's hopes and fears, 177-80; again invited for Brittany winter but stays in Paris, 179; depressed himself, he gets rallying cry from Gauguin, 180; confident talk—when with Gauguin—about Madagascar, 184, but raises objections at a distance, 185-6; tells Gauguin of Theo's madness, 194; grows lukewarm about Madagascar, 194; first signs of envy—complains that he is not being taken seriously, 194; changes his style, 195; disagrees with Gauguin about Vincent exhibition, 195; definitely withdraws from Gauguin's tropics scheme, 201; begins his campaign against Gauguin, 201-2; not at Gauguin farewell dinner, 205; does not write to Gauguin in Tahiti, 215; attends Gauguin's soirées at rue Vercingetorix, 240-1; writes article attacking Gauguin—Gauguin's reaction, 265-266; Gauguin refuses to exhibit with him, 266
Bernard, Madeleine, 94, 130, 134, 135, 137, 142, 143, 150, 168, 170, 180, 184, 244, 265
Bertin, 15, 17, 22, 32, 37, 61-4, 66, 80, 83, 204, 235
Bible, The, 38, 151, 187, 262, 279
Bing, 113
Bishop of Atuona, 273-5, 279, 280, 284
Bizet, 190
Blake, 278
Bolivar, 19
Bonnard, 165, 238, 285
Botticelli, 156, 175, 274
Bouillot, 49, 50, 73, 76, 77, 79, 98, 109
Bouillot, Mme, 77

Bracquemond, 84, 95, 98, 99
Brandes, 70, 82, 83, 247

Cabanel, 58
Caron, Mme, 230, 285
Carrel, Armand, 22
Carrière, Eugène, 198
Cazals, 198
Cézanne, 49, 52, 53, 66, 68, 91, 109, 124, 135, 154, 165, 173, 185, 198, 202, 204, 235, 238, 240, 285
Chamaillard, Ernest de, 172, 177, 178, 241, 242, 244
Chaplet, 85, 95, 98, 108, 109
Chaudet, Léon, 257
Chazal, André, 19-22, 24, 38, 162
Chazal, Antoine, 19, 38
Colin, Paul-Emile, 187
Collarossi, Académie, 40, 66, 111, 172, 230
Cormon, Ecole, 93, 94, 110, 112
Corot, 43, 259
Courbet, 37, 43, 58, 94, 156, 216
Courtois, 72
Cuvier, 248, 249

Daubigny, 151
Daudet, 151
Daumier, 37, 49, 151
Debussy, 46, 134
Degas, Edgar, meets Gauguin at Nouvelles Athènes—description, 48; thinks well of Gauguin's work, 51; possible influence on *Etude de Nu*, 53, 59, 126, which he likes, 58; wealthy but difficult, 76; reproves Gauguin at Dieppe, 78; the only Impressionist to sell, 79, 98; insists that the name Impressionist be dropped, 83; his comment on Seurat's *Grande Jatte*, 83; impressed by Gauguin's canvases at last exhibition, 85; helps Gauguin to go to Pont-Aven, 86; praised by Gauguin to disciples, 91; thinks well of Gauguin's Pont-Aven studies, 97; Gauguin's child studies "not like Degas", 126; he buys a Gauguin Brittany picture, 138, and Gauguin hopes that his friends will do likewise, 139; Gauguin believes he is Vincent van Gogh's *bête noire*, 151, 154; his work discovered by the Nabis, 165; buys *La Belle Angèle*, 169, 201; a photograph of his *Arlequin* always kept by Gauguin, 175, 218, 274; criticises Gauguin's figure work—his advice, 179; Gauguin's "his work lacks heart", 179; buys Gauguin Martinique canvas, 201; Pissarro's *canard*, 203; his influence acknowledged by Gauguin, 204; his work makes money for Durand-Ruel, 231; he persuades Durand-Ruel to exhibit Gauguin's Tahiti canvases, 232; his explanation of the Tahiti style, 237, which he admires, 238; he buys Gauguin's copy of *Olympia*, 249
Delacroix, 37, 54, 112, 115, 156
Denis, Maurice, 164, 165, 187, 197, 265, 266, 270
Desnaunay, 189
Dreyfus, 204
Dupuygodeau, 90
Durand-Ruel, 37, 49, 62, 64, 94, 231, 232, 235, 236
Durrio, Francisco, 240

Erikson, Ida, 240
Estrup, 17

Fauché, Léon, 110, 161-3, 181
Fénéon, Félix, 84, 164
Filiger, Charles, 172, 175, 187, 189, 190, 194
Fontainas, André, 262, 263, 277
Fourel, "Mère", 76
Fra Angelico, 175

Gad, Ingeborg, 38, 183, 184
Gad family, 17, 34, 35, 38, 67-9, 71, 73-5, 77, 80, 118, 122, 177
Gauguin, Aline, 39, 50, 60, 130, 205, 259, 260, 266, 286
Gauguin, Aline-Marie (née Chazal), 20, 22-4, 26-32, 70, 259
Gauguin, Clovis, 22-4, 26
Gauguin, Clovis (Jnr.), 54, 60, 73, 76-83, 86, 95, 97-9, 109, 116, 228, 270, 271
Gauguin, Emile, 39, 50, 184, 205, 228, 231-4
Gauguin, Jean, 61
Gauguin, Isidore (Zizi), 27, 30, 232
Gauguin, Marie (later Uribe), 22-7, 30, 31, 78, 79, 97, 100, 101
Gauguin, Mette Sophie (*née* Gad), early years, 17; meets Gauguin in Paris, 15, and falls in love, 15-33; dismay at his past, 21, 26, 32, and inability to understand him in the present, 33-4, but she gladly becomes engaged, 36, and married, 38; bears first child, Emile, 39; humours Gauguin's attempts to paint, 40; birth of Aline, 50; uneasiness at Gauguin's increasing devotion to painting and his painter friends, 50-1; birth of Clovis, 54; she forbids

Gauguin, Mette Sophie—*continued*
models in the house, 54, and apparently dismisses Justine after painting of *Etude de Nu*, 59; birth of Jean, 60, and Paul (Pola), 61; reaction to Gauguin's decision to leave Bertin, 62-3; presses him to move to Copenhagen after the Rouen fiasco, 67; affected by her family's attitude to Gauguin, 68, 71, 73; a quarrel followed by his departure for Paris, 73; analysis of her relations with him, 74-6; she reproaches him and complains to mutual friends, 77, 79; anxiety for Clovis, 81, 95; more complaints and talk of suicide, 82; she is given all Gauguin's news, 83; offer to come to Paris rejected, 84; does not respond to his enthusiasm for a home at Pont-Aven, 89; is ill, 89; further reproaches, 95; her self-pity, 98; meets him unsuccessfully before he leaves for Panama, 100, fetches Clovis and takes many of Gauguin's pictures, 109; demands money, 102; sends no birthday greetings, 103; her silence hurts him, 105, and her complaints when letters arrive in Martinique, 106; continued lack of faith in his work, 108; her letters "always have an *arrière pensée*", 109; asks Gauguin to Copenhagen after his first good sale of pictures, 116-17; her reasons and his reply, 118-19; she complains of loneliness, 122, and of his silence, 123; sends birthday greetings and a self-pitying letter, 123-4; receives (from Arles) money from Gauguin and news of his growing stature in art world, 149-50; rejects his offer to visit Copenhagen, 161; is given a description of life in Le Pouldu, 171-2; regards his now customary bunch of press cuttings without enthusiasm, 173, confirmed, she thinks, by his confession that he cannot sell, 175; more complaints, more demands for money, and a reprimand, 176; her lack of imagination, 177; she does not reply and he is unhappy, 183, but resists chance to score off her, 183-4; sends him photographs of children, he invites himself to Copenhagen but she is cautious and demands money for Emile's first communion clothes, 184; is given his news and replies to another suggestion of Copenhagen visit with a suggestion that he "drop his affectation of paternity", 196, leading to another squabble, 197; receives press cuttings of Mirbeau article and another affirmation of love, 200; analysis of this, 200-1; more cuttings arrive—about Drouot sale and its success, 202, and she agrees to Copenhagen visit—a temporary accord, 205, which vanishes on her side when he leaves for Tahiti with remnant of proceeds—sends bitter letter, 206; hears lyrical praise of Tahiti from him, mingled with excuses and explanation, 207-8; he replies to her savage letter, but her view of him as artist-money-maker is changing, 215; she thinks him unwise to leave France—his answer, 215-16; sends more photographs of children but does not encourage his hopes of family reunion, 216-17; receives his canvases for exhibition with explanation of *Manao Tupapau*, 219-20; writes only three short notes in two years, 223; visits Paris to collect Gauguin canvases—his jealousy of Morice—her rigid attitude, 224-5; she begins to sell his work but sends him only photographs of children—his comments, 225-8; ignores his letter from Marseilles, 230, and letter and telegram from Paris, 231; eventually tells him that Tahiti pictures have not sold and refuses to come to Paris to greet him, 232, refuses a second invitation after he has inherited Uncle Zizi's money—her anger and explanation to Schuff—disastrous effect on Gauguin, 232-5; invites him, later, to Copenhagen, but too late, 235; hears of "artistic success" of his new exhibition, 238; is reproached by him for writing only about money, 246; reputed visit of Gauguin to Copenhagen and of her refusal to accompany him to Tahiti, 246-7; declines to reveal what pictures she has sold, 247; he gives her 1500 francs, 247, she demands six thousand, 250, and says "you *must* shift for *yourself*", 250-1; writes only notes dealing with money, 253; thinks him "criminally selfish"—his comment, 254; her complaints of poverty proved untrue, 258; is asked not to write again, 259, but sends news of

Gauguin, Mette Sophie—*continued*
Aline's death—Gauguin's reply, 259; she does not send birthday greetings, he breaks with her, 259-60; tries but fails to tell him of death of Clovis—her reasons, 270-1; complaints after Gauguin's death—then acceptance of his greatness, in public, but complete inability to understand him remains, 285-6

Gauguin, Eugène-Henri-Paul, born 1848, 22-3; maternal ancestors, 18; maternal grandmother, Flora Tristan, 19-21; mother, 22; father, 22-3; early years in Lima (1851-5), 23-6; schoolboy at Orléans (1855-65), 27-9; goes to sea (1865-71), 29-31; joins the firm of Bertin, 31-2; description of, 16; meets and falls in love with Mette Gad (1873), 15-17, 33-6; meets Emile Schuffenecker (Schuff), who interests him in painting (1871), 37-8; marriage (1873), 38, and domestic life, 39; meets his painter brother-in-law Fritz Thaulow (1874), 40; attends evening classes at Académie Collarossi, 40; interest in painting increased by his guardian Gustave Arosa, 40; a painting accepted by the Salon (1876), 40; he meets Camille Pissarro, 41-6; begins to meet and paint after the Impressionists and to buy their canvases, 46-9; takes lessons in sculpture from his landlord Bouillot (1877), 49-50; Mette's view of his growing absorption in painting, 50-1; exhibits with Impressionists (1880), 51; Huysmans' comments on his work, 51; painting holiday with Pissarro, Cézanne and Guillaumin (1881), 52-3; paints *Etude de Nu* (1881), 53-9; again exhibits with Impressionists (1882) but makes no progress, 59; effect of failure—he decides to leave Bertin and set up as painter (1883), 59-61; moves to Rouen (1884), 63-5, but fails, 66, and agrees to Mette's request that they go to her home in Copenhagen (1884), 66-7; the Gad family disapproves, 67-8; he becomes a commercial traveller but his passion for painting grows, 68-9; increasing friction with Gads, 69-72; failure of his first solo exhibition, 72-3; more trouble and he leaves suddenly for Paris with his son Clovis (1885), 73; analysis of relationship with Mette, 74-6; hard times in Paris, 76-81; becomes a bill-sticker, 81; acrimonious correspondence with Mette, 81-3; again exhibits with Impressionists (1886), 83, has moral but not financial success, 83-5; takes up pottery with Chaplet, 85; goes to Pont-Aven in Brittany, 86, settles into Pension Gloanec, 88; proud isolation, 89-90, changes with arrival of disciples including Charles Laval, 90-1; his advice, 91-2; arrival of Emile Bernard, 92-5; returns gloomily to Paris at end of season, 95-6; sells nothing and again suffers hardship, 98-9; sails for Panama with Laval (1887), 99-101; his hopes fade, 100, and he is forced to work as navvy on canal diggings, 102; with Laval's help they get to Martinique, 102, which at first seems absolute heaven, 102-4; he plans to bring out his family, 102-3, and paints well, 104, until he and Laval go down with fever, 105; despair mingled with satisfaction at progress of his painting, 105-6; works his passage back to France, 107; more disappointment in Paris, 108-9; mitigated by admiration of small group meeting at Theo van Gogh's gallery, 109-111; talks with Vincent van Gogh, 111-16; purchase of picture by Theo offsets dissension with Schuff, 116-17; decision to return to Pont-Aven clarifies relations with Mette, 117-19; birth of the Ecole de Pont-Aven (1888), 120-2, 124-6; more exchanges with Mette, 122-4; his work advances—child studies, 126-7; Vincent invites him to Arles, 127-9; reappearance of Bernard with sister and effect on him—he paints *Vision Après le Sermon*, 130-3; synthetic-symbolism, 133-5; and *cloissonisme*, 135; idols appear in his work, 136; he meets Paul Sérusier and announces famous dictum, 136-8; prolonged hesitation—to Arles or not? 138-42; he decides to go, 142-3; arrival in Arles (1888), 144, where he puts Vincent and his house in order, to Vincent's great pleasure, 144-51; beginnings of trouble, 151-6, ends in decision to leave, Vincent's abortive attack and self-mutilation, 157-9; analysis of relationship with Vincent, 159-60; return to Paris—a good portrait group and first lithographs,

Gauguin, Eugène-Henri-Paul—*continued* 161-2; the Volpini exhibition (1889), 162-6; Javanese village and the reminiscences of Mme Redon re-kindle his longing for tropics, 166-8, but by *force majeure* he returns to Brittany, 168, where he turns to portraiture, 169, is joined by Meyer de Haan, 170, and paints many great works, 171; moves to Le Pouldu, 171-2, where disciples join him, 172-5, yet he remains dissatisfied because of lack of sales, poverty, 175-80; returns to Paris (1890), 180; joins the Symbolist group, 181-3, but still hungers after tropics and tells Mette so, 184-5, as well as more plans after forced return to Pouldu, 185-6, but life and work in Brittany prove unexpectedly pleasant, 187; effect on him of Vincent's suicide and Theo's death, 193-4; he decides to go to Tahiti, 195-7; arranges sale at Hotel Drouot (1891), 197; the Mirbeau article, 199-200; success of sale, 201-4; reasons for leaving France, 204-5; visit to Copenhagen and temporary accord with Mette, 205; farewell dinner at Café Voltaire, 205; he leaves—anger of Mette, 206; favourable first impression of Papeete, 207, does not last—he rents a hut at Mataiea, 210; his pleasure, 210-11, but cannot work, seeks "vahine" and finds her in Tehura, 211-13; begins to work well, 213-14, 220; sends canvases to Mette, 215-16; Tehura inspires the *Manao Tupapau*, 218-20; disadvantages of Tahiti life appear, 221-5; he decides to leave, 225-6; arrives Marseilles penniless (1893), 229; in Paris with loan from Sérusier, 230; hears nothing from Mette, runs out of money, 231; is rescued by legacy from Uncle Zizi, 231-2; invites Mette to Paris, she refuses, he consoles himself madly, 232-5; exhibition of Tahiti paintings fails, 235-9; his reaction—in clothes, 239-240; companion (Anna), 240, and life in new *appartement*, 240-1; he tires of idleness and after Brussels visit returns to Pont-Aven (1894), 241-2, where he paints well, 243, but is ruined by Anna, 243-4, breaks ankle, is laid up for months, deserted, and has his *appartement* rifled, 244-5; decides to return to Tahiti, 245-6; organizes another Drouot sale (1895), 247; exchange of letters with Strindberg, 247-9; the sale fails and after disagreement with Mette he leaves France, 249-251, having contracted syphilis, 251; rents land and builds hut at Punaria, 252-3, and lives with new vahine, Pahura, 253-4, but health gets steadily worse, his loans unrepaid, his letters unanswered, 254-5; paints well in spurts (1896), 256; death of his daughter leads to final break with Mette, 259-60; attempts to kill himself after painting *D'Où Venons-Nous?*, 261-4; paints *Les Seins aux Fleurs Rouges* (1899) after much suffering, 265-7; begins to write anti-government, anti-mission, pro-islander articles in *Les Guêpes*, 267-8, then launches his own paper *Le Sourire*, 268, which collapses after a few months (1901), 269; the dealer Vollard buys his work, 270; death of his son Clovis unknown by him, 270-1; moves to Hiva-Oa in the Marquesas, 271-2; buys land and builds hut, 273-4; insults the Bishop and scandalises the foreign colony, 274-5; deceptive burst of health and good work, 275, followed by increasing illness, 276; writes *Avant et Après* (1902), 277-9; more exchanges with Bishop, 279, almost bedridden, he is deserted, 280, but still champions the oppressed islanders with memoranda —to the governor, magistrate and colonial inspectors, 281; is convicted of libel and sentenced harshly, 282; his defiance, 282-3; last weeks and death (1903), 283-4; triumph after death and statement of faith, 285-6

Gauguin paintings mentioned in the text:
- *Arearea*, 220
- *Arearea No Varua Ino*, 243
- *Baigneur*, 173
- *Bonjour Monsieur Gauguin*, 171, 175, 242
- *Christ Jaune*, 135
- *Contes Maoris*, 170
- *Cour de Ferme au Pouldu*, 187
- *Deux Bretonnes sur la Route*, 243
- *Environs du Pouldu*, 171
- *Etude de Nu*, 55-60, 126, 133, 215
- *Femme à la Vague*, 163, 171
- *Femmes Maoris*, 104
- *Ferme à Pontoise*, 51
- *Intérieur d'Atelier*, 59
- *Jeunes Bretons Debout*, 171
- *La Barrière*, 171

La Belle Angèle, 169, 201
La Falaise, 126
La Gardienne de Porcs, 171
La Gardienne de Vaches, 171
La Sente du Père Dupin, 51
La Siesta, 220
La Vision Après le Sermon, 132, 133, 137, 201, 202
Le Calvaire, 135
Le Christ du Jardin d'Oliviers, 135
Les Blanchisseuses, 243
Les Bretonnes, 142, 149
Les Meules, 187
Les Négresses, 104
Les Seins aux Fleurs Rouges, 253, 266
Manao Tupapau, 218, 219, 249, 258, 262
Nafea Fo I Poipo, 220
Nevermore, 258
Nirvana, 170
No Te Ana Se Rive, 253
Otahi (Seule), 220
D'Où Venons-Nous? Que Sommes-Nous? Où Allons-Nous?, 261
Paysage à Viroflay, 40
Paysage de Bretagne, 243
Paysage Décoratif, 136
Pastorales Tahitiennes, 214, 237
Petit Breton, 171
Petit Breton à l'Oie, 171
Poèmes Barbares, 256, 264
Pommiers de l'Ermitage, 51
Pommiers de Vaugirard, 51
Rêverie, 213
Tahitienne, 213
Tahitiennes Nues sur la Plage, 220
Ta Ma Tete, 264
Te Aa No Areois, 264
Te Arii Vahine, 256
Vahine No Te Tiare, 213
Gauguin, Paul (Pola), 61
Gérard, Judith, 241, 244, 250
Gérôme, 43
Gide, 190
Ginoux, M. and Mme, 146, 148, 149
Giotto, 156, 195
Gloanec, Marie-Jeanne, 87, 88, 91, 96, 109, 110, 121, 122, 124, 130, 140, 169, 172, 242, 243, 246
Goncourt, Edmond de, 151
Gordon, Charles George, 64
Goupil gallery (Boussod and Valadon), 94, 114, 116-8, 165, 166, 182, 194, 231
Granchi, 90
Guillaumin, 49, 52, 63, 68, 76, 78, 85, 97, 110, 150, 163, 204, 231, 236

Haan, Meyer de, 170, 172, 175, 177-80, 185, 187, 189, 194, 195, 201, 205, 245
Heegaard family, 17, 34, 67
Heegaard, Marie, 15, 17, 39, 81, 86
Henry, Mlle Marie, 172, 174, 175, 187, 194, 242
Hugo, 206
Huysmans, 51, 58, 59, 164, 167

Ingres, 91, 151, 154, 218

Jobbé-Duval, 51, 76, 79, 82, 85, 87, 98
Jobbé-Duval, Mme, 76, 79, 82
Jongkind, 49, 98
Joyant, Maurice, 228, 230, 231
Julian, Ecole, 124, 136-8, 165, 171, 188, 189
Juliette, 186, 196, 200, 232, 240
Justine, 54, 56-9

La Fontaine, 237
Lamartine, 206
Laval, Charles, meets Gauguin at Pont-Aven and is at once a disciple, 90; his work a pale shadow of Gauguin's, 92; difference between his attitude and Bernard's, 95; accompanies Gauguin to Panama, 99; paints portraits and earns the fare for both to Martinique, 102; down with fever, tries to kill himself, saved by Gauguin, 105; in hospital at St Pierre, 107; rejoins Gauguin in Pont-Aven and shares his money, 129; falls in love with Madeleine Bernard, 130; painting in Bois d'Amour when Gauguin gives Sérusier his famous instruction, 137-8; fans Gauguin's desire for the tropics, 139; Vincent complains of his influence over Gauguin, 141; chosen for Volpini exhibition, 150, 163; his talk of tropics begins to annoy Gauguin, 166, who declines to include him in a future expedition, 167-8; secret engagement to Madeleine Bernard, 168; a gossip?, 168; at Le Pouldu with Gauguin, 172, but Gauguin criticises his idleness, 178; plan to winter in Brittany falls through, 179; returns to Pouldu the next summer, 187, but leaves before winter, 194; early death, 244
Leclercq, Julien, 198, 240, 241
Lefèvre, Jules, 58, 165
Leroy, Alfred, 41
Loiseau, 189
Loti, 195, 208, 239
Louis Napoleon, 23
Louise, 88, 122, 171

Maeterlinck, 206
Maillol, Aristide, 260
Mallarmé, 167, 182, 183, 190, 198, 205, 206, 238, 240, 262, 283
Manet, 37, 46-9, 60, 62, 91, 175, 196, 218, 248, 274
Manzi, 238
Marchand, Captain, 268
Marie le Pape, 88, 122
Massenet, 190
Matisse, 176, 285
Maufra, Maxime, 188, 189, 242
Maupassant, 152
Meissonier, 154, 164, 200
Memling, 241
Michael Angelo, 91, 195
Mignet, 22
Millet, 112, 154, 216
Mirbeau, Octave, 197, 199-201, 207
Molard, William, 241, 244, 250, 252, 254
Molard, Mme, 241, 244, 250
Monet, 37, 41, 45, 48, 49, 51, 58, 59, 64, 83, 85, 94, 98, 127, 148, 163, 165, 204, 231, 236
Monfreid, Georges-Daniel de, description, 110; meets Gauguin—his admiration, 111; seen occasionally at Theo van Gogh's gallery, 110; included in Volpini exhibition, 163; growing friendship with Gauguin—helps him, 181; lends Gauguin his studio, 196; Gauguin gives him portrait of Juliette, 196; gradually takes place of Schuff, 196; trouble with his wife, 196; chief correspondent with Gauguin in Tahiti, 210; becomes sole recipient of Gauguin's news, 214-15; Gauguin describes *Manao Tupapau* to him, 219-20; receives many complaints from Gauguin of neglect by others, 222-3; Gauguin tells him of the effect of Tahiti life, 223; sends money to Gauguin, 225; his limitations, 226; sends more money to Gauguin, 226-7; arranges for Gauguin to pick up money on return to France, 230; is on his yacht when Gauguin arrives, 231; Gauguin tells him of decision to return to Polynesia for good, 245; Gauguin gives him relics from rue Vercingetorix, 250; he visits him often, 251; is told of his disease, 251; divorces his wife—Schuff's criticism, 254; Gauguin writes often to him—mostly cries of distress, 254; Gauguin sends Tahiti canvases to him, 256; he counsels patience, 257; Gauguin tells him to give canvases to Mette, 258; receives full description of *D'Où Venons-Nous*, Gauguin's symbolic canvas depicting the plight of the island race, 261-3; tries to arrange Gauguin exhibition, 265; Gauguin expresses his wishes to him, 266; a good friend to Gauguin—how he helped him, 269-70; tells Gauguin that his work is in demand, 270; discourages Gauguin's wish to return to France or Spain, 276; Gauguin tells him about *Avant et Après*, 277; Gauguin's comment to him after libel sentence, 282; Gauguin's last note to him, 283
Monticelli, 112, 115, 154
Moréas, Jean, 198
Moret, Henri, 175, 178, 179, 187, 188, 194
Morice, Charles, 181-3, 197-9, 206, 222-226, 228, 235, 236, 240, 242, 245, 254, 258, 263, 270, 271, 281, 282
Mürer, Eugene, 63, 64
Murillo, 126, 127

O'Conor, Roderick, 90, 187, 188, 242, 245, 250

Pahura, 253, 254, 258, 271
Picasso, 176, 285
Pissarro, Camille, meets Gauguin, 41; driving force in organization of Impressionist exhibitions, 41; Arosa buys his pictures, 49; description, 44-6; effect on Gauguin, 46; introduces Gauguin to Impressionists at Nouvelles Athènes, 46-9; Gauguin takes to his pupil Guillaumin, 49; his pictures bought by Gauguin, 49; is invited to Gauguin house, 49; Mette's view of him, 50; invites Gauguin to exhibit with Impressionists—Gauguin's exhibits show his influence, 51; Gauguin spends painting holiday at his house, 52; his penchant for gossip leads to trouble, 53; his moderate view of Gauguin's talent, 53, which seems confirmed after 1882 exhibition with Gauguin's Pissarroesque canvases, 59; Gauguin spends another painting holiday with him after break with Bertin, 62; "do something revolutionary", 63; he sends enthusiastic reports from Rouen, 63; dismay at Gauguin's plan to follow him—differences between them, 64-5; hears from

Pissarro, Camille—*continued*
Gauguin in Copenhagen, 68; too poor to help Gauguin in Paris, 76; flirts with Seurat technique—more differences with Gauguin at Dieppe, 78; thinks a Schuff still-life "terrible" at last Impressionist exhibition, 83; heated defence of neo-Impressionism leads to dissension, 85-6; Gauguin praises his work to disciples at Pont-Aven, 91; quarrels with Gauguin at Nouvelles Athènes, 97-8; he criticises Gauguin's work but admits his growing influence, 99; Gauguin insists that he be left out of Volpini show, 150; his fury when Aurier defends Gauguin—attack on Gauguin, 202-4; Gauguin acknowledges (later) his debt to him, 204; gigantic sneer when Gauguin leaves for Tahiti, 206; Gauguin criticises his work, 216; his protest at Gauguin's Tahiti canvases, 237-8
Pissarro, Lucien, 64, 83, 131, 203, 238
Proudhon, 19
Puvis de Chavannes, 151, 175, 247, 248, 261, 263, 274

Raphael, 68, 91, 151, 282, 283
Redon, Odilon, 167, 195
Redon, Mme, 167, 184, 208
Rembrandt, 58, 70, 156, 174, 218, 274
Renoir, 37, 48, 49, 51, 58, 59, 64, 79, 83, 85, 126, 127, 163, 236
Rimbaud, 133, 134, 268
Rodin, 167, 182, 198
Roujon, 250
Roulin, 144, 146, 148, 158, 240
Rousseau, J.-J., 30
Rousseau, Th., 151, 156
Roussel, K.-X., 165, 238
Roy, Louis, 110, 163
Rubens, 174, 241

Saint-Simon, Comte de, 20
Sand, George, 21
Satre, Mme, 169, 170
Schuffenecker, Emile (Schuff), meets Gauguin at Bertin—his admiration, 37; encourages him to look at pictures and try his hand at painting, 37; trusted by Mette, 38, who lives near him, 39; Gauguin's first child named after him, 39; persuades Gauguin to take evening classes at Académie Collarossi, 39-40; follows Gauguin to the Salon, 50, and in the Impressionist manner, 51; henpecked by his wife, 51; reassures Mette about Gauguin's love of painting, 51; his talk of leaving Bertin a possible encouragement to Gauguin—but the two men very different, 62; recipient of Gauguin's confidences from Copenhagen, 68, 72-3; helps to found Salon des Indépendants and invites Gauguin, 69; prospers and helps Gauguin in Paris—but his wife is difficult—Gauguin predicts break up of marriage, 77; is introduced to last Impressionist exhibition—Pissarro's criticism, 83; Gauguin gives him remarkable description of effect of Brittany on his work, 89; painting at Concarneau, he gives Emile Bernard introduction to Gauguin, 92; praises Gauguin's pottery, 95, 98, and finds him "a little hovel" in Paris, 95-6; more help to Gauguin, 98; sends him money in Martinique, 106; unwisely leads Gauguin to believe that Chaplet will develop big business, 108; introduces De Monfreid to Gauguin, 111; tactless attempts to sell Gauguin's Martinique work provoke quarrels, 116-17; sends money to Gauguin in Brittany, 122; hears that Gauguin is going to Arles and gets the fare from Theo van Gogh, 142; commanded by Gauguin to arrange exhibition for "little group of pals", 150; again offers Gauguin a bed on the return from Arles—the family portrait, 161; shows a certain genius in arranging the Volpini exhibition, 162-3; entertains Gauguin's friends, 166; meets Redon at the Châtelet, 166-7; more trouble between Gauguin and Mme Schuffenecker—his trials in marriage, 168; is given Gauguin's news from Le Pouldu, 175, 178; offers penniless Gauguin the fare to Paris and puts him up—but Gauguin is soon put out by his wife, 180-1; loses his place as Gauguin's best friend, 181, 196; prospers in many directions and Gauguin asks him to finance Madagascar plan—his reaction, 185; "his banality is frightful", 195; temporarily annoys Mette (with whom a correspondence has developed), 196; Gauguin's view of him, 197; Mette complains to him of Gauguin, 206; he reproaches Gauguin (in Tahiti) for being self-

Schuffenecker, Emile (Schuff)—*continued* willed, 216; complains to Mette of Gauguin's bad character, 223; friction with wife increases—he helps Mette to collect Gauguin canvases, 225; more criticism of Gauguin to Mette—Gauguin's comment and complaint that he had not offered him the fare to France at interest, 228-9; Mette continues to criticise Gauguin to him, 233-4; afraid to disapprove of Gauguin face to face, 240-1; employed by Mette as advocate for her constant demands for money from Gauguin, 253; Gauguin on his hypochondria, 254; champions Mette to Gauguin while criticising his own wife, 254; again helps Mette to take Gauguin Tahiti canvases, 258; divorces wife and refuses to forward letter from Mette to Gauguin, 270-1
Schuffenecker, Mme, 37-9, 51, 77, 116, 161, 168, 181, 254, 271
Segatori, 114
Séguin, Armand, 172, 177, 181, 187, 188, 194, 242, 244, 245, 250
Sérusier, Paul, description, 136-7; meets Gauguin reluctantly but is impressed, 137; paints in Bois d'Amour and is instructed by Gauguin—an historic moment, 137-8; preaches Gauguin to his fellow Nabis at the Ecole Julian, 165; he and Maurice Denis lead them to Theo van Gogh's gallery, the Volpini, Tanguy's shop, 165; rejoins Gauguin at Pont-Aven—his scepticism conquered, 171; follows him to Le Pouldu, 172; they share a bedroom, 175; he comes to Pouldu the next summer, 187; description of him by Maufra, 188; he propagates a Sérusian version of Gauguin at Pont-Aven, 194; not at Gauguin's farewell dinner, 205; writes once to Gauguin in Tahiti, 223; sends money to penniless Gauguin at Marseilles, 230, and refers him to Paris friend for further loan, 231; founds his own school at Pont-Aven—Gauguin's mordant comments, the friendship ends, 242; Gauguin forbids the "Sérusier-Denis band" to exhibit with him, 265; "What does it matter if I'm the pupil of Bernard or Sérusier!", 266
Seurat, 78, 83, 85, 86, 94, 97, 150, 153, 154, 203, 237
Shakespeare, 38, 187, 278
Signac, 78, 83, 86, 97, 150
Sisley, 45, 49, 64, 83, 85
Strindberg, 240, 247, 248

Tanguy, "Père", 49, 52, 113, 114, 165, 184
Tehura, 212-4, 217-25, 227, 229, 253, 264
Thaulow, Fritz, 38, 40, 41, 50, 70, 78, 183
Thérèse, 274
Thiers, 22
Tioka, 279, 280, 283, 284
Titi, 207-9, 211
Toulouse-Lautrec, 110, 112, 114, 162
Tristan y Moscoso, Flora, 19-22, 24, 31, 33, 269
Tristan y Moscoso, Don Mariano, 19, 24
Tristan y Moscoso, Don Pio, 23-5, 27
Turner, 70

Uribe, Juan, 31, 79, 97, 100, 101

Van Gogh, Theo, 94, 109, 111, 113-17, 127, 128, 138-43, 145-7, 149, 151, 155, 157, 159, 160, 163, 165, 166, 170, 178, 179, 181, 182, 191, 193-5, 215, 228
Van Gogh, Vincent, Emile Bernard praises him to Gauguin—description, 94; his veneration for Gauguin after Martinique, 111; his background, sufferings and enthusiasms, 111-12, 114; Gauguin mocks his Dutch heroes, 112, but perceives an original painter in him, 112-13; his influence on Gauguin, 113-14; outlines his plan for Impressionist studio in south of France, 114; his need of a companion, 115; Gauguin discourages his offer, 116; he goes to Arles, 127; repeats his offer after hearing of Gauguin's hardships in Brittany, 127; Gauguin accepts—reasons why, 127-9, then procrastinates, 129; his criticisms of "biblical interpretations" of Gauguin and Bernard, who "has probably never seen an olive tree", 135; three-cornered correspondence between him, Gauguin and Bernard—exchange of self-portraits, 138-9; his hysterical need of Gauguin—he continues to press him to come to Arles, but Gauguin is absorbed by thoughts of tropics, 139; Gauguin tries to postpone the inevitable without offending Theo, 140; he

Van Gogh, Vincent—*continued*
refuses Gauguin's and Theo's suggestions to go to Brittany, 141; his letters veer between criticisms of Gauguin and overmastering longing for him at Arles, 141; decorates yellow house in Gauguin's honour, 141; helped by Theo, Gauguin reluctantly joins him, 142-3; effect on him of Gauguin's company—at first wholly good, 144-7; he paints to Gauguin's directions, 147-8; his good work, 148-9; he and Gauguin at the brothel, 149; his uncharacteristic amenability—his happiest moment, 150-1; beginnings of differences, 151; his fears of losing Gauguin, 151-2; envy of Gauguin's success with women, 152; Gauguin tries to change his views on painting—fierce arguments, 153-4; he behaves strangely, 155; promises amendment when Gauguin threatens to leave, 155, but a visit to Montpellier gallery arouses fresh incompatibilities, 156; Gauguin finishes his portrait, 156-7; his reaction—Gauguin prepares to go, 157; he threatens to attack Gauguin—mutilates himself, 158; in hospital, 159; attitude to Gauguin, 159; analysis of their relationship, 159-60; in asylum at St Rémy—does not exhibit at Volpini but defends Gauguin, 163; correspondence with Gauguin—offers him furniture from yellow house—hopes to live with him again—understands his dissatisfaction with life in Brittany, 177-8; makes painting after Gauguin sketch, is ill because of it but happy when Gauguin praises it, 191; tells Aurier, writer of first article on his work, that he should praise Gauguin before him, 191; finds Gauguin letter gloomy, 191; moves to Auvers, invites himself to Brittany but Gauguin temporises, 191; kills himself—Gauguin's comment, 192; effect of his death on Gauguin, 193 ff.

Verkade, Jean, 189
Verlaine, 133, 134, 182, 197, 198, 206, 223, 240
Vernier, 280, 281, 283, 284
Virgil, 68
Vollard, Ambroise, 266, 270, 275
Volpini, 162, 163, 236, 265
Vuillard, 165, 238, 285

Wagner, 175
Willemsen, 189
Wollstonecraft, Mary, 20

Ziem, 151

Printed in Great Britain
by T. and A. Constable Ltd., Hopetoun Street,
Printers to the University of Edinburgh